BLURRING
THE COLOR LINE

THE NATHAN I. HUGGINS LECTURES

BLURRING
THE COLOR LINE

The New Chance for a More Integrated America

RICHARD ALBA

HARVARD UNIVERSITY PRESS

Cambridge, Massachusetts, and London, England

2009

Library of Congress Cataloging-in-Publication Data

Alba, Richard D.
   Blurring the color line : the new chance for a more integrated America /
Richard Alba.
      p.   cm.—(The Nathan I. Huggins lectures)
   Includes bibliographical references and index.
   ISBN 978-0-674-03513-3 (cloth : alk. paper)   1. United States—Race relations.
2. Minorities—United States.   I. Title.
   E184.A1A447   2009
   305.800973—dc22   2009012154

In memory of my parents,
Richard (né Diego) Alba (1915–1945) and
Mary Theresa O'Sullivan (1914–1974),
who, though their lives were too short,
exemplified boundary blurring at its best

Contents

Acknowledgments

This book originated in an unexpected invitation. Sometime in the summer of 2006, I received a letter from Henry Louis Gates, Jr., probably the best known African-American intellectual in the United States and someone whom I had not met, inviting me to present the Nathan I. Huggins Lectures at Harvard, which are sponsored by the Du Bois Institute there and honor the original occupant of the university's W. E. B. Du Bois Professorship. At first, I thought there must be some mistake—how could Henry Louis Gates possibly have identified me for this role? And what could I, who have spent the better part of my career writing about the assimilation of immigrant groups, contribute to the intellectual atmosphere at the nation's leading center of African-American studies? But my initial skepticism yielded eventually to the recognition that invitations of this sort provide opportunities to break free from some of the confining conventions of scholarly writing. The longer I thought about it, the more I saw the invitation as an opening to knock down some of the taken-for-granted compartmentalization in the study of racial and ethnic groups in American society and to think boldly, but also rigorously, about the relationship of past changes wrought by assimilation, broadly construed, to future prospects for the erosion of white/nonwhite divisions. When I read the writings of Nathan Huggins in preparation for the lectures and found that he, like me, was comfortable with analytic categories that recognized similarities across racial lines, I felt confident that I had chosen an appropriate direction.

I presented the lectures on three consecutive days in March, 2008. As I have experienced on other occasions, the Harvard community is uncommonly generous and engaged. I was very gratified by the number of Harvard faculty and graduate students who took time out of their demanding schedules to attend some or all of the lectures and by the warm and sympathetic reception the lectures received from them. The attentiveness and responsiveness of my Cambridge friends and colleagues helped me to see more clearly what I had accomplished and what was still lacking. Their critiques, suggestions, and questions, which continued well after the lectures both in correspondence and in personal meetings, prodded me to reshape the argument into a structurally robust form. Among those whose attentions in Cambridge and afterward stand out in my mind are: Michael Aronson, Christopher Bail, Kimberly DaCosta, Nathan and Lochi Glazer, Corina Graif, Evelyn Brooks Higginbotham, Jennifer Hochschild, Christopher Jencks, Michèle Lamont, Helen Marrow, Gwen Moore, Robert Putnam, John Stone, Van Tran, Mary Waters, and William Julius Wilson. Dell Hamilton, the Assistant Director of the Du Bois Institute, was a most cordial host during my time in Cambridge.

Spurred on by the reception of the lectures in Cambridge, I saw the argument as meriting more than the usual volume that comes out of a lecture series and quickly worked up a full-fledged book manuscript. Michael Aronson, the Harvard University Press editor who had previously worked with Victor Nee and me on *Remaking the American Mainstream* (2003), enthusiastically embraced my idea for the book and made the path smooth at the Press. Numerous colleagues read parts or all of the manuscript and gave me the benefit of their evaluations and suggestions. I am especially indebted to Nancy Foner and Mary Waters—both read the book manuscript in its entirety and presented me with detailed comments and then, at my request, reread some parts that had been substantially revised. In addition, I profited from readings of the entire manuscript by Nancy Denton, Jennifer Hochschild, Victor Nee, Donald Tomaskovic-Devey, and an anonymous Harvard University Press reviewer. Others responded with reactions and comments to an article-length version of the argument; they include Ira Katznelson, Michèle Lamont, Mara Loveman, Helen Marrow, and Douglas Massey. Robert Putnam's pointed remarks to multiple presentations of the basic argument called my attention to some strengths I seemed to be neglecting.

I rehearsed the argument in a shortened form in a number of venues and got more helpful reactions back in return. Among the places where I made presentations are Bellagio, the Beijing Forum, the City University of New York, the Economic School of Paris, Göttingen University, Leipzig University, the Manchester-Harvard workshop, Princeton University, Russell Sage Foundation, the University at Albany, UC-Berkeley, and Vanderbilt University. Among those who provided useful suggestions or encouragement are Irene Bloemraad, Michael Burawoy, Samantha Friedman, Michael Hechter, Donald Hernandez, Gary Gerstle, John Mollenkopf, James Nazroo, Alejandro Portes, Tim Smeeding, and Gillian Stevens. Alex Haslam and David Wagner advised me about the relevant literature in social psychology.

I could not have completed the manuscript without solid technical support. At the time, I was the Director of the Center for Social and Demographic Analysis at the University at Albany, where I could count on an excellent staff for the necessary census data work. I am grateful to Dr. Hui-shien Tsao and Dr. Ruby Wang for their efforts in this respect. I must also acknowledge the financial support for this research infrastructure provided by the University as well as by a grant from the National Institute for Child Health and Human Development (5R24HD044943–05). Jeffrey Napierala helped me by constructing the graphs of the occupational distribution. At Harvard University Press, Hilary Jacqmin helped me to surmount various hurdles, and Elizabeth Gilbert smoothed out the rough spots in my prose. I am grateful also to Martin Tulic for compiling the index.

I am an incessant cannibalizer of my own writings, believing that if I have already formulated something in a way that pleases me, I shouldn't be forced to rewrite it in a less satisfactory form. I am grateful therefore to Victor Nee and to Harvard University Press for their permission to reuse several paragraphs from *Remaking the American Mainstream* in the current volume.

Finally, I must make a bow to the role that my family has played for me over several decades. Without the solid foundation of happiness and emotional fulfillment that Gwen, Michael, and Sarah have given me, I would not be able to pour into my intellectual work the intensity that I do, nor would I find as much pleasure in it. I feel especially fortunate to enjoy their love and can only hope that what I give in return is commensurate with what I receive.

BLURRING THE COLOR LINE

> . . . for the problem of the Twentieth Century
> is the problem of the color-line.
>
> —*W. E. B. Du Bois,*
> *The Souls of Black Folk (1903)*

> There are, I suspect, qualities of common experience and
> character that make us more like one another than like the
> peoples in the lands of our forebears. Despite what they
> may suspect, an Afro-American and the grandson of a Pol-
> ish immigrant will be better able to take things for granted
> between themselves than the one could with a Ghanaian
> or Nigerian and the other could with a Warsaw worker.
> They, like all other Americans except Indians, are sons of
> a migrant experience to the "new world" and have shared a
> continual interface with one another. It has been a rather
> harsh, bitter, and strained relationship, but it has existed and
> has been a central element in their consciousness.
>
> —*Nathan I. Huggins, Revelations:*
> *American History, American Myths (1995)*

> It is a rare and intriguing moment
> when a people decide that they are the instruments of
> history-making and race-building.
>
> —*Nathan I. Huggins, Harlem Renaissance (1972)*

Paradoxes of Race and Ethnicity in America Today

With the ascent of an African American for the first time to the presidency in 2009, the United States might seem to have finally put its tortured history of slavery and racism behind it. Many commentators greeted Barack Obama's candidacy and victory as transformational events and as confirmation of tidal shifts that, they presume, have quietly been taking place below the surface of the turbulent sea of racial attitudes. The election gave Eugene Robinson, an African-American columnist at the *Washington Post,* the experience of "how some people must have felt when they heard Ronald Reagan say, 'it's morning again in America.'" Robinson basked in the "new sunshine," which "feels warm on my face." *New York Times* columnist Thomas Friedman, who is white, declared Obama's victory to be the "final chapter of America's Civil War," an ending coming, he noted, nearly 150 years after the first shots were fired. "We awake this morning to a different country," he concluded immediately after the election; and, though acknowledging that the "struggle for equal rights is far from over," he wanted every child, citizen, and new immigrant to know that "from this day forward everything really *is* possible in America." Many savored the fact that Obama garnered a higher percentage of votes cast by whites than had a number of white Democratic candidates. Writing just after he clinched the Democratic nomination, the *Washington Post*'s Anne Appelbaum posed the question, "Will Americans vote for a black man?" The election result seemed to justify the audible note of triumph in her answer: "Yes, Americans will vote for a black man."[1]

Yet American race relations remain as paradoxical as they have been throughout the country's history. Coinciding with Obama's rise on the national political scene came the racially inflamed events in Jena, Louisiana, which led to a nationwide civil-rights campaign after six black high-school students were charged with attempted murder for beating up a white youth following a series of racial confrontations at school and elsewhere. The one-sided actions of the local justice system, which climaxed in the conviction of one of the black students by an all-white jury (a conviction that was subsequently set aside), seemed to evoke the Jim Crow South. Yet as commentator Orlando Patterson pointed out in the pages of the *New York Times,* "the Jena case is hardly a throwback to the 1960s, but instead speaks to issues that are very much of our times."[2] In particular, the case points to the submerged iceberg of black incarceration, which has expanded rapidly since 1980. On any given day, one of every eight black men in their late twenties is locked up in the nation's prisons and jails, and many more are under supervision by the correctional system, on probation or parole. According to The Sentencing Project, the lifetime risk of a prison term is approaching one in three for black male youth. Once they have criminal records, their employment possibilities sink like a stone thrown into a deep lake. An extraordinary historical reversal in the life prospects of African-American men is highlighted by a straightforward comparison of moments just two decades apart: as the twenty-first century opened, more black men were in prison than were attending college; in 1980, the situation was the reverse and by a lopsided three-to-one margin. For the black community, imprisonment has become an affliction far greater than it ever was in the pre–civil-rights era. The United States has become the world's leader in putting its own citizens behind bars, and this incarceration has had a disproportionate impact on ethno-racial minorities, who make up 60 percent of prisoners.[3]

For those who study the racial divide systematically, the resilience of inequality and segregation thus seems a truer characterization of the contemporary United States than does the vision of transcendence inspired by a singular candidate for the presidency. Throughout this country's history, one of its most notable features has been the critical role that race and ethnicity play in determining the life chances of Americans, whether these are a matter of where they dwell, how much education they get, what kinds of jobs they do, whom they marry, or even how long they live—and, one should add, whether they go to prison and for how long.[4] Even in the early nineteenth century, visitors were struck not just by the contradiction between democracy and slavery but by the plight of free blacks; according to Alexis de Tocqueville,

> In almost all the States where slavery is abolished, the Negroes have been given electoral rights, but if they show up to vote, they risk their lives. If they are oppressed, they may complain, but only whites are to be found among the judges. The law opens the jurors' bench to him, but prejudice keeps him out of it. His son is excluded from the school where the descendent of Europeans comes to learn. In the theaters, he cannot, for the price of gold, buy the right to take his place beside his former master. In the hospitals, he sleeps separately. The black is allowed to pray to the same God as the whites, but not to pray to him at the same altar. He has his own clergy and his own churches. The doors of heaven are not closed to him: nevertheless, inequality hardly ceases at the border of the other world. When the Negro is no longer, his bones are cast aside, and the disparity of conditions persists even in the equality of death.[5]

An enormous literature in the social sciences demonstrates the continuing potency of the country's ethno-racial divisions. In terms of the black-white divide, the most salient social boundary in the United States, numerous differentials in life chances have remained stable for several decades, since the close of the civil-rights era, or at most show painfully slow improvement. One well-studied instance concerns residential location, which not only determines who the neighbors will be, but what the "quality" of the neighborhood is, where this may be reflected in crime rates, the adequacy of the schools, or other ways. Research on segregation reveals the basic stability of these black-white differentials for more than half a century and indicates that racial inequalities are produced by a combination of individual-level discrimination and institutional mechanisms anchored in the practices of the real-estate industry and the policies of largely white suburban communities. In addition, the process known as "invasion-succession," or more colloquially, "white flight," makes neighborhood integration unstable, even sometimes fleeting. Although the level of residential integration is slowly improving—according to 2000 Census data, the average value of the prime index of segregation had fallen modestly during the 1990s, from 69 to 65—the segregation of blacks remains substantially higher than that of other population groups, and the rate of its decline is so glacial that it will take a century for segregation to become a minor phenomenon.[6]

Many other indices of black-white inequality have proved equally stubborn when it comes to amelioration. The ratio of black-to-white median family income scarcely budged from the early 1970s to the end of the century, when it ticked upward a few notches. The median income of black families currently hovers at about two-thirds of its equivalent among whites. Poverty affects a substantially higher fraction of blacks than of whites, and the disparity is striking for children: in 2006, a third of black children lived in poverty, compared with a tenth of white children. The largest economic inequality between the races concerns wealth, the indicator that is most telling about the long-term prospects of individuals and families: recent research estimates that white families on average possess about seven times more assets than black families do.

There is still a notable discrepancy in life expectancy despite recent improvements, as whites outlive blacks on average by five to six years. In the case of incarceration, however, the situation of African Americans, especially men, has gotten much worse in recent years. The degree of racial inequality has become stunning: among men in their early thirties at the end of the twentieth century, about 20 percent of blacks had served time in prison, compared with just 3 percent of whites.[7] Other indices of life chances that display marked racial inequalities could be cited, but the point is clear: whenever a valued resource or status is involved, blacks are considerably worse off than whites.

The ethno-racial divides of the United States put not only African Americans at a disadvantage. American Indians and Hispanics are on average also significantly worse off than white Americans. Despite the wealth that some tribes have acquired through the settlement of land claims or the establishment of gambling casinos and other enterprises, American Indians are the poorest of the broadly defined ethno-racial groups in the United States: more than a quarter have incomes below the poverty line, and the poverty rate is much worse among those living on reservations. Some of the poorest places in the United States in fact are reservations. The poorest county according to the 2000 Census was Buffalo, South Dakota, home to the Crow Creek reservation; and other South Dakota counties that house reservations regularly rank high on the list of the poorest as well. Because of poverty, chronic health problems including alcoholism and inadequate health services, the life expectancy in some of these places is much lower than elsewhere in America, and for some tribes it does not exceed 45 years.[8]

Hispanics now form the largest minority population in the United States, and their numbers are increasing rapidly because of immigration and higher fertility, the latter as much a consequence of their concentration in youthful ages as of higher average family size. According to the 2008 projections of the U.S. Census Bureau, they could account for nearly one of every three Americans by the middle of the century. Yet in terms of basic socioeconomic indicators, they remain well behind white Americans, even after their families have been present in the country for several generations. Indeed, the lack of visible progress across the generations born in the United States has raised doubts about whether Hispanics can ever catch up. For example, at the end of the twentieth century, the median household income of Hispanics who were born in the United States was about $40,000, 73 percent of white household income, but it made little difference how many generations their families had resided on American soil. The poverty rates for Hispanic children are also quite high—27 percent in 2006—though they are somewhat lower than is the case for black children. During the 1990s, Hispanic residential segregation increased, albeit slightly, but it was thus moving in the opposite direction from slowly declining black segregation. The increase was undoubtedly a consequence of high levels of immigration, since immigrants usually are drawn to neighborhoods of co-ethnics by virtue of the social networks that assist them during the early phase of settlement. Hispanic youth are also vulnerable to incarceration. One analysis found that, in 2000, 8 percent of U.S.-born Mexican-American young men were institutionalized. While the figure is lower than the incarceration rate for black men, it is much higher than the 1–2 percent of young men in general who were confined in prison at that time.[9]

Given such data, scholars who study ethnicity and race incline toward the view that a durable ethno-racial order exists in the United States, with whites occupying the top position, African Americans at the bottom, and others somewhere in between.[10] One implication of such a hierarchy is that many minority individuals find it difficult to escape the social constraints imposed on the members of their group, especially when they come from poor families or those handicapped in other ways, as for instance by the undocumented status of immigrant parents.

Yet it may be a mistake to view our current ethno-racial inequalities as enduring. We know that fundamental changes to ethno-racial cleavages can take place; this is recorded in the history of assimilation, to which many Americans point as proof of the ultimate openness of their society. That such changes can occur even when racial visibility is involved is indicated by the Asian-American experience over the course of the twentieth century. When the century opened, Asian Americans were racially excluded from any meaningful participation in mainstream American society. Asian immigrants were handicapped by the racial bar in American citizenship law, which prevented them from naturalizing as citizens; and legislation soon blocked any further immigration from the "Orient." In some states like California, marriages between Asian Americans and whites were forbidden by antimiscegenation laws. But during the second half of the century Asian Americans broke free from their mooring in a position of racial disadvantage and rose to high average levels of education, occupational status, and income as well as to widespread acceptability among white Americans. Intermarriage rates, mainly with white American partners, have soared to the point that about one of every two young U.S.-born Asian Americans marries a non-Asian. This change in status has not yet eclipsed all stereotypes about Asian Americans, such as those of the "model minority," whose members are expected to be high achievers despite their racial visibility, and of persons who are "forever foreign" no matter how long their families have been in the United States. But the changes have been profound, nevertheless.[11]

In truth, the changes involved in assimilation can be more radical than most Americans now appreciate, for assimilation ultimately affects the way that group differences are perceived. This sort of assimilation has had an especially strong impact on some once-denigrated European groups, such as Irish Catholics and those from southern and eastern Europe. In order to appreciate the magnitude of assimilatory change, which has caused the distinctions based on different European origins to fade to the point of near invisibility in much of social life, it is important to recognize how our "eyes," our perceptions, have been altered as a consequence. To view the differences with the eyes of today is to view them anachronistically because they have been reduced so dramatically; we need to recover the perceptions of witnesses of the time, if we are to have an appreciation of what the distinctions meant, say, a century or more ago, when the immigrations from Ireland or from southern and eastern Europe were cresting. The historical record provides abundant testimony that many native white Americans saw the new immigrants as fundamentally different kinds of human beings. The iconography that visually represented these distinctions frequently depicted the new immigrants as physically distinctive and inherently inferior or undesirable. It depicted them, in other words, as racially different.

That iconography was particularly coarse in the late nineteenth and early twentieth centuries. Consider the racial aspects of the caricatures of the Irish that were prevalent in nineteenth-century cartoons, for instance. As historian John Higham describes, the Irish were typically portrayed with "a pug nose, an underslung jaw, and an air of tattered truculence usually augmented by whiskey." In fact, they were commonly presented as subhuman, even bestial—a "simianized Paddy," according to Lewis Curtis, Jr.[12]—as in the drawings of the most famous political cartoonist of the nineteenth century, Thomas Nast, whose cartoons in *Harper's Weekly* influenced the course of American politics in the 1870s and 1880s. One of Nast's well-known cartoons of the Irish depicts a riotous celebration of St. Patrick's Day and pivots on a strong visual contrast between the policemen, whose Anglo-American features seem to convey a level-headed intelligence, and the Irishmen, who despite their fancy dress, including top hats, appear apelike and threatening (see Figure 1.1). Most twenty-first-century viewers, for whom this iconography of the Irish has been lost because our perceptions of the group have been so altered by its assimilation to the mainstream, probably wonder what to make of the distinctive but uniform appearance Nast gives the Irish. Surely, Nast knew that not all Irishmen looked alike. But one can make sense of his iconography if one sees it as his depiction of the inner—and probably, in his eyes, intrinsic—nature of the Irish. Like a number of observers on both sides of the Atlantic in the late nineteenth century, Nast viewed the Irish and African Americans as equivalent in their intellectual and moral inferiority, and another of his best-known cartoons portrayed the two as balanced on a scale (Figure 1.2). Nast was not alone among American caricaturists in portraying the Irish as lower on the tree of humanity than were northern European Protestants. Cartoonists working in *Puck* and *Judge,* such as Frederick Opper and James Wales, also mined this vein of racialist imagery.[13] And the stereotype of the simian Paddy was repeated on the other side of the Atlantic, among the British cartoonists working for *Punch,* for instance.

Today, one could hardly get more American than to be of Irish descent. Since the 1970s, when social surveys began to measure the ethnic backgrounds of later-generation Americans, we have known that Irish Catholics are among the most successful groups in the United States, in socioeconomic and other terms. In 1976 Andrew Greeley observed that, after Jews, Irish Catholics were the best educated group among whites. They are also highly integrated into the white population, as is indicated by their low degree of residential segregation. One study of the New York City area, where ethnic neighborhoods persist for a long time and segregation among groups tends to be quite high in general, found that, in 1990, the index of segregation of persons of Irish ancestry from other whites was only about 22 (on a scale that goes from 0 to 100). By contrast, the segregation of blacks from whites in that year was over 80 and that of Hispanics from whites was nearly 70.[14]

Another index of the integration of the Irish into the American core is the widespread embrace of an Irish identity. As Michael Hout and Joshua Goldstein observe, when the Census Bureau asked in 1980 for the first time a subjective question about ethnic identity, 40 million Americans claimed to be wholly or partly Irish, placing that ancestry among the top three, along with British and German. Hout and Goldstein ask how 4.5 million immigrants from Ireland, the great majority of whom came between 1820 and 1920, could have given rise in such a

RUM. BRUTAL ATTACK ON THE POLICE. "THE DA

Figure 1.1. "The Day We Celebrate," St. Patrick's Day, 1867, according to American political cartoonist Thomas Nast. (*Harper's Weekly*, April 6, 1867, courtesy of American Antiquarian Society)

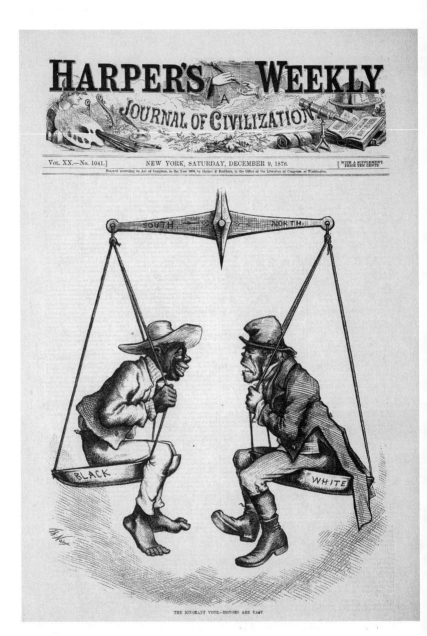

Figure 1.2. "The Ignorant Vote: Honors Are Easy" by Thomas Nast. (*Harper's Weekly*, December 9, 1876, courtesy of American Antiquarian Society.)

short historical period to so many Irish Americans.[15] Their answer combines the prevalence of intermarriage across ethnic and religious lines by Irish Americans with the tendency of the descendants of such marriages to continue to identify as Irish. That tendency implies that there is some degree of desirability attached to an Irish identity and that no great social cost involved.

The perceptions of other Americans also register this change in position of the Irish group. Since the mid-1920s, sociologists have measured a social distance scale of ethno-racial groups that is based on the willingness of respondents to tolerate varying degrees of closeness to individuals from different groups, from accepting them into the family, to living next to them, to allowing them to immigrate to the United States. When this scale was first measured in the mid-1920s by its inventor, Emory Bogardus, the shift in position of the Irish was apparently well under way; in the eyes of his respondents, the Irish headed a list of what were then perceived as European immigrant groups and were separated by only a short distance from the American core groups identified as "English," "Americans (U.S. whites)," and "Canadians." They held their position at or near the top of the immigrant-group section of the scale throughout much of the twentieth century, but in the most recent measurement of it, in 2001, they are now tied with the "Canadians" and the "British."[16]

To appreciate the potential of the American future, we must understand how this transformation in the status of Irish Catholics, along with that of the descendants of southern and eastern European immigrants, took place. I am thus asking: how did assimilation on a mass scale, a process that took place decisively in the quarter century following World War II, occur? Moreover, could anything similar happen to currently disadvantaged minorities, who are non-European and therefore racially distinct? These are the two questions I will seek to answer in this book.

I will focus the investigation of the second question on black and Hispanic Americans, by far the two largest groups that suffer from

ethno-racial disadvantages. Their large size within the American population is an asset for the statistical portion of the analysis, because it
facilitates the detection of differences across subgroups, such as birth
cohorts. My focus does not deny the existence of other disadvantaged
groups such as American Indians. (Another reason I do not analyze
American Indians is that the tendency to identify with this group has
risen sharply since the 1960s, as more and more Americans of mixed
heritage declare themselves to be American Indian rather than something else on the Census and other questionnaires.[17] This phenomenon could potentially confound the analysis of other changes over time.)
African and Hispanic Americans are also the prime exemplars of two
types of minorities: one is largely a non-immigrant-origin population
descended from ancestors who were brought to the United States forcibly as slaves, though with an admixture of recent immigrants from
Africa and the Caribbean and their descendants; the other, a largely
immigration-derived population, though containing subgroups of individuals whose ancestors became U.S. Americans through military conquest, at the ends of the 1846–1848 war with Mexico and the 1898
Spanish-American War.[18] I refer to these groups as "populations" to un-
derscore the diversity within them, as they themselves contain group divisions based, for example, on different national origins, as between, say,
Mexican and Cuban Americans. Because of data limitations, I will not
be able to do justice to this diversity in my analysis.

A pivotal concept in my account is that of a "social boundary."[19] The
theoretical ideas surrounding the concept invoke not just the social distinctions that are the foundations for ethno-racial group inequalities, but
the social forces that create, maintain, and, when necessary, reinforce
these distinctions and the hierarchies they entail. But these ideas also
yield insights into the circumstances under which boundaries recede in
salience and play a less significant role in the lives of those positioned on
their disadvantaged side. Using these ideas, I critically examine the most
widely accepted explanation among historians of white-ethnic assimila-

tion, the so-called whiteness perspective, and find it informative but ultimately inadequate. This explanation depends on a conceptualization of the disadvantaged positions of the Irish, Italians, and Jews as inhering in their problematic racial position as "in-between groups," to use the apt characterization of James Barrett and David Roediger.[20] In short, their membership in the white race was doubtful, and the challenge they therefore confronted, according to this perspective, was to gain full acceptance as whites. Once that was attained, the barriers to their full integration presumably fell away.

The whiteness perspective does help us to understand the processes of social ascent by the descendants of once-despised European immigrant groups like the Irish, but it does not explain their mass assimilation in the middle of the twentieth century. This perspective suffers from two blind spots: one is that these groups' ethno-racial disadvantages cannot be understood solely in racial terms, for they had important ethnic and religious elements. The fading of these elements from our understanding of potential sources of disadvantage and social cleavage is a result of the process of mass assimilation, not its precondition. The second problem becomes apparent once we bring the boundary concept into the frame. A sociological commonplace is that privileged groups defend the boundaries that separate them from the less fortunate. Why, then, did native-born white Protestants, overwhelmingly of northern and western European backgrounds, so easily accede to the mass assimilation of previously disadvantaged religious minorities whose ancestors were looked down upon because of their countries of origin? Why didn't white Protestants protect their privileged positions against these newcomers?

My answer is that the advance of these groups was much less threatening than it might have otherwise been because of what I call "non-zero-sum mobility." Such mobility occurs when members of lower-situated groups can move upward without affecting the life chances of the members of well-established ones. (A zero-sum situation exists, by definition, when the gains of some must come at the expense of others.)

The economic expansion after World War II, in part a consequence of the global dominance of the victorious and largely undamaged United States, enabled the members of the rising groups to obtain much more education and better jobs than their parents had without any sacrifice on the part of native white Protestants. In fact, many of the Protestant young people were surpassing their parents, too.

Non-zero-sum mobility is key to a complex of factors that I argue, on inductive and theoretical grounds, was sufficient to bring about the massive incorporation of the white ethnics; and it holds, I claim, a special significance in general for the possibility of fundamental ethno-racial change. Might a period of non-zero-sum mobility in the near future allow changes to soften boundaries that we currently see as rigidly racial, like those disadvantaging African Americans and Hispanics?

I believe the answer is "yes." Pessimism about the prospects for socioeconomic mobility in the near future is rampant, largely premised on economic structural changes that are thought to limit chances for minorities to move up the ladder, to say nothing of the deep worldwide recession at the end of the century's first decade.[21] But the departure of the massive baby-boom generation from the labor market, which will occur during a roughly twenty-five-year period through the early 2030s, has not been factored into the picture. The baby boomers are heavily white and well educated, and they dominate many of the best-paying occupations. Their departure could open up the labor market in a way that has not been true since the middle of the twentieth century.

The retirement of the baby boomers is a certainty, but its consequences are not. One point of uncertainty is whether other economic changes, for example, the off-shoring of jobs now based in the United States, could blunt the potential for upward mobility among African Americans and Hispanics. No definitive answer exists when such a sociologically and economically complex future is being predicted, but I give reasons to think that the huge magnitude of the job openings associated with the departure of the baby boomers will make non-zero-sum mobility a major opportunity for American society, as well as for many Americans, in the near future.

Other difficult questions arise when we consider the degree to which ethno-racial minorities will benefit from future non-zero-sum mobility. I provide evidence that minorities are already penetrating the top tiers of the U.S. labor market in much larger numbers than in the past. In this respect, an important process of integration is already under way, driven largely by demographic shifts in the cohorts of young adults entering the labor market. However, when the correspondence between educational attainment and labor-market position is taken into account, as well as the earnings of individuals in different occupations, it is apparent that white men remain very privileged. Were minorities to be the primary beneficiaries of non-zero-sum mobility, however, ethno-racial inequalities on the top rungs of the labor market might be very much reduced, according to the scenario I present.

But will they in fact be the primary beneficiaries? Among the contingencies that must be considered are the other groups—working-class whites, future high-skilled immigrants, and white women—who might be able to take advantage of the new opportunities. I argue that the potential of the first two groups to fill the vacancies created by the baby boomers' departure is modest. Women, however, especially white women, in part because of their recently attained educational edge over men, are likely to be major beneficiaries of future mobility opportunities. Yet according to my projections, they are quite unlikely to be able to satisfy all of the demand for highly educated workers. Hence the United States must look to young minorities in order to satisfy future needs for highly skilled workers and to fill the slots in the labor market coming open because of the baby boomers' departure. Young minorities stand out among the underutilized groups in the population because their proportion among the young adults entering the workforce will increase rapidly in the decades to come. The non-zero-sum mobility of the near future offers an unusual opportunity to repair some of the worst injustices of American society.

The principal barrier to the greater utilization of blacks and Hispanics in the upper tiers of the workforce remains the large educational gap, particularly in education after high school, that separates them on average from whites. The non-zero-sum mobility of the mid-twentieth century included an educational catch-up by disadvantaged ethnics, some of whom—the children and grandchildren of southern Italian immigrants are the best-documented example—had posted weak school records to that point. I consider the possibility that a similar catch-up could help African and Hispanic Americans and argue that, given the demonstrated deficiencies in the schools many of them attend, substantial policy changes, accompanied by a manifest national commitment to true equality of educational opportunity, would make a large dent at the very least in educational inequalities.

Whether there will be much greater integration in the future depends on more than non-zero-sum mobility. It also is contingent on what further opportunities are opened to minorities who are upwardly mobile in educational and occupational terms and, in particular, whether mobility, which is likely to mean greater integration in the world of work, also brings about greater integration outside of it. Toward the end of the book, I consider the evidence on this question, which generally supports the linkage of socioeconomic ascent with broader social inclusion. Minorities who are better situated socioeconomically are also more residentially integrated with whites, and for Hispanics (and Asians) greater social inclusion is also evidenced by higher intermarriage rates. Yet a similar socioeconomic gradient in intermarriage is not apparent for African Americans, and it is but one indicator of a persisting and troubling racial divergence in patterns of social integration. Asians and those Hispanics who are light skinned encounter much less difficulty in translating improvements in their socioeconomic position into social proximity to white mainstream Americans than do darker-skinned Americans. This pattern is long-standing, and it indicates the need for continued attention to the difficulties faced by African Americans, Afro-Caribbeans, and dark-skinned Hispanics, even if a period of sustained non-zero-sum mobility allows many among them to move upward socioeconomically.

Despite the uncertainties that are inevitable in projecting several decades ahead, there is merit in envisioning what a future of greater integration might look like. To begin with, it will not be a mirror image of the wholesale incorporation of the white ethnics in the post–World War II decades. Too much has changed in American society for that to happen—most important, the degree of economic inequality is considerably greater today than it was then, when the United States experienced an unusual period of compressed income inequality. The relatively high inequality of the early twenty-first century, a match to the "Gilded Age" of a century ago, will condemn a substantial part of the population to poverty or near-poverty. Given that race functions in the United States in a way that inflicts greater risks on darker-skinned Americans, the large bottom of the income and wealth distributions means that there will be many black and Hispanic, but fewer European, Americans looking upward from these precincts.

Nevertheless, there will be much more ethno-racial diversity at the middle and higher levels of the United States within the next few decades. The demographic changes taking place in the young-adult population guarantee this, but the diversification could be accelerated by non-zero-sum mobility. I argue that the concept of blurred boundaries is helpful for thinking about what this greater diversity might involve at the experiential level for whites and minorities. As opposed to unambiguous and rigid "bright" boundaries, blurred boundaries entail zones of ambiguity, allowing some minority individuals to present themselves at times as belonging to, or at least comfortable on, the non-minority side. Obama's political persona exemplifies this boundary blurring, and this fact contributes to the sense that his victory represents at least a partial breakthrough. Such boundaries, I argue, mean that minority individuals with the appropriate social and economic "credentials" will have more control over their ethno-racial social identity. Rather than having it imposed on them by whites, often in a racially exclusionary manner, they will have more ability to determine the occasions and manner of its presentation. For some minorities, then, what we view today as a racial distinction could become more like an ethnic one.

In sum, the future in a more integrated society is likely to be paradoxical, but not in the same way as the past and present. The concentration of nonwhites in the bulging bottom of the American social structure will coexist with an increasing fluidity of ethno-racial boundaries in the middle and upper reaches of the society. But this is not a reason to deny the significance of the possibilities for achieving a more integrated America. Progress is often made in lurches rather than by continuous advance, and one must be wary of allowing unattainable ideals to spoil achievable gains. In this respect, no one has yet improved upon Voltaire's caution that "Le mieux est l'ennemi du bien"—the best is the enemy of the good.

2

The Puzzle of Ethno-Racial Change

Ethno-racial change was central to the American experience during the twentieth century. The civil-rights movement and the attainment by African Americans of the status of full citizens, if not of fully equal ones, are but the most prominent part of the century's story in this respect. Two other changes are less visible to many Americans today because they were achieved with less overt struggle; but they are not in any sense less central. These are the rise of once despised and legally handicapped East Asians to social acceptability for many white Americans, and the assimilation of the descendants of Irish Catholic and southern and eastern European Catholic, Jewish, and Orthodox Christian immigrants into what then became a white American mainstream, as opposed to one defined in terms of Protestant religion and northern European ancestry.

All of these changes demonstrate that ethno-racial hierarchies, at least in democratic, economically dynamic societies, are less rigid than they are sometimes thought to be. But they leave a crucial question unanswered—how does change occur? The achievements of the civil-rights movement were made possible by a mass movement dedicated to political struggle against the institutions and legal structures of racism.

That struggle, which primarily took place in the South and was often greeted with officially sanctioned violence that was repugnant to many white Americans, resulted in legal changes during the 1950s and 1960s that represent what are perhaps the highest achievements of the Congress and the Supreme Court during the entire century. Yet these legal changes, transformative though they were, fell short and could not satisfy the yearnings of African Americans for full equality and rapid improvement in their lives, and the decade of the 1960s, when the climactic successes of the civil-rights movement were achieved, closed with race riots that left the black sections of many American cities in flames.

By contrast, the other major ethno-racial changes of the century occurred more quietly. This is not to say that they lacked the dimension of political struggle and legal challenge. Jews, for example, legally and politically confronted many of the barriers in their way, such as anti-Semitic quotas limiting their access to elite colleges and to medical schools; and Asian Americans, who suffered from many of the same legal disabilities imposed on nonwhites as black Americans did when the twentieth century opened, benefited in major ways from the civil-rights legislation of the 1960s. But the balance of forces behind these changes was different and involved other dimensions, which are situated deep in social structures and culture, where they are less detectable by the naked eye and therefore often go unobserved. These are the dimensions to which I want to pay attention in this and the next chapters, for I will argue that we can learn from what took place in them about the potential for change in coming decades.

The Story of the Century

If we could travel back in time to the beginning of the twentieth century, we would find an America very different from the one we experience at the beginning of the twenty-first. In the South, African Americans were subordinated to Jim Crow, which confined every aspect of their lives, condemning them to live in substandard housing unless they were servants in the homes of wealthy whites, to work in the most menial of jobs, to behave in a servile manner toward any white they encountered no matter humble his or her status, and, if they were male, to avoid at risk to their lives any contact with white women that could be misinterpreted as implying familiarity or intimacy. It goes without saying that African Americans were deprived of any political power; though formally entitled to vote, a variety of devices such as poll taxes and literacy tests applied in a racially discriminatory manner reduced their voting power to virtually nil.[1] This racist caste system was sanctioned by the U.S. Supreme Court in the 1896 Plessy v. Ferguson decision, which found that "separate but equal" facilities met constitutional tests. Threats to this system were countered with violence: between the 1880s and the 1920s, dozens of lynchings occurred annually in the South.[2]

Conditions were better in the North, where racism was not encoded in law and was also less crude. Yet African Americans were largely confined to residential ghettoes once their numbers began to increase early in the twentieth century, and they rarely could find jobs that ranked any higher than the bottom rungs of the labor market. They were perceived as economic competitors by immigrants from Europe and their descendants, who eventually controlled many unions and through them access to jobs. The right to vote was mostly respected, but the political machines that dominated northern cities allotted blacks only tiny dollops of the fruits of electoral power. Even in the North, black children attended segregated schools, though the segregation was informal, not legally mandated, and the education provided was undoubtedly better than that found in southern schools reserved for them.[3] Nor was the servility expected by whites of blacks in the South a requirement for survival in the North, and the expectations of a better life, combined with mechanization and other changes in southern agriculture, fueled a large-scale, decades-long migration to the North by southern African Americans, starting in the second decade of the century.

The 1954 Supreme Court decision Brown v. Board of Education, which reversed Plessy v. Ferguson, and the civil-rights legislation of the 1960s dismantled the legal foundations of the Jim Crow regime and inaugurated an era of greater integration and opportunity for African Americans. The subsequent changes have been enormous. Since the Voting Rights Act of 1965, for example, which finally secured the electoral rights of blacks and other racial minorities, the number of black elected officials has soared. According to the Joint Center for Political and Economic Studies, in 2000 there were more than 9,000 black elected officials throughout the United States, a sixfold increase since 1970.[4] The post-civil-rights period has featured much greater opportunity for African Americans to earn postsecondary and professional credentials, especially outside of historically black colleges and universities, and one consequence has been an expansion of the black middle class. Yet the aspirations for racial equality that drove many of the participants of the civil-rights movement have not been attained. Inequality between whites and blacks, as the first chapter observed, is still substantial in magnitude and well entrenched, anchored among other places in the residential segregation that remains a very visible pattern in many regions of the United States. It implies, for one thing, that black children will usually attend schools that are less well endowed with resources and highly skilled teachers than are the schools typically attended by white children and, for another, that they will be exposed to much higher risks, for example, of criminal involvement as well as of victimization, as they grow up.[5]

The case of Asian Americans demonstrates convincingly that a more thoroughgoing racial change is possible.[6] At the beginning of the twentieth century, this group too suffered from severe legal liabilities imposed on the basis of racial distinction. These began with restrictions on their ability to enter the United States and to become citizens. When Chinese men from Guangdong province began to immigrate to the West Coast after the discovery of gold in California in 1848, they were quickly perceived by white workers as racial inferiors and as economic competitors who could undercut wages. It was not long before the Asians were the targets of the movement for immigration restriction, and the first restrictive law, the Chinese Exclusion Act, was enacted in 1882. The ability of Chinese immigrants to influence this legislation was nil, because, given the racial restrictions on naturalization—first, to "free whites" by virtue of the original naturalization act of 1790 and, then, to whites and blacks after 1870—they were unable to gain American citizenship until the middle of the twentieth century. (Their children, few in number in the early 1900s, were, however, U.S. citizens by virtue of the Fourteenth Amendment.) Once the gates closed on immigration from China, those men who lacked the means to return to their homeland were forced to spend their remaining years as bachelors in Chinatowns.[7]

The story of Japanese immigration, which began later, exhibits some distinctive features against a background of fundamental similarity. Unlike the Chinese, the Japanese entered agriculture and soon dominated the production of numerous California crops, such as berries. In 1907–1908, the administration of Theodore Roosevelt arrived at the so-called Gentlemen's Agreement with the government of Japan to limit further immigration, though the agreement allowed the entry of wives and hence the Japanese were able to maintain a family life denied to the Chinese. However, whites' perception of unwanted economic competition from a group they deemed racially inferior led to further restrictions, especially in California, whose legislature passed Alien Land Acts in 1913 and 1920 that aimed to deprive Japanese farmers of land ownership and limit their opportunities in agriculture.

All immigration from Asia (other than from the Philippines) was excluded by the restrictive legislation of the 1920s, and the Asians remaining on the U.S. mainland continued to suffer legal and social impediments—for example, through antimiscegenation laws and restrictions on the professions they could enter—through the middle of the twentieth century. The World War II internment of all of the Japanese on the West

Coast is rightly viewed as the most notorious illustration of Asians' severe racial disadvantages during this period. The internment made no distinction according to citizenship (equivalent to U.S. birth because of the racial provisions of naturalization law), not only depriving the Japanese of liberty but imposing irretrievable property losses on them. The decision of the U.S. government to round up an entire nonwhite group stands in sharp contrast to the decisions involved in the internment of limited numbers of Germans and Italians. While these latter decisions may also have been unjust in some cases and were made in a climate of suspicion fed by wartime anxieties about fifth columns, they were nevertheless based largely on the characteristics and behavior of individuals, rather than on group membership per se.

Yet the position of Asians has changed fundamentally in the intervening decades. The bar to the naturalization of Asian immigrants was finally lifted by legislation in the early 1950s, and Asian Americans were beneficiaries of the civil-rights legislation and court decisions of the 1960s. To give just one example, the 1967 Supreme Court decision in the marvelously named case Loving v. Virginia swept away the last of the antimiscegenation laws by vacating the conviction of a white man and a black woman for violating Virginia's law, and in the process contributed to the rise in Asian-white intermarriage rates. And the civil-rights emphasis during the 1960s on eliminating the last vestiges of legal distinctions in terms of race and national origin led to the fundamental revision of immigration law in 1965. By scrapping for good the national-origins quota system and the nearly absolute barriers to Asian immigration, the new law opened the United States to immigrants from anywhere in the world and made a large-scale inflow from Asia possible.[8]

Today, due partly to the subsequent immigration of many Asians with high levels of human capital, the educational and occupational status of Asians compares very favorably with that of white Americans, and their household incomes are substantially higher on average than those of whites. The socioeconomic advantage of Asians is not entirely due to immigration, however; and the Japanese, who have not received nearly as much immigrant inflow as the other Asian groups, are a suitable index of racial upgrading for the descendants of the Asian immigrants of the late nineteenth and early twentieth centuries. Their socioeconomic profile is as favorable as that of any group in the United States: according to the 2000 Census, for example, the median family income in households headed by Japanese Americans was, at $70,800, 40 percent higher than that for the nation as a whole.[9] The labor-market discrimination against the Japanese began to relent during the 1960s under the impact of civil-rights legislation, among other forces. Because the educational attainment of U.S.-born Japanese Americans had been consistently higher than that of whites since the early twentieth century, the second and third generations were poised to break through into the upper reaches of the labor market once the bar of discrimination was lowered.[10]

It is not necessary to enter into the debates over whether a glass ceiling limits the entry of Asian Americans into highly paid managerial jobs or whether Asian Americans can fully assimilate to see that race plays a far more modest role for them today than it once did.[11] The current substantial levels of intermarriage between Asian and white Americans are compelling evidence of the diminished salience of race—about half of young U.S.-born Asian Americans marry whites[12]—and again the Japanese case demonstrates this quite convincingly for the descendants of the immigrants of a century ago. Using 1990 Census data, Victor Nee and I found that, between two cohorts born in the United States four decades apart, the rate of Japanese-American intermarriage went from about 5 percent to nearly 70 percent.[13] Among the children born during the 1980s to Japanese-American parents, 63 percent had mixed ancestry, and typically the other ancestry was Euro-American of some variety; during the 1990s, the rate rose further to 68 percent. These percentages indicate quite literally the erosion of a racial boundary in that the clarity of the phenotypic differences on which it is based is being clouded by intermixing.

The expansion of the white population in the middle of the twentieth century—and indeed the view that whiteness trumps ethnic bases of division among Americans of European ancestry—offers another compelling instance of ethno-racial change. Many immigrant-origin groups that are now unquestionably included in the mainstream white population did not start out that way. In the late nineteenth and early twentieth centuries, Irish Catholics and southern and eastern European Catholics, Orthodox Christians, and Jews were initially viewed as both ethno-religious *and* racial outsiders by native white American Protestants and occupied an in-between position in U.S. labor and housing markets.[14] Religious and other ethnic distinctions were central to their social inferiority. These groups entered a society whose mainstream was resolutely defined in religious, as well as racial, terms: as Christian in the post-Reformation sense. Anti-Catholicism and anti-Semitism had been threaded through the fabric of American history since the earliest English colonists. The anti-Semitism faced by Jewish immigrants and their children in the United States is still remembered; the anti-Catholicism much less so.[15] But a New England primer from the late seventeenth century, which instructed pupils to "Abhor that arrant Whore of Rome,/ And all her blasphemies;/ And drink not of her cursed cup,/ Obey not her decrees," gives a taste of the antipathy that many Americans felt toward the Catholic Church.[16] From the early nineteenth century until the middle of the twentieth, anti-Catholicism was a major political, cultural, and intellectual force in American life, as white Protestant Americans feared that their society and its institutions would be submerged under the flood of Catholic immigrants, whose religion was held to be inimical to democracy. From the 1830s on, an anti-Catholic literature developed in the United States to which some distinguished Americans contributed—for instance, in 1835 the painter and inventor Samuel F. B. Morse published *Foreign Conspiracy against the Liberties of the United States* to denounce the dangers of Catholicism. During the twentieth century, anti-Catholicism contributed not only to the drive to restrict immigration but also to the resurrection of the Ku Klux Klan.[17]

There were also racial aspects to the "in-between" position of these groups. The derogatory language that was routinely applied to southern and eastern European immigrants and their families—for example, "hunkie" and "guinea"—betrayed their problematic racial situation; and the contrast to these slurs was often the racial norm, "white." As just one example, the historian David Roediger cites the case of an applicant for a blast-furnace job who was told, "only hunkies work those jobs, they're too damn dirty and too damn hot for a white man."[18] The color significance of these terms was nowhere better registered than in the "guinea" slur for Italians, which ultimately derives from the history of slavery, as it refers to the west African coast as well as to the black bondsmen and women who came from there.[19]

Scientific racism alleging the inherent inferiority of the immigrants provided a major rationale for the restrictive immigration legislation of the 1920s and its national-origin quotas. While that restriction was certainly not equivalent to the virtually complete exclusion of Asian immigrants in the Johnson-Reed Act of 1924, it was nevertheless severe. For instance, apart from the years of World War I, during the first two decades of the century, immigrants from Italy averaged nearly 200,000 per year, but the national-origin quotas imposed by the legislation, when fully implemented in 1929, limited annual entrants from Italy to less than 6,000—in other words, about 3 percent of the prior level of immigration.[20] The strategy behind the quotas was to set the immigration clock back to the time before the large-scale arrival of the southern and eastern Europeans at the turn of the twentieth century. To that end, the final quotas were based on estimates of the ethnic origins of the American people ("white" being taken for granted) in 1920. To develop the estimates, a demographic study was conducted under the aegis of the American Council of Learned Societies to establish the contribution of the different European nations to the white American mix at that date. The crucial question the study had to address concerned the national origins of white Americans in 1790![21]

The racial undesirability of the newest immigrants was presumed to have been established as scientific fact. One of the earliest applications of IQ testing was an attempt to demonstrate the intellectual inferiority of the southern and eastern European immigrants, and the hypothesis was believed to have been confirmed.[22] The widespread view of these immigrants among educated white Americans is conveyed in a 1914 essay on "American blood and immigrant blood" by one of the founding fathers of the new discipline of sociology, E. A. Ross.[23] Among other things, he wrote:

> It is fair to say that the blood now being injected into the veins of our people is "sub-common." . . . You are struck by the fact that from ten to twenty per cent are hirsute, low-browed, big-faced persons of obviously low mentality. Not that they suggest evil. They simply look out of place in black clothes and stiff collar, since clearly they belong in skins, in wattled huts at the close of the Great Ice Age. [Pp. 285–6]
>
> "The Slavs," remarks a physician, "are immune to certain kinds of dirt. They can stand what would kill a white man." [P. 291]
>
> The Northerners seem to surpass the southern Europeans in innate ethical endowment. Comparison of their behavior in marine disasters shows that discipline, sense of duty, presence of mind, and consideration for the weak are much more characteristics of northern Europeans . . . Among all nationalities the Americans bear the palm for coolness, orderly saving of life, and consideration for the weak in shipwreck, but they will lose these traits in proportion as they absorb excitable mercurial blood from southern Europe. [Pp. 295–6]

The last is, of course, all the more remarkable for having been published a few years after the *Titanic* disaster and without the merest whiff of irony.

Today these characterizations have an antiquated air that belies their meaningfulness into the middle of the twentieth century. An indirect indicator of their former durability is the youthful age of the scholarship that has demonstrated the erosion of the social and cultural differences that could sustain the stereotypes—the work dates to the 1980s. The children of the southern and eastern Europeans began to close the socio-economic gap with other white Americans with the cohort born in the 1925–1935 decade, which came to maturity after World War II. But it was really only with the postwar birth cohorts that the gap fully closed.[24] The assimilation the second and third generations underwent was expressed in a mobility that whittled away at the social foundations of ethnic distinctions—diminishing the cultural differences that serve to signal ethnic membership to others and to sustain ethnic solidarity; bringing about a rough parity of life chances to attain such socioeconomic goods as educational credentials and remunerative jobs, while loosening the attachment of ethnicity to specific economic niches; shifting residence away from central-city ethnic neighborhoods to ethnically mixed suburbs and urban neighborhoods; and fostering relatively easy social intercourse across ethnic lines. Not surprisingly, the rates of intermarriage involving these groups rose sharply in the postwar period to the point that intermarriage became the rule and endogamy the exception. Under conditions of socioeconomic parity and frequent boundary crossing, ethnicity itself took on a voluntary character and ethnic identity became an option, exercised only occasionally by many, rather than an inescapable categorization imposed from the outside.[25]

In this chapter and the next, I will focus the discussion of ethno-racial change on the Irish and the southern and eastern Europeans, because their cases offer a better fit in important respects to the contemporary circumstances of nonwhite groups than do the other twentieth-century instances of change. The European immigrant groups were much larger than the Asian ones because of the immigration restriction from which Asians suffered; size matters because it is related to the degree of threat perceived by the majority.[26] Moreover, the Asian second and subsequent generations exhibited exceptional educational attainment, while apart from eastern European Jews, the educational successes of the second generation of the European immigrant groups were quite modest. For some of them—the Italians, one of the largest of the groups, are noteworthy in this respect—problems at school, such as early dropout rates and delinquency, were widely noted at the time.[27] Consequently, in the second generation, a substantial portion of the new immigrant population was concentrated in the urban working class, and it was possible to envision some of these groups not rising much above that level in subsequent generations.[28] This social position lent itself to a perception of permanent inferiority vis-à-vis the white Protestant middle class. Even the differences in legal position, where the advantages of the European groups might initially seem to make them less useful as a prototype, have a contemporary relevance. For, while the social status of the new immigrant populations as white was in doubt, their legal claim to the rights of whites never was. Unlike the Asian immigrants, the European immigrants could naturalize, and this access to the voting booth gave them a significant degree of political influence and all that it brings, including a modicum of government jobs.[29] And unlike Asian and African Americans residing in many states, the members of the new European populations could marry other whites; although intermarriage by the new populations with whites of northern and western European ancestry may have been uncommon at first, it gradually increased.[30] Yet, in the end, this legal parity with the racial majority is an advantage for the analogy to the present because the legislation of the civil-rights era swept away the legal foundations for racial distinctions. In this respect, contemporary racial minorities operate in a world that more resembles that of the early twentieth-century European immigrant groups than that of the legally marginalized nonwhites of that period.[31]

The Telling Case of the Irish

Our perceptions of groups like the Irish have been altered profoundly as a consequence of ethno-racial shifts, as the forgotten iconography of Thomas Nast's caricatures of the Irish illustrates. Many native white Americans of the nineteenth century saw the Irish, as they did later the immigrants from southern and eastern Europe, as fundamentally different kinds of human beings. The onetime vitality of these social distinctions based on religion and ancestral place of origin in Europe has been lost to us, because the ethnic origins involved have been deprived of most of their role in everyday life and have become only occasionally visible; they are more and more muddled in any event by the extensive marriage across nationality and even religious lines among whites.

These shifts pose problems for the common conceptions of race and ethnicity, found not only in the scholarly literature but also in common discourse. According to these ideas, racial and ethnic groups are distinct types: racial groups derive from widespread perceptions of innate, ineradicable characteristics and are typically identifiable on the basis of phenotypic features, while ethnic groups arise from shared understandings about "ancestry," where this involves a perception of common origins or roots. Ethnic distinctions do generally appear to be mirrored in "objective" social and cultural features, such as occupational, language, and/or religious differences between members of an ethnic group and others, though the nature of these may change over time without necessarily eroding the distinctions.[32] This definition of a racial group in no way assumes that humanity can be meaningfully divided into "races" with distinctive biological endowments—that assumption is almost universally rejected by social scientists—but rather posits that people often act as if it can. According to a formulation that has become almost a social-science cliché, race is a "social construction," implying that it is indeed mutable, though its transformation into ethnicity is not usually assumed to be part of this mutability.[33]

The analytical distinction between racial and ethnic groups is bolstered by what is today called "race theory," which envisions the origin of racial distinctions in the waves of European colonization and exploitation of peoples around the globe that commenced with the voyages of discovery in the fifteenth century. Put simply, racism as worldview and ideology is seen as arising as a solution to a moral dilemma, for the domination and exploitation of others could be morally justified if they could be viewed as inferiors.[34] Prior to European colonization, race theory argues, the conquest and enslavement of one people by another lacked the essential ingredient of racism, an ideology of ineradicable differences between human groups that justified the subjugation of one by another. A specifically Western development, the Enlightenment, may have contributed to racism. The Enlightenment's radical challenge to established social hierarchies such as that between noble and commoner made the problem of justifying the exploitation of others more acute, necessitating more elaborate rationales. For instance, the manifest contradiction between slavery and the view that "all men are created equal" and "are endowed by their Creator with certain unalienable rights," enshrined in the U.S. Declaration of Independence, spurred southern slaveholders and their ideologues to formulate complex arguments rooted in biology, the Bible, and philosophy to justify the system from which they benefited.

Race theory holds that the racism of prior centuries has given rise to racial distinctions that have enormous staying power and are qualitatively different from ethnic differences. However, the theory's exponents have generally failed to acknowledge similar dynamics in operation in the past among any groups that are viewed today as white.[35] The English subjugation of Ireland, a process that took centuries and that was accomplished with brutality, especially once the conflict took on the color of a religious war, is a particularly striking case. Starting in the seventeenth century, the efforts to dispossess the Irish of their lands and settle English and Scots colonists in their place accelerated. The Cromwellian conquest in the middle of the century was accomplished with the wholesale slaughter of the defeated garrisons and populations of some towns, most infamously at Drogheda, and the shipment of prisoners of war to other English colonies as bond-labor; other Catholics were encouraged to migrate elsewhere in Europe or to North America. At the end of the century, Catholic resistance finally collapsed, and the victorious Protestants imposed the so-called penal laws in order to secure their dominance. These laws treated the Catholics as a legally inferior population in most aspects of civil and religious life and thus divided the country into two populations with distinct regimes of rights—for example, Catholics could not carry arms and could neither vote nor serve in Parliament nor at the bar; nor could they own horses worth more than £5. Intermarriage was strongly discouraged by the penalties imposed on the Protestant partner. By the beginning of the eighteenth century, Catholics, who had owned most of the land a century before, had been largely dispossessed; they owned only 14 percent of the land in 1703, and their share fell to 5 percent by 1776.[36] The stage was thus set for the Famine of the mid-nineteenth century, which was made possible by the tiny amounts of land most Irish families were restricted to and their resulting dependence on the potato as their primary source of calories.

Though the distinctions involved in English dominance over the Irish may seem from today's perspective to be essentially ethnic, because they primarily involved religion and language, the colonization of Ireland was accompanied by a conceptualization of the Irish as racial inferiors, a characterization that took on the veneer of science during the Victorian period.[37] In the mid-nineteenth century, visual depictions of the Irish as subhuman or racially equivalent to Africans were common, as the cartoon in Figure 2.1, which comes from *Punch* and depicts a brutish Irish partisan as one in a row of threatening colonials. This caricature is no different in its principal iconic features from the drawings of the cartoonists across the Atlantic. The English view of the Irish throughout the nineteenth century, at a time when Irish Catholics formed a major portion of the immigrant stream arriving in the United States, was little different from their view of other subject peoples in the Empire: the Irish were held to be childlike, if somewhat violent, wards incapable of governing themselves. Victorian-era scholarship contributed its measure to this racism. Anthropologists and ethnologists set about laying an empirical basis, in cephalic measurements, for example, for a scientifically founded belief in the racial distinctiveness of the Celt: they dubiously located this distinctiveness in such features as a prognathous, or projecting, jaw. Historians charted the histories of the different "races" found in

TIME'S WAXWORKS.

(1881 *JUST ADDED TO THE COLLECTION.*)

Mr. P. "HA! YOU'LL HAVE TO PUT HIM INTO THE CHAMBER OF HORRORS!"

Figure 2.1. A simian Paddy joins the line-up of colonial representations. (*Punch,* December 31, 1881.)

the British Isles, counterpoising the democratic virtues of the Saxon ancestors of the English against the distinctly lesser qualities of Celts.[38] The scholarly view of the Irish could be quite demeaning, especially when expressed in private. For instance, one of the best-known Cambridge historians of the late nineteenth century, Charles Kingsley, wrote to his wife while on a visit to Ireland in 1860:

> But I am haunted by the human chimpanzees I saw along that hundred miles of horrible country. I don't believe they are our fault. I believe there are not only many more of them than of old, but that they

are happier, better, more comfortably fed and lodged under our rule than they ever were. But to see white chimpanzees is dreadful; if they were black, one would not feel it so much, but their skins, except where tanned by exposure, are as white as ours.[39]

The comparison of the Irish to Africans, especially to Hottentots, then held to be one of the lowest branches on the human tree, was common to the racialist literature of Victorian England.[40]

The similarities between the iconography of the Irish in late nineteenth-century America and that prevailing in Victorian England are no accident. The racist depictions of the Irish as an inferior type of human spread easily from one side of the Atlantic to another, facilitated by the orientation of many well-born Americans of Protestant British ancestry toward England for intellectual and cultural inspiration. Common adjectives applied to the Irish in mid-nineteenth-century America were "*low-browed* and *savage, groveling* and *bestial, lazy* and *wild, simian* and *sensual,*" which were also frequently used with reference to blacks; it was common also to hear the Irish described as "niggers turned inside out."[41] This convergence has led one historian of "Anglo-Saxonism" to remark on the nearly simultaneous emergence in both countries of its racist doctrines, especially in "the period from the mid-1860's to the mid-1890's."[42] Yet today this iconography has been largely lost (save for the affectionately styled mascot of the University of Notre Dame), as has the racist view of the Irish that lay behind it.

Additional Complexities of Race and Ethnicity

The mutability of racial position exhibited by the Irish in the United States—that is, that a group perceived as racially different at one point in time can mutate into an ethnic group—indicates a need to rethink aspects of the standard conceptions of race and ethnicity.[43] The earlier-cited standard definitions of these concepts highlight identifiability as the key to any system of racial and ethnic distinctions and inequalities:

the group membership of an individual has to be detectable to others, so that they know what attitude to take, what behavior to exhibit, toward him or her. The identifiability of racial and ethnic groups is commonly thought to differ, in lay discourse as well as in social science, in that racial membership is immediately visible, even for individuals encountered in passing, whereas ethnic membership must usually be detected, often by questioning about names and social origins, and hence is typically known only for those close enough to be acquaintances.[44]

Among the problems with the neatness of this division between two types of groups is that racial groups obviously possess social and cultural characteristics that under some circumstances may help others to identify their members ("black English," which can identify African Americans speaking on the telephone),[45] while members of ethnic groups can have physical features that betray or confirm their group affiliations (for example, Italian olive skin, Jewish noses). Hispanics, about whose position in this scheme the scholarly literature is divided, epitomize this problem. On the basis of the standard social-science definitions, they are most rigorously treated as an ethnic population, identified by family origins in the countries of Latin America and/or a family heritage of speaking Spanish. Underscoring the ethnic character of the Hispanic population is its diversity with respect to racial characteristics, for it includes individuals with European appearances no different from those found in the white mainstream. Nevertheless, many, probably most, of its members are distinguishable from white Americans by their darker skin color, body type, and indigenous or African facial features, and therefore in a statistical sense Hispanics can be viewed as a group that is racially distinctive.[46] (About half of Hispanics self-identify as "white" on the U.S. Census; how many of them would be viewed as "white" by other Americans is not known.)

But equally important, our common conceptions have connotations that do not necessarily correlate well with one another when we widen our focus from their application to present-day American society. For example, there is the common view that, according to our contemporary understanding of the American experience, ethnic distinctions, unlike racial ones, do not give rise to rigid systems of stratification. The case of the Catholic/Protestant cleavage in Northern Ireland is a convincing counterexample, since there is no racial aspect to this deep division through the middle of a society. Because of the general cultural and physical similarity between the members of the two groups, individuals casually encountering one another at a neutral site might find it difficult to visually "read" each other's communal membership. Nevertheless, the distinction can be maintained because of rigid social segregation. The groups live mostly in separate neighborhoods, attend different schools, and belong to different sports clubs and other associations. Assimilation from one side to the other is rare, as is indicated by a very low intermarriage rate.[47]

We also tend to think of nonwhite race as involving imposed status—for example, Americans of African descent cannot fully escape the disadvantages of being black unless they are fortunate enough to be able to pass as white—while ethnicity generally entails a voluntary attachment to a group, since ethnics have the option of full assimilation. Yet the history of European anti-Semitism shows that members of a group who, from the standpoint of the standard definitions, form an ethnic group can also suffer from disabilities imposed on them by others. To be sure, at many times and in many places, Jews could convert to Christianity and perhaps escape persecution, but conversion was a radical step that detached an individual or family from a community and, in any event, was often suspect in the eyes of Christians.

The standard definitions of race and ethnicity have their value, especially when it comes to analyzing the realities of racial inequality in present-day American society. However, we need to recognize that multiple dimensions are implicated in the distinction between these concepts, regardless of how we define them; and these dimensions correlate imperfectly with each other across space and time. Hence, for the purposes of the discussion here, which will focus on the potential mutability of race-like distinctions, race and ethnicity may be better viewed as poles in a multidimensional space. For that reason I will often refer to them with a single encompassing term: ethno-racial.[48] Most African Americans are located at the racial pole since they are readily identifiable solely on the basis of skin color. Many individuals, however, including some African Americans and members of other groups, are located in the middle of the space, where identifiability depends on a bundled mix of characteristics, social and cultural as well as physical: accents, dress, names, residential locations, and schools attended can all play a part in everyday identification of where people "belong." The characteristics that typically go into the bundle can change over time, as can the way they are seen: the Irish were no doubt readily identifiable to native white Protestants during the nineteenth century, and this distinctiveness contributed to the view that they were intrinsically different; but Irish ancestry tends to be encountered among Americans today in complex ethnic mixes that obscure facile distinctions. Intermarriage, it need hardly be said, can loosen the connection between phenotypic characteristics and group membership in the next generation.[49]

Reframing the Question in Terms of Social Boundaries

In considering how ethno-racial distinctions that were prominent during the first half of the twentieth century between the then visible immigrant populations and native whites could have virtually disappeared by the century's end, we gain perspective from the elevation afforded by abstraction. Especially helpful is the concept of a social boundary, by which I mean a social distinction that individuals make in their everyday lives and that shapes their actions and mental orientations toward others.[50] Such a distinction is typically embedded in a variety of social and cultural differences between groups that give a boundary concrete significance (so that those on one side think of those on the other, "they are not like us because . . ."). Ethno-racial boundaries usually (but not inevitably) have a hierarchical character: one side holds superior status and has greater access to the social and economic resources that matter for life chances and for social life in general. In this case, it is typical for those on the superior side to justify their position in moral terms: the others are lacking in the characteristics that would make them either successful or deserving.[51]

The mechanisms that generate and maintain hierarchically ordered boundaries are multiple.[52] However, for our purposes we can view them in terms of three broad types. There are those that create and preserve differential access to resources—generating, for example, inequalities between groups in the levels and qualities of schooling. When for instance during the 1920s Jews started to be competitive in large numbers for places in elite Ivy League colleges, these institutions imposed admissions policies, including outright quotas, to restrict their entry and preserve the character of these schools as a training ground for the Protestant elite. There are, in addition, mechanisms that promote social distance between groups, in the form of residential segregation, for example. When groups that are separated by a social boundary have little contact with one another, it is easy for each side to believe stereotypes about the other and to practice discrimination. At Princeton in the era of restrictive admissions, Jews were not admitted to the eating clubs that were at the core of the college's social life, because they were the places where permanent bonds were being formed among Gentile young men.[53] Finally, there are the ideological or symbolic mechanisms by which superior groups justify their position, both to themselves and, if they can, to others. In the era of restrictive admissions, the elite white Protestants who saw the Ivy League schools as critical sites for transmitting privilege to their children scorned academically talented Jewish youngsters in moral terms, as selfish "grade grubbers."

As is often the case with ethno-racial boundaries, the immigrant–native boundaries of the early twentieth century mixed racial and ethnic elements—that is, the sense of difference felt by natives was linked both to characteristics of the new groups that were widely perceived to be inherent and "natural" in origin and to those that could be considered more malleable. But questions immediately arise: Were not these distinctions built principally on characteristics that were, in fact, malleable, whatever the native whites of the time may have believed? How difficult would it have been for the children and grandchildren of the denigrated European immigrants—namely, the Irish and the southern and eastern Europeans—to cross the boundary that separated them from the white mainstream of the early twentieth century? If we assume that the phenotypic differences between them and native whites were ultimately small—and this assumption holds for the majority of cases but not for all (for example, those southern Italians with dark skin tones)—then would not boundary crossing have been simply a matter of name changing? In fact, there was a great deal of name changing in the immigrant and second generations in order to fit more easily into the native white social and business worlds, and more than a little cosmetic surgery to dispose of "ethnic" facial features.[54] But other changes would have been required as well, not least in religion. Religion was an important communal demarcation between the new immigrant populations, who were Catholic, Orthodox Christian, and Jewish, and native whites, who were overwhelmingly Protestant. At a time when the United States defined itself as a Christian nation in the post-Reformation sense, the religious distinctions were critical to the palimpsest of social distinctions and differences from which the new immigrant/native white divide was constructed. There can be little doubt that the antipathy felt by native whites toward the new immigrants was anchored to a considerable extent in anti-Semitism and anti-Catholicism. The doubts felt by many Protestant whites about Catholics and Jews survived the end of mass immigration in the 1920s. The widespread belief, for example, that Catholics were unsuited to a democratic order because of their subservience to ecclesiastical authority lingered into the second half of the century and was believed by many well-educated Protestant whites; this view was underscored by Paul Blanshard's best-selling book, *American Freedom and Catholic Power*, which appeared in 1949, and it played a notorious role in John F. Kennedy's 1960 campaign for the presidency.[55]

Boundary crossing was certainly possible, but it was also risky. That is, one could throw oneself into the personal transformations seemingly required for acceptance by the white Protestant majority without gaining it; and, since those transformations not only signaled a rejection of one's origins but in some sense demanded it, they carried the risk of the loss of attachments to family, friends, and community. While success beyond that attainable on the ethnic side of the boundary was possible, so was a double loss. This sort of boundary, involving a distinction that is widely noted and associated with inequality in life chances, I have elsewhere called "bright." It is typical of bright-boundary situations that crossing from the disadvantaged side to the advantaged one involves a risk-laden personal transformation, a process akin to a conversion. Not everyone is willing to chance it. The counterpoint is a boundary that is "blurred" in the sense that, for some set of individuals (generally members of the ethnic minority), location with respect to the boundary is indeterminate or ambiguous. Under these circumstances, assimilation to the mainstream may be eased insofar as the individuals undergoing it do not sense a rupture between participation in mainstream institutions and familiar social and cultural practices and identities; and they do not feel forced to choose between the mainstream and their group of origin.[56]

Philip Roth's novel *The Plot against America* is instructive about the experiential qualities of a world governed by bright boundaries. That Roth gives the family at the center of the story the identity of his own family and places himself as a main protagonist reveals the autobiographical intent behind the blatantly fictional plot—the reader is to understand that some qualities of the experiences portrayed are the novelist's, the way he remembers things. The story is set in 1940, and the Roth family of that era lives its intimate social life in an almost hermetically sealed Jewish world of relatives and friends who share the same ethnicity and religion. Relations with Gentiles do occur, but they are strongly colored by their boundary-spanning character, and the Roths are always aware of their own vulnerability in a Christian-dominated society. Indeed, the entire social world is viewed by the family in terms of a Jewish/Christian division. The one character who denies the dangerous power of these boundaries and mixes freely in the Christian world, Rabbi Bengelsdorf, is shown in the end to have been a fool.[57]

That the bright boundary between native white Protestants and new immigrant groups continued to operate for the second generation in this period is demonstrated by Irvin Child's well-known study of the Italian-American second generation in New Haven during the late 1930s. Child depicted its members as hemmed in by a psychological double bind: if they attempted to assimilate, they risked being rebuffed by the WASP majority while undermining or losing their ties to co-ethnics because of apparent disloyalty; if they chose loyalty to the Italian group instead, they largely gave up on the chance to improve more than marginally their social and material situation. Child found many of them to be "apathetic"—his term—unable to choose between these two risky options. As one of his respondents plaintively expressed the dilemma:

> Then a lot of times in the show you see Mussolini on the screen and they all start to razz him. Then I feel, "How the hell do I stand?"[58]

Yet, during the second half of the twentieth century, it became apparent that the position of these once-despised groups had shifted fundamentally. In contemporary parlance, they had been fully incorporated as whites. Without question, they caught up over time to other whites in terms of socioeconomic position and integrated with them in suburbs and through intermarriage.[59] This parity was brought about not so much by frequent boundary crossing as it was by a dimming of the once-bright boundaries, which faded in their significance for the life chances of the members of the new immigrant populations and for the quality of their everyday lives. Distinctions based on ethnicity and religion ceased to be as all-important as they had been. It is this remarkable shift in a short period of time that gives the white-ethnic groups a potentially paradigmatic status for the contemporary era.

The Difficulties of Explanation

We do not yet have a satisfactory account of how this boundary dimming occurred. Assimilation processes have been and remain profoundly important in the United States. But assimilation theory, at least in its canonical, most widely known form, is not adequate as an explanation. The canonical account, best expressed in Milton Gordon's classic book from the 1960s, *Assimilation in American Life,* envisions assimilation as an individualistic process, whose major stages are governed by generational position with respect to immigration and by socioeconomic mobility. Assimilation thus appears to be a constant ongoing process that accelerates with each generational transition, from the first or immigrant generation to the second and from the second to the third.[60]

There is considerable truth in the canonical approach: certainly, the white ethnics displayed a generational march in the direction of assimilation. But the approach fails us when it comes to two salient features of the mid-twentieth-century incorporation of the white ethnics into the American mainstream: first, the rapidity and scale of mass assimilation; and, second, the receding of ethno-religious boundaries among whites. The gradualism and ahistorical character of the canonical approach cannot explain how white-ethnic assimilation occurred on a mass scale in a few decades following World War II, nor can it address how it swept up two groups, the Irish and Italians, that differed so greatly in their main periods of arrival as well as in their general acceptability to other white Americans at that point. Since large-scale Irish immigration began in the middle of the nineteenth century and its equivalent for the Italians came a half century later, the Irish should, by the logic of the theory, have assimilated considerably ahead of the Italians. To be sure, by the middle of the twentieth century, the Irish were positioned ahead of their Mediterranean co-religionists—they were more likely to have college credentials and professional educations and they occupied positions of significant political power (including those within the Catholic Church)—but they were still a very distinct ethnic group and segregated in largely Catholic social and even professional worlds.

The receding of ethnic and religious distinctions that had previously been prominent on the social landscape is even more of a puzzle for canonical assimilation theory. Because the theory is formulated in terms of individual assimilation, it implies that assimilatory change is largely one-directional: that is, the individuals who are assimilating refashion themselves to fit into the mainstream, discarding most aspects of their ethnic culture and replacing them with their mainstream equivalents.[61] Thus conceived, assimilation appears to be a form of boundary crossing—individuals move from one side of the boundary to the other through a process that can be likened to conversion—and it is unclear what significance assimilation of this sort has for the qualities of the boundary itself. Without question, assimilation does often occur as boundary crossing, and during the first half of the twentieth century, one could reasonably claim that assimilation generally had this character, as many ethnic individuals changed their names, for example, in order to improve their fit to the requirements of mainstream jobs. However, as the mass assimilation of the postwar period unfolded, it became less and less necessary for assimilating individuals to make such drastic changes. Hyphenated identities, which had been scorned in the early twentieth century (Presidents Theodore Roosevelt and Woodrow Wilson famously thundered against "hyphenated Americanism"), came into vogue, and many ethnics perceived no contradiction between, say, keeping ethnic names and some ethnic practices and operating within the mainstream. As Matthew Frye Jacobson has observed, "Ellis Island" identities replaced "Plymouth Rock" ones, as the ideal of Anglo-Conformity was dethroned and the mainstream opened up.[62] Hollywood serves as a suitable indicator: if a previous generation of stars felt compelled to change their names in order to wipe away any traces of their ethnic origins (as when Margarita Cansino became Rita Hayworth and Emanuel Goldenberg became Edward G. Robinson), the stars of a new generation, who may have changed their names for aesthetic reasons, boldly broadcast their ethnicity—consider Robert De Niro, Al Pacino, and Barbra Streisand—and drew strength from the "authenticity" of ethnic roots. These developments are a signal that boundaries were blurring and, consequently, assimilating individuals did not feel intensely pressured to choose between the mainstream and ethnic identities (at least, certain socially acceptable and largely symbolic aspects of them).[63] It is this boundary blurring that allowed ethnic and religious boundaries to fade into the background, because, as more and more individuals with visible ethnic and religious identities pressed into the mainstream, the significance of the boundaries as social dividing lines came more and more into question.

Another widely accepted explanatory framework has been developed in recent decades by historians working under the rubric of "whiteness." This historical narrative is ultimately rather straightforward and quite satisfying in some respects: some of the European immigrant groups, it begins, were not accepted as fully white when they arrived in the United States.[64] Their problematic position in the black-white racial order was compounded by their initially humble position in labor-market and social terms: the work they did at first was not seen as fitting for whites, and they lived next to and intermingled with African Americans. The challenge they faced was to gain acceptance as members of the dominant race. This they did partly through their own efforts, as they struggled upward by putting distance between themselves and blacks. The Irish, for instance, are often cited for the development of an intense hostility toward African Americans, which climaxed violently in the New York Draft Riots of 1863, when mobs that included many Irish immigrants attacked blacks. On a more day-to-day basis, the Irish often refused to work alongside blacks, leading to the exclusion of African-American workers from some occupations in northern cities.

But the European immigrant groups were also greatly helped by their legal position, for they were legally "white," a status that gave them a variety of rights and privileges that were denied to nonwhites. The European immigrants could become American citizens and thus gain access to the ballot box. They were in fact courted for their votes by politicians in northern cities and thereby gained tangible benefits in terms of municipal jobs and contracts along with electoral and appointed positions. And because they were not subject to antimiscegenation laws, they could achieve a social integration that flowed from their being candidates for marriage with other whites.[65]

Considerable weight is also placed in this narrative on the racially differentiated consequences of New and Fair Deal policies, as entailed in the legislation and implementation of such innovations as the Federal Housing Authority, the Social Security Act, and the GI Bill, which in their totality gave advantages to ethnic whites in a variety of domains that were withheld from the great majority of African Americans. The original Social Security Act had pernicious consequences for racial division because its pension provisions left out agricultural and domestic service, where many blacks but few whites labored.[66] And New Deal housing policy was intended to restart the housing industry during the Depression but ultimately contributed to the growth of racial disparity. Most important, the policies of the Federal Housing Authority, by guaranteeing mortgages, enabled an expansion of homeownership among whites, including the ethnic whites, and contributed after the war to the exodus of many ethnics from their urban neighborhoods and their participation in the Euro-American mixing that took place in the newly developing suburbs. At the same time, by redlining areas occupied by African Americans or under threat of undergoing a racial shift from white to black, these policies not only failed to challenge residential segregation but reinforced it. Ultimately, they have been shown to have contributed mightily to the inequalities between whites and blacks because of the large role played by homeownership in the wealth accumulation of many whites.[67]

The political scientist Ira Katznelson has recently characterized the relevant laws and policies as "affirmative action" for whites, and these measures certainly benefited ethnic whites, such as Italians, who were given the same privileges as whites of northern European backgrounds.[68] This statement applies, for instance, to the GI Bill as a form of covert affirmative action for whites. The GI Bill assisted millions of working-class men to gain college educations and enter the middle-class world of work. But, in the main, these were white Americans, who traced their ancestry to somewhere in Europe. To begin with, black men did not have the same opportunity as white men to serve in the military (and, if they did, they served in segregated units, which were often assigned low-status tasks); and many had not graduated from high school. Even when they could legitimately aspire to a college education, black veterans were generally confined to black colleges, which had relatively few places compared with the nonblack sector of higher education, which expanded rapidly to accommodate the white veterans coming back to school. The accumulation of these advantages meant, according to Katznelson, that "the gap in educational attainment between blacks and whites widened rather than closed. Of veterans born between 1923 and 1928, 28 percent of whites but only 12 percent of blacks enrolled in college-level programs. Furthermore, blacks spent fewer months than whites in GI Bill schooling."[69] Among the other measures taken to integrate veterans, the program of Veterans Administration mortgages had a similarly disproportionate racial impact.

Viewed in its totality, the whiteness account has provided a convincing set of answers to one of two fundamental questions about how white ethnics moved from their humble station as quasi-racial outsiders to the position of insiders in a white American mainstream. The literature settles the question of how the southern and eastern European groups, along with Irish Catholics, who initially seemed scarcely more advantaged than blacks in U.S. cities, moved decisively ahead of them.[70] The skids were apparently greased on the ethnics' behalf—by citizenship and antimiscegenation laws and by federal policies, which for instance helped their residential mobility and integration but not that of African Americans. And white ethnics themselves made strenuous efforts to separate themselves from nonwhites, especially African Americans; these efforts may have made the situation of African Americans worse and certainly contributed to blocking any possibility of substantial African-American advance in northern cities, at least through the middle of the twentieth century.

Where the analyses are less satisfactory, however, is on a second question: how were the white ethnics able to attain parity and integration with native white Protestants, the defining core of the American mainstream a century ago? Why, in other words, did the United States evolve by the second half of the twentieth century toward a two-group division, white versus nonwhite (and, in most places, black), rather than a three-tier one, with the white ethnics remaining in between? Legal equality, we know, is compatible with social inequality, so the legal and institutional explanations of the whiteness literature are insufficient to answer this question. An incident during the presidency of Franklin Roosevelt, who took the first steps to bring numbers of white ethnics, at least the Jews and the Irish Catholics among them, into high-level governmental posts, drives home the point that the citizenship of the ethnics could easily have remained second-class. At a 1942 lunch, Roosevelt declared to Leo Crowley, an Irish Catholic New Deal official, "Leo, you know this is a Protestant country, and the Catholics and Jews are here under sufferance. It is up to you to go along with anything I want."[71]

The point of the second question is to challenge the facile, common explanation of white-ethnic assimilation—namely, that they were, in the end, white. Yes, they were, but the explanation presumes a social world that only came about *because of* the assimilation of groups such as Irish and Italian Catholics and eastern European Jews, a world in which race so overshadowed the ethnic differences based on national origin and religion that they were rendered scarcely visible. How such a dramatic decline in the visibility of what had been powerful social distinctions can occur is *the* critical question about ethno-racial boundary change, because it highlights the processes by which a hierarchically ordered boundary, one that seals off the privileges of a core group, loses its salience and its power to exclude.

3

Solving the Puzzle: A New Theory of Boundary Change

American society could have developed quite differently in the twentieth century. If we could look toward the second half of the century from the perspective of 1950, we might well predict a more complex ethno-racial stratification, especially in the urban North, than was found by century's end. Instead of race as the paramount distinction, with the binary between whites and nonwhites looming over the social landscape and casting other ethno-racial distinctions into deep shadow, a three-strata system might have emerged, with ethnic and religious distinctions among whites remaining salient and corresponding with prominent social differences. In this counterfactual scenario, the Catholic groups that, in the immigrant generation, occupied en masse the lower rungs of the labor market would have populated an intermediate stratum, situated between Protestant whites above, or at least the middle and more elite classes among them, and nonwhites below. The place of Jews is more uncertain in this scenario, because by mid-century they were already pressing into the professions in large numbers; however, one could expect them to have faced continued exclusion from the social milieus of elite white Protestants.

In fact, the sociological literature of the mid-twentieth century frequently portrayed some of the Catholic ethnic groups, the Italians above all, as constituting such an intermediate stratum, as not just concentrated in the working class but unlikely to rise above it. This depiction reflected the socioeconomic realities of the time. But in explaining them, the studies detected cultural differences between Catholics and others that seemed fateful and certainly could have served to differentiate them within institutions such as schools. One of the best known of numerous studies was published by Bernard Rosen in the *American Sociological Review*.[1] Rosen noted that "ethnic groups with Roman Catholic affiliation have moved up less rapidly than non-Catholic groups," but his explanation had ultimately more to do with the secular aspects of origins. Crucial, according to his argument, is whether the ingredients of an "achievement syndrome," including an activist stance toward the world, individualism, and future orientation, are inculcated by a group's cultural heritage. Analyzing survey and social-psychological data that indicated that Americans of Italian and French-Canadian origins trailed the other white groups in his sample in these respects, Rosen pointed to the formative influence of "Old World" experiences of each group: the members of the Catholic groups "came from agrarian societies or regions in which opportunities for achievement were strictly curtailed by the social structure and where habits of resignation and fatalism . . . were psychologically functional."[2] This interpretation was echoed in the findings of other sociologists and social psychologists, for example, Fred Strodtbeck's identification of attitudes nurtured in family interaction as the source of Jewish–Italian American differences in social mobility. Herbert Gans's famous study of the Italian Americans of Boston's West End, *The Urban Villagers,* also portrayed the Italians as seemingly locked into a working-class situation, though his interpretation placed less weight on cultural causes and more on the similarity between their class positions in southern Italian villages and in American cities.[3]

Rosen's analysis was inspired by the work of Harvard psychologist

David McClelland, who formulated the achievement-syndrome concept and developed tests to measure it. McClelland traced its roots to child-rearing practices and found broad differences between Protestant and Catholic families in this respect. Protestant families encouraged more independence, and Protestant children exhibited more of the desirable achievement syndrome as a result. McClelland blamed the Catholic deficit on "the view toward authority and control which is consciously promoted by the church, [which] has had what is probably an unintended consequence on the child-rearing practices of Catholic parents."[4] In other words, Catholic parents were too respectful of authority, and they hemmed in the autonomy of their children in order to teach them to respect it, too. Catholicism was also indicted in one of the best-known mid-century sociological studies of religion in America, *The Religious Factor*, by Gerhard Lenski, published in 1961. Discussing the apparent underrepresentation of Catholics in scientific careers, Lenski pointed to the "basic intellectual orientation which Catholicism develops: an orientation which values obedience over intellectual autonomy."[5]

The view that the Catholic ethnics were somehow different did not disappear, as one might think, in the early 1960s after the election of John F. Kennedy to the presidency. During the turmoil in urban America associated with the civil-rights challenges in northern cities of the 1960s, arose another image of the ethnics as an intermediate stratum, an image that had wide resonance as an understanding of the urban resistance to African-American advance (and to anti–Vietnam War sentiment). A spate of books on the "white-ethnic" problem appeared in the 1970s and typically equated "white ethnic" with "working class" and with "Catholic." A few, such as Michael Novak's *The Rise of the Unmeltable Ethnics*, presented a positive story about the survival of gritty ethnicity; but most, even when sympathetic to the plight of working-class ethnics, portrayed them as traditionalists mired in a class and ethnic milieu and standing in the way of change and thus, implicitly, of social progress.[6] These works assumed that the white ethnics, because of their lack of mobility, were the whites who were left behind in many nonsouthern cities as other whites moved to the suburbs; consequently, they were the buffer—quite literally, in spatial as well as in social terms—between poor blacks and other minorities concentrated in the inner city and middle-class whites settled in suburbia. Because of their adamant refusal to share their neighborhoods with minorities, the white ethnics constituted the new face of racism.[7]

This view of the white ethnics, a term that, it should be remembered, covered the southern and eastern Europeans, along with the Catholic Irish, points toward an alternative pathway along which American society, at least in the formerly industrial cities of the Northeast and Midwest, could have developed, but did not. Current explanations of white-ethnic assimilation, such as those found in the whiteness literature, fail to address why this pathway was not taken, why groups that were once disparaged not just in racial terms but also in ethnic and religious ones were ultimately assimilated fully into the mainstream. In a sense, the whiteness strand of explanation has a teleological character: it assumes that a social world like that of the United States in the late twentieth century, where race overwhelms other ethno-racial distinctions, was already operational when the immigrant ancestors of the white ethnics were arriving. In such a world, it appears that the essential question about the immigrants and their children was which side of the racial dividing line they would ultimately fall on. However, the weakness of other ethno-racial distinctions at the end of the twentieth century came about because of the mass assimilation of the white ethnics and cannot help in explaining it.

Prior to the late twentieth century, great weight was placed on ethno-religious distinctions that now have been absorbed into the American mainstream. (The hyphenated term is appropriate to the mid-twentieth-century fusion of the dimensions involved.) These distinctions could well have led to an enduring social cleavage. As late as 1960, most Catholic children received some or all of their education in a separate parochial system (which had been erected to protect them from the Protestant influences of the state-supported system in the middle of the nineteenth century). This was especially true in those parts of the United States where the European immigrants had settled in large numbers. The school records of many Catholics thus identified them, and their separation from non-Catholic children during the school day created a social distance from others, since the schools children attended integrated them in different play groups, sports teams, and other extracurricular activities. The political scientist Robert Putnam observes that, in his Ohio hometown during the 1950s, everyone knew who was Catholic and who was Protestant, especially since the Catholic children attended parochial schools; this was a major divide when it came to friendship, dating, and marriage.[8] Jews, to be sure, were equally identifiable in mid-twentieth-century America as a result of such features as names and social networks and were excluded from many Protestant-dominated social settings, such as resorts and country clubs.

Any doubt that ethno-religious distinctions could have served as the foundation for a social cleavage in post–World War II America dissolves with a look at Europe today, where the divide between Muslim immigrants and their children, on the one hand, and Christian and secular Europeans, on the other, is gaping and shows no signs of closure in the near future. This cleavage has tangible ramifications for the socioeconomic placement of the generations raised in Europe, for the children of North Africans and Turks are on average well behind their western European peers in educational credentials and labor-market position. The analogy of Europe today to the United States during the first half of the twentieth century is all the more intriguing because the stereotypes about Muslims held by Europeans—for example, that they allow religion to intrude into domains where it does not belong—are similar to the ones applied in the past to Catholic immigrants by American Protestants.[9] And those who are skeptical of the viability of a three-tier social system need only look at Latin-American societies, where it is common to find such a system, with individuals of European ancestry at the top, those of indigenous or African descent at the bottom, and a middle stratum where most persons of racially mixed ancestry *(mestizos)* are located; the racial order of Brazil is an example. That a group of European origin can constitute the middle layer is demonstrated by the Portuguese in Hawaii. When Portuguese laborers immigrated to Hawaii in the late nineteenth and early twentieth centuries, they were not accepted as members of the dominant white, or *Haole,* population, even though they were officially classified as Caucasians. Unlike the cases of the southern and eastern Europeans on the mainland, the social disadvantages stemming from this original exclusion have lingered, resulting in demonstrable inequalities.[10]

Because social boundaries other than racial ones were widely available and charged with hierarchical meaning, one has to ask why native white Protestants did not draw on them to exclude the newer groups from entry into the social settings where the native group was dominant. Such a system would not have meant an end to all assimilation, as long as it took the form of one-way conversion to Anglo-American cultural and social forms by modest numbers of individuals.

A long-standing, plausible hypothesis is that the initiation of contacts between socially disparate groups leads to competition and the reinforcement of social boundaries to keep the members of the lower-standing group in their place.[11] This hypothesis is bolstered by recent research in social psychology. One strand in modern social psychology, social identity theory, demonstrates the investment that humans have in group identities. Such identities generally function in terms of contrasts to other groups, as individuals seek to distinguish themselves from others. For members of high-status, more powerful social groups, contrasts to other groups can easily invoke stereotypes affirming the value of their own groups and denigrating others. A group identity becomes active, or salient, when it is seen as relevant to a situation, and the salience of a higher-status group identity is very likely to rise sharply in a context where other groups appear to be moving upward and entering settings from which they have previously been absent. In this vein, research in organizations shows that members of higher-status work groups commonly resist, and members of lower-status ones generally welcome, mergers of the two. Resistance to mergers stiffens when the division of social resources may be altered, when members of higher-status groups have reason to fear giving something up to the newcomers. This idea is strongly supported by the central findings from another major strand of social psychology, realistic group conflict theory, which has provided the intellectual foundation for research since famous experiments conducted in the 1950s by Muzafer and Carolyn Sherif showed the ease with which a group division could be conjured into life. One recent study in this tradition examined North Americans' attitudes toward immigration and found them to hinge on whether immigration is viewed in terms of a zero-sum competition, a perception that was manipulated in the research. When the perception was heightened, attitudes toward immigration became highly unfavorable. This effect was much greater in predicting attitudes than was a measure of generalized prejudice, suggesting that attitudes toward outgroups may not be so much determined by previously fixed evaluations as by responses to changes in the relative position of groups.[12]

That humans cling tenaciously to the smallest shreds of status and privilege is a commonplace observation. One could imagine that this tendency would be counteracted by contacts between members of different groups, leading to greater familiarity and a lowering of prejudices and suspicions about each other. But this idea, famous as the "contact hypothesis," has been the subject of reams of social-psychological research that shows it to hold only under certain restrictive conditions, including the equal status of the individuals who are interacting and the existence of a cooperative rather than competitive relationship between them. In contradiction to the hypothesis, Robert Putnam has assembled evidence to demonstrate that increasing racial and ethnic diversity in U.S. communities reduces social capital as well as generalized trust, though paradoxically it is not just the social capital that bridges different groups that is diminished but also the within-group, bonding social capital. The implication is that increasing racial and ethnic diversity, at least initially, provokes growing isolation, not the expansion of social connections anticipated by the contact hypothesis.[13]

History and sociology provide numerous examples of privileged groups that, upon the arrival or social ascent of a new group that might threaten their position, act to fortify boundaries in order to reduce the threat and to secure their privileges.[14] It is probably easier to see such fundamental dynamics through examples that are far away rather than close at hand, where familiarity with the complexity of detail can overwhelm clarity. Consider then the divisions between immigrant minorities and natives in the French educational system: in France, as in the United States, the dominant ideology, deemed "Republicanism" there, emphasizes equality of opportunity and assimilation; but by comparison with the United States, the educational system is far more subject to the control of the national state and is formally more egalitarian. Nevertheless, researchers have found that many French parents and school administrators pursue on-the-ground policies to reconstruct the privileges that the egalitarian policies of the state would deny.[15] For instance, in order to establish tracks within schools to separate middle-class French students from immigrant students and others from disfavored backgrounds, schools in some areas have introduced classes in unusual second and third languages, such as Japanese or classical Greek, where knowledgeable parents place their children. Middle-class parents also have the knowledge to take full advantage of a complicated and controversial system for assigning students to schools, the *carte scolaire*, in order to avoid having their children attend schools with many children from immigrant and poor families; when it is not possible to avoid this, they send their children to private schools (which also receive state financial support in France). These and similar actions work to subvert not only the formal

equality among schools, in levels of funding, for example, but the policies of the state that seek to reduce educational inequalities. Thus the
efforts of native French parents to further differentiate students on the
basis of their social origins can be seen as a response to the policies of the
state to make access to the "bac," the indispensable credential for university education, more widespread.[16] Consequently, it is not surprising that
the children from immigrant families are rarely found at the elite level
of the French postsecondary system, the *grandes écoles,* equivalent to the
Ivy League, whose graduates are more or less guaranteed well-paying,
prestigious careers; and that, though these children do attend universities in large numbers, they are not commonly in the curricula with the
best prospects in the labor market. The inequalities between the native
French and others that are constructed through the educational system
are compounded by discrimination in a labor market that does not provide enough good jobs for young people, nearly a quarter of whom are
unemployed. The children of immigrants have a higher likelihood of
unemployment and of underemployment, placement in jobs below their
level of qualification, than one can account for by their educational credentials. High percentages of them believe that they are the victims of
discrimination at the hands of employers. This discrimination targets,
according to them, their distinctive names more than any "racial" feature.[17]

But we do not need to look very far to see that under the right circumstances, native white Protestants in the United States could respond
to the new immigrant groups in ways that reinforced the boundaries between the native group and the newcomers. This is evident in the restrictions that were imposed on the admission of Jews to Ivy League
colleges during the 1920s, restrictions that, in disguised forms, lasted
until the late 1950s.[18] (It was much less necessary to restrict the entry
of Catholics, who, concentrated in working-class strata, had generally
lower levels of educational attainment in the first place and, when they
attended college, could do so at Catholic institutions of higher educa-

tion.) In doing so, the Protestants exploited the principal mechanisms by which a powerful, established group can reinforce the social boundary against a new group: increasing the symbolic valence of the boundary by stereotypes that reduce the apparent moral worth of the newcomers; excluding them from, or at least restricting their entry to, arenas where privileges are forged and bestowed ("hoarding opportunities," in the trenchant language of Charles Tilly);[19] preserving social distance from the new group, to prevent its members from achieving the subtle cultural knowledge (for example, sartorial style, rules of polite behavior) and close bonds to be able to emulate the established group and to insert themselves in its midst; and in general maintaining inequalities that help to position groups in a rank order of superiority and inferiority.[20]

One significant aspect of the restrictive-quota episode is that the social distinctions drawn by establishment Protestants between themselves and the upwardly mobile Jews they perceived as threats had a largely ethnic, rather than racial, character. The key contrast, in other words, was not between whites and Jews—or, more accurately put, it was rarely posed in such terms—but rather between the social and moral codes of two distinct ethno-religious groups. Jews were depicted as excessively ambitious in academic terms, and therefore as poor social mixers and deficient in terms of the ideal for students, that of the "all-around young man." Frequently enough, the administrators implementing the restrictive policies appealed for assistance to Jewish alumni, apparently with the notion in mind that the "better class" of Jews would not want to see their alma mater overrun by social inferiors. This notion seems to imply that the problem was viewed, at least partly, as one of insufficient acculturation rather than one of intrinsic characteristics that give offense. However, even when Jews were admitted as students, they would usually be excluded from inner circles where the social and cultural requisites for subsequent privileges were bestowed, such as the eating clubs at Princeton or Yale's Skull and Bones secret society. What the restrictive admissions policies of Ivy League institutions demonstrate is that the boundaries between native white Protestants and the new immigrant populations could survive the weakening or disappearance of the racial element; they could be reconstructed on ethno-religious terms.

That such boundary-reinforcing behavior was not limited to the white Protestant elite is highlighted by the brief efflorescence of the Ku Klux Klan during the 1920s, including in northern cities with many recent immigrants, such as Chicago and Detroit. This second life of the Klan, unlike its first one in the rural South during the late nineteenth century, was not aimed exclusively at African Americans, but took in Catholics, Jews, and recent immigrants among its multiple targets. Catholics in fact were the principal enemy for Klansmen in these years, according to historian Kenneth Jackson, who has written authoritatively about the urban Klan. According to him, "among Klansmen in almost every state and section, the most basic and pervasive concern was the Pope," and the Klan insisted "upon the impossibility of being both a good Catholic and a good citizen" and therefore "opposed all Catholic candidates for political office." The Klan declared that "America is Protestant and so it must remain."[21] Its program included support for "one hundred per cent Americanism," a formula that required the immigrants and their children to discard all aspects of their ethnic cultures, and for Prohibition, seen by some Protestants as needed to extirpate the alcohol-oriented cultures brought by the immigrants.

The lower-middle-class Klan movement did not survive the 1920s, and it is plausible therefore to see it as a xenophobic reaction during the final spasm of mass immigration from Europe. Once the portals for immigration were largely shut by the immigration restriction law of 1924, the Klan's *raison d'être* ceased. Moreover, its crude intolerance and anti-modernism were rejected by many mainstream white Americans of the time. But the second life of the Klan nevertheless demonstrates that a white Protestant identity could be a basis for exclusionary organization under the right circumstances.

So the critical question, then, about the social ascent of the so-called white ethnics can be reformulated as: under what conditions are boundaries relaxed in way that that newcomers can assimilate in large numbers? What seems apparent is that boundary relaxation is most likely when competition between groups is reduced, in particular, when the threat to the position of previously privileged groups is diminished; for otherwise they have a strong incentive to reinforce boundaries and protect their privileges.[22]

The Boundaries Relax for White Ethnics

The restrictions on the admission of Jews to elite colleges and universities fell away during the late 1950s and 1960s. An initial loosening set in during and after World War II, encouraged by the shrinking of the application pool because of wartime manpower requirements and the odium attached to blatant anti-Semitism in the war's aftermath. The top colleges of the Ivy League are a barometer of this opening up. At Princeton, "long a bastion of anti-Semitism," according to Jerome Karabel,[23] the enrollment of Jews reached 6–7 percent in the late 1940s, a figure that, while low in relation to the proportion of Jews in any potential pool of qualified applications, was at least double what it had been a decade earlier; and it continued to climb, to about 14 percent by the late 1950s. At Harvard, which despite a quota had generally admitted more Jews than Yale or Princeton, the Jewish proportion was 25 percent by the early 1950s. At Yale, the breakthrough came in the early 1960s and in response to charges of anti-Semitism by members of the Yale community. The growing religious diversity at elite colleges did not mean that they had abandoned their self-defined role as the channel between privileged WASP origins and equivalent adult status. Far from it: the leaders at these schools sought to preserve as much as possible an admissions system that allowed them to usher in disproportionate numbers the children of privilege. In the process, they devised a scheme that has been widely influential among selective colleges and universities: disdaining purely academic criteria, it gives a large role to subjective assessments of the applicant's potential contribution to the campus and in subsequent life through "leadership" and other hard-to-quantify talents. It also provides special portals of admission for the children of alumni ("legacies") and athletes. A system of this sort allows a great deal of administrative discretion in the admissions process. While conceding considerable space to the meritocratic demand for the admission of children from nonelite origins, it preserves the historic role of the elite colleges as an intergenerational transmission belt for privilege.[24]

More generally, the socioeconomic position of young white Americans of recent immigrant origins surged forward in the couple of decades following World War II. The educational record, for instance, of the children of southern and eastern European immigrants improved with each new cohort born in the United States, reflecting historical changes in educational opportunities. But since those same opportunities were also open to young Americans of British ancestry, the gap between the two did not close very much until the cohort born in the 1930–1945 period, whose members reached maturity after the war. In the prior cohort, born in 1915–1929, the gap in college attendance showed an approximately 50 percent advantage for young men of British background over their ethnic counterparts and a two-to-one British advantage among women. For those born in 1930–1945, the gap was reduced to less than 10 percent among men and about 20 percent among women. In the next cohort, born after the war, it disappeared.[25]

The rapid gains of southern and eastern European ethnics in education, which were accompanied by occupational rises, movement away from urban ethnic neighborhoods and into the suburbs, and increasing intermarriage, cannot be explained by the generational transition from the second, made up of the children of immigrants, to the third, the grandchildren, because the 1930–1945 cohort came too soon after the period of mass immigration from southern and eastern Europe to contain many third-generation individuals. The generational transition did matter for the white-ethnic assimilation story, but its timing doesn't coincide with the educational breakthrough. Nor can the gains be explained by the presence of many Jews among those who traced their ancestry to eastern Europe. Although the educational achievements of eastern European Jews far outshone those of Christian (mainly Catholic) southern and eastern European ethnics during the first half of the twentieth century, the college attainment of cohorts of Italian Americans, a group with a low educational starting point that was not, as were many eastern European groups, divided between Christians and Jews, shows an even stronger convergence than that described above.

Dramatic as the improvements in white ethnics' situation may have been, they did not eliminate all resistance to their ascent. In this respect, one has to reject a highly oversimplified narrative of white-ethnic assimilation that is frequently encountered today, usually in the company of a contrast posed between contemporary immigration and that of past eras. This narrative presents post–World War II ethnic successes as largely the fruit of individual efforts in a system that was by then quite open to whites regardless of their ethnic backgrounds; it overlooks the hurdles that still existed in the form of organized discrimination against them. The whiteness literature represents one version of this narrative, for once the ethnics were accepted as whites, the barriers preventing them from entering the mainstream presumably fell.

Two groups, Jews and Italians, the largest in the massive wave of southern and eastern European immigration, complicate this story, for sizable groups of members of both, in quick succession in the two decades following the end of the war, came under suspicion for activities harmful to society and became the subjects of state surveillance and police and judicial actions. Jews were prominent among the targets of the anticommunism fervor of the 1950s (though some elite white Protestants were also caught in the nets fabricated by Senator Joseph McCarthy and his supporters during the Red Scare).[26] McCarthyism's witch hunting heavily affected those industries and professions, such as

Hollywood and teaching, where Jews were concentrated; and hence they figured disproportionately among the thousands who lost their jobs or were blacklisted. In the arts and in entertainment, some of the notable victims of blacklisting included Leonard Bernstein, Aaron Copland, Howard Fast, Lillian Hellman, Arthur Miller, Zero Mostel and Edward G. Robinson, all from Jewish backgrounds.[27] The execution of Julius and Ethel Rosenberg on charges of atomic spying undoubtedly crystallized in the minds of many Americans an association between Jewishness and membership in the Communist Party and other left-wing organizations.

Italian-American communities, now increasingly composed of second-generation families, came in for intense suspicion shortly afterward, when southern Italians were singled out by government policy as the source of the nation's organized-crime problem. The identification of organized crime with the culture of a single group began in earnest with the Kefauver hearings in the U.S. Senate in 1951, which claimed the existence of a national crime group, the Mafia. It intensified after police broke up an organized-crime conclave in Apalachin, New York, in 1957 and following the congressional testimony of Joseph Valachi, a onetime Cosa Nostra insider, in 1963. The apogee was attained in the 1967 Report of the President's Crime Commission, which in its chapter on organized crime identified the "core" of that problem as constituted by twenty-four Italian-American crime families, whose structure, it declared, "resembles that of the Mafia groups that have operated for almost a century on the island of Sicily."[28]

The involvement of some Jews and some Italians in the Communist Party and organized crime, respectively, is not in question. But what is telling about each case is that a perception of threat was met with a veritable crusade by parts of the American establishment against a target that was defined—to a significant extent in one case, that of communism, and to a very large extent in the other—in ethnic terms. The danger seen as emanating from some of each group's members was depicted as extreme, potentially threatening the nature of American society as it then existed. Domestic communism was viewed as aiming to subvert American democracy. In the case of Italian-American organized crime, the equivalent view is epitomized by the title of a well-known book written at the time by an eminent criminologist—*Theft of the Nation,* by Donald Cressey, whose cover featured a black handprint over the dome of the Capitol. These threats, political radicalism and crime, were ones that Americans had historically identified with foreign and immigrant influences;[29] indeed, the fears about them had contributed to the political support for immigration restriction during the 1920s. A significant consequence of these suspicions for the mobility and integration of group members was intense surveillance of ethnic communities by the police and the FBI. Moreover, suspicion was cast more broadly than the small group of Communist Party members, in the one case, or the initiates in Cosa Nostra families, in the other. The mere suggestion of an association with the wrong person or group was often sufficient to taint a career, especially one in the public eye. "Fellow traveler," synonymous with "pinko," was a term of opprobrium during the 1950s applied to individuals who, though not Communists, supposedly sympathized with some of their views (which could, in some parts of the United States, be as innocent as support for African Americans' civil rights). Into the 1990s, suspicions of Mafia family connections spoiled the attempts of a number of Italian-American politicians to gain higher elective office.[30]

The organized efforts of the groups themselves to break down remaining barriers also show that resistance did not simply disappear in the immediate postwar years. Jews were in the vanguard of these efforts, and their legal and political successes undoubtedly paved the way for others. For example, the lowering of discriminatory barriers to admission to elite universities and to professional schools was hardly accomplished in the fashion of an upbeat Hollywood ending, whereby privileged groups experienced a change of heart and welcomed previously scorned newcomers into their midst. Jewish organizations had to cam-

paign against the use of religious and racial criteria in admissions; they
pressed the case for antidiscrimination legislation especially in New York
State, where a number of prestigious, exclusionary institutions, such as
Columbia and Cornell, were located. An initial success was achieved in
1946, when the New York City Council adopted legislation threatening
the tax-exempt status of nonsectarian colleges and universities that dis-
criminated on the basis of race or religion. Columbia was thereby forced
to revise its admissions procedures, and some other schools, seeing the
handwriting on the wall, did the same. New York State followed with an
antidiscrimination statute in 1948. That these laws were in fact successful is demonstrated by, for example, the increase in the Jewish percentage
among New York's medical students from 15 percent in 1948 to about
50 percent by the mid-1950s.[31]

The position of the previously excluded white groups shifted profoundly, as they went within a couple of decades from being disparaged
outsiders, tinged with elements of racial inferiority, to viable candidates
for inclusion in what had been a white Protestant mainstream. One indicator of this shift is the rapid decline of the most virulent anti-Semitic
prejudices in the decade after the war's end, since attitudes toward Jews
were a sensitive barometer of intolerant attitudes toward white ethnics
more generally. One survey question that was repeated periodically—
"Have you heard any criticism or talk against the Jews in the last six
months?"—measured the extent to which anti-Semitic sentiments were
openly discussed, and undoubtedly allowed respondents who harbored
such sentiments themselves to report them without having to acknowledge personal responsibility. During and immediately after the war, a
majority of Americans—the high-water mark was 64 percent in 1946—
answered the question affirmatively. But in the late 1940s and the early
1950s, the number giving this response plummeted: by 1951, it was
down to 16 percent; and in 1956, it was only 11 percent.[32] Even if some
of this decline came from respondents telling interviewers what they
thought the interviewers wanted to hear, it still represented a dramatically rapid change in norms.

Another indicator is the growth of marriage across religious lines, which was limited in the prewar period. Religious intermarriage doubled in frequency for the southern and eastern European groups, who were overwhelmingly Catholic and Jewish, between those cohorts born in the United States before 1916 and those born between 1916 and 1930, most of whom would have married during and after the war. For the latter group, a third married across religious lines. This intermarriage was mainly an affair of Catholics marrying Protestants, for Jewish intermarriage did not begin its steep climb until the 1960s. The proportion of the religiously intermarried continued to rise among subsequent cohorts, reaching half among those born during the 1960s. The soaring of intermarriage indicates that religious boundaries, which were relatively impermeable in the prewar period, became much less so after the war.[33] The inevitable conclusion is that the once almost insurmountable differences associated with religion had receded in salience for many Americans.

How can one understand these profound shifts in the position of the white ethnics? White racial status does not guarantee equality, for ethnic distinctions can still be in play, especially in a society like that of mid-twentieth century America, where religious differences were notable and religious identities, encoded for instance in names and schools attended, were usually easy to ascertain. Moreover, white Protestants held a superior status that they should have had reason to protect. Analyzing poll data collected in 1939 and 1940, on the eve of the war, Hadley Cantril verified the better socioeconomic positioning of white Protestants vis-à-vis Catholics, especially once the South, where there were few Catholics anyway, was discounted:

> The ratio of Protestants in a population group tends to increase with the economic status of the group. Conversely, the ratio of Catholics in a population group tends to decrease with the economic status of the group. A higher concentration of Protestants and a lower concentration of Catholics in the middle and upper economic groups is likely to

be found among the persons in these groups who have had the most formal education.[34]

While Cantril's findings indicate that there were plenty of Protestants to be found in the same socioeconomic strata where Catholics were concentrated, they also highlight the advantages held by the better-educated Protestants who were situated at higher income levels. Had his data permitted the identification of the southern and eastern Europeans among the Catholics, an even more sharply edged stratification would have become evident. That would also have been true given denominational affiliations among Protestants. While the members of some denominations such as the Baptists were no better off in socioeconomic terms than the average Catholic, others such as Methodists and Presbyterians held clear advantages at the time. Writing two decades later, in the early 1960s, sociologists Albert Mayer and Harry Sharp concluded, based on a study of Detroit, a city with many white ethnics, that "most Protestant denominations far exceed the Catholics in economic standing."[35]

Apart from the individualistic assimilation and whiteness approaches, other potential explanatory factors have been proposed. A frequently invoked one takes as its point of departure the restrictive immigration laws of the 1920s, which sharply curtailed the immigrant flow (which would have declined precipitously during the 1930s because of the Depression, in any event). The cutoff of immigration has generally been credited with spurring the assimilation of the immigrants and their children because, for one thing, it interrupted what had been the steady stream of new arrivals into immigrant communities, thus drying up the human springs that were renewing these communities and their cultures. Historian David Roediger, one of the creators of the whiteness approach, argues that the end of mass immigration reduced native whites' fear of being overwhelmed by hordes of new immigrants and their children, and this in turn allowed for a decline in the intensity of the stereotypes against them during the 1930s. The changes observed in public school classrooms by the 1930s are consistent with his claim, for the zealotry of the Americanizers had abated by then and the immigrant cultures of many schoolchildren were being presented in more positive ways.[36] This explanation has a contemporary resonance, for similar measures have been advocated in recent years as a means of stimulating the assimilation of new immigrant groups (especially, of course, by those who have seen it as lagging, such as the eminent political scientist Samuel Huntington).[37]

It is quite plausible that the four-decade hiatus in mass immigration starting in the mid-1920s contributed to the cultural assimilation of the southern and eastern Europeans. However, the potency of an immigration halt to render lower-status immigrant-origin groups much more acceptable to a dominant native one is questionable. A few counterexamples raise doubts: the downturn in immigration during World War I due to the interruption of transatlantic ship traffic and the mobilization of many young Europeans for the war did not lead to a decline in stereotypes and prejudice; in fact, the wartime period and the few years afterward produced some of the worst xenophobia the United States has ever seen. Even more telling are the cases of Asian-American groups. Although immigration from Asia was completely closed off over a period of several decades beginning with the Chinese Exclusion Act of 1882 and ending with the Johnson-Reed Act of 1924, stereotypes of Asians did not lose any of their intensity until well after World War II.

Moreover, the acceptability of Asian Americans to whites has been rising in tandem with immigration from Asia. Both developments date to the 1960s, the period of the civil-rights legislation that opened the door to Asian-American socioeconomic advance and also of the changes in immigration law that allowed large-scale immigration from Asia for the first time since the nineteenth century. Consequently, the entrance of Asian Americans into largely white milieus—into elite colleges and universities and middle-class, suburban neighborhoods, as well as into families through intermarriage—has been increasing at the same time as the immigration from Asian countries. The Chinese are a particularly revealing case, for during the latter part of the twentieth century, the social advance of a later-generation group of Chinese Americans could in principle have been impeded by the large volume of Chinese immigration from the mainland, Taiwan, and elsewhere in Asia, especially since this immigration contained a substantial working-class component that clustered in established or newly founded Chinatowns. But this did not happen.

Another factor that could be associated with the postwar fluidity of boundaries among Euro-Americans lies in the remarkable reduction of income inequality that characterized the middle of the twentieth century, which has been labeled the "Great Compression" by economic historians.[38] According to the data of economists Thomas Piketty and Emmanuel Saez, the high level of income inequality that characterized the United States during the early part of the twentieth century was gradually reduced during the New and Fair Deals, a period not only of government policies aimed at assisting middle- and low-income Americans but also of unusual union power, and reached its nadir in the quarter century beginning with the Eisenhower administration.[39] In addition, since the education of young Americans was advancing rapidly and there was little or no immigration to feed the bottom of the labor market, the wages of unskilled workers rose appreciably. This reduction in inequality, which during the early part of this period was most pronounced among whites, presumably would have produced a perception of greater parity among whites with different ethnic origins, thus reducing the salience of any ethnic (or quasi-racial) distinction.

The Great Compression may have some relevance, but it is highly doubtful that it would by itself have been sufficient to dull what had been a bright boundary between native white Protestants and the new immigrant populations, because that distinction was rooted as much in status perceptions as in socioeconomic ones, to borrow a key sociological distinction that dates back to one of the discipline's founders, the German Max Weber.[40] Status considerations are fundamentally a matter of "social honor," and as such they can survive a reduction of economic differences. Such a reduction may even enhance them because of the threat to the status position of a privileged group implied by the closing of the economic gap previously separating it from its inferiors. The point is borne out by the anti-Semitic admissions policies imposed at Ivy League colleges during the 1920s. They were needed not because Jews were seen as the economic or academic inferiors of white Protestants; indeed, if anything, it was more that the reduction of these differences between the groups made Jews into more threatening status competitors. Hence, the prevalent denigrating stereotypes cast Jews as *nouveaux riches,* as those who have not acculturated to the norms of the social milieus that their newly acquired economic status should entitle them—they were pushy, given to vulgar display, and so forth. Accordingly, while some exceptions may have been made in extraordinary cases, Jews as a group were held to be unworthy of entry to the white Protestant establishment, and on a broader scale, the same standard could have been applied by middle-class white Protestants to the Italians and the other southern and eastern European groups that were ascending economically in the postwar period. Indeed, it was.

An Explanation

With any complex historical process, a variety of unique factors contributes to the outcome and cannot be easily disentangled from it. Hence one should not rule out the relevance of the partial explanations I have just cited, to say nothing of the whiteness and individualistic assimilation approaches. But none of them, singly or in combination, is an adequate answer to the question posed earlier within the conceptual framework of boundaries: why didn't native white Protestants take steps to fortify the boundaries that separated them from ethnic, non-Protestant whites? The changes in income do suggest a solution to this puzzle, for it was not just that income inequality declined: at the same time, average real income was growing. Thus the decline in income inequality, which lifted previously disparaged groups closer economically to native whites, may not have been perceived as a threat since incomes of the latter were rising. From their individual perspectives, their life chances and those of their children were not diminishing, but improving.

The key to the relaxation of boundaries in the mid-twentieth century, I argue, lies in three conditions that are sufficient to account for it. One can be described as "non-zero-sum mobility."[41] By definition this does not require downward mobility by members of more privileged groups in order for upward mobility by members of less privileged groups to take place; hence it is less likely to raise the specter of threat to established privilege and an intensification of competition along racial and ethnic lines. The arrival of large numbers of academically talented Jewish students at the Ivy League colleges in the 1920s is a contrasting case: one of zero-sum mobility, at least in the perceptions of establishment whites. They perceived the places going to Jews as ones that would not be available to them and to their sons (daughters not being relevant in this period), and in their eyes, if the Jewish share of the student body rose high enough, then the colleges might be lost as places where the social and economic privilege of a new generation of establishment Protestants could be minted. A common axiom of the time was that this had happened at Columbia, which was abandoned by the WASP establishment once the Jewish fraction had risen beyond the threshold of acceptability.[42]

A second condition must work in tandem with non-zero-sum mobility: the ability to convert socioeconomic advance into social proximity to the dominant group. One of the most consequential expressions of this proximity in the United States is residential integration with the majority population, for this not only tends to engender equal-status contacts across boundaries but gives members of a minority access to the spatially based resources and amenities that are normally under the control of the majority—good schools, safe streets, and so on. Residential integration is probably most consequential for the children of a minority group, who are able to attend better schools and to form interethnic and/or interracial friendships; as a result, they are able to gain the social skills (and confidence) necessary for success in mainstream settings as adults. More generally, social proximity under conditions of equal socioeconomic status provides the most favorable context for the kinds of intergroup relationships that the contact hypothesis envisions as breaking down barriers and demolishing stereotypes.

A third condition may not be as central as the other two but, at a minimum, it enhances their effectiveness: namely, a revision of the ideological or symbolic underpinnings of a boundary to acknowledge that members of the minority may have the same moral worth as the members of the majority. Such a revision in the beliefs held by at least a portion of the majority (it is typical that an enlightened vanguard accepts moral equality with the minority well ahead of the majority's mass) makes the arrival of upwardly striving ethnic-minority members more acceptable than it would previously have been. Those with enlightened views may take on the role of moral entrepreneur and act in ways to spur change—by reminding their recalcitrant co-ethnics of the moral imperatives implied by the democratic ideals they hold sacrosanct, facilitating the entry of minority individuals into spheres from which they were previously excluded or protecting them when their presence in such sites is challenged.

These three conditions were manifest in abundance during the three decades beginning with World War II, the period when white ethnics were able to enter the mainstream in large numbers and the boundaries that had previously made them outsiders receded in salience. There was enormous non-zero-sum mobility in the middle decades of the twentieth century, as indicated by the transformation of the college and university system, for in a period of just three decades, 1940–1970, it quintupled in size and thus accommodated a much higher fraction of the college-going age group than before. In the well-known formulation of

Martin Trow, higher education went from being an elite system to a mass one, in just a single generation.[43] In 1940, just before wartime manpower requirements drew down student populations, the number of students enrolled in colleges and universities stood at 1.5 million, a mere 9 percent of the 18- to 24-year-olds. By 1970, the number had exploded to more than 7 million and nearly a third of the 18- to 24-year-olds were involved. This expansion was not simply fueled by the GI Bill, which may have helped to ignite it in the immediate postwar period, for it persisted more or less continuously from the late 1940s through the 1960s, long after the effects of the GI Bill had subsided.

It is admittedly harder to specify in detail how the elite sector of higher education fits with the story of the creation of non-zero-sum mobility. Certainly, it was not the case that Harvard, Princeton, and Yale expanded in proportion to the overall postsecondary sector. What then allowed greater openness to take place by the 1960s, when Jews and Catholics became much larger fractions of the entering classes than they had been before?[44] I suggest that two consequences of the basic expansion could have played a role: one is that the overall expansion and the shift to a mass system supported the rise of a meritocratic ideology that proved hard to resist, and the other is that the investment by government in higher education allowed some other universities, mainly in the public sector, to attract star faculty and rise to elite status, thus expanding overall the number of institutions viewed as belonging to the top tier. This spread of elite status to institutions in such places as Berkeley and Ann Arbor, along with the rise of non-Ivy privates like Swarthmore, relieved some of the pressures on the top Ivies and provided alternatives to upper-middle-class families.

Occupational mobility grew in tandem with the expansion of the educational system. (Had it not, then the egalitarian consequences of the expansion of the education system might have been blunted, as ethnic privilege would have reasserted itself in the transition from school to the labor market.) Much of this mobility was generated by a far-reaching transformation of the American workforce, which narrowed or closed out some occupational slots while opening up others, and thus reshaped economic opportunity over time. A comparison of 1930 and 1970, a period that covers the century's economic extremes from the Great Depression to post–World War II prosperity and also spans generations—the work lives of, say, southern and eastern European immigrants and those of their children and/or grandchildren—suggests the rough dimensions of this process. In this forty-year period, the percentage of the national workforce in agricultural pursuits declined precipitously, from 21 to 3 percent, thus forcing many grandchildren and great-grandchildren of earlier immigrants who had settled in rural areas into more urban lines of work. Further, even though the overall proportion in blue-collar and service occupations hardly changed, remaining at slightly less than 50 percent, significant realignments were taking place within these categories: in particular, unskilled laborers, a category that included many of the immigrants in the early part of the century, declined sharply from 11 to 4 percent of the labor force. Last, white-collar occupations expanded robustly, from 29 to 45 percent. Moreover, nearly half of this increase was concentrated in the generally high-ranking occupations of the professional and technical category, whose share of the labor force doubled, going from 7 to 14 percent.[45]

A consequence of such massive shifts is structurally engendered mobility, as a substantial proportion of each new generation entering the workforce is more or less constrained by a drastically altered regime of opportunities to take jobs different from those held by its parents. For the children and grandchildren of many immigrant groups, the most significant aspect of the occupational transformation is that it entailed a sharp contraction at the lower end of the occupational spectrum and a corresponding expansion in its middle and upper reaches. Jobs in the sectors where the immigrants and perhaps the second generation had established themselves—Italians on the docks, for instance—were growing scarcer. (A common conception, or perhaps misconception, is that the European immigrants and their children found jobs predominantly in the manufacturing sector, which provided them with economic ladders because of wage improvements due to unionization and because of mobility internal to firms. However, Roger Waldinger's research shows that this is only partly true and some groups, like the Italians, were not well represented in manufacturing jobs.)[46] The choice for ethnic youth was clear: get enough education to advance to the white-collar jobs that were proliferating; find a place, frequently through kin connections, in one of the skilled trades; or face diminished economic prospects.

The second condition, namely, the ability to convert socioeconomic advance into social proximity to the dominant group, was in its way also a by-product of non-zero-sum mobility in the middle of the twentieth century. That is, it was associated with the drastic reorganization of residential space, characterized by the emergence of many new suburban communities where white families of diverse ethnic origins could buy homes and mix. As Herbert Gans describes the residents of one of these early new suburbs in his classic, *The Levittowners*, "thirty-seven percent reported being of Northern European origin (English, German, or Scandinavian); 17 percent were eastern European (mostly Russian Jewish with a scattering of Poles); 10 percent, Irish; 9 percent, Southern European (mainly Italian), and the remainder a heady mixture of all of these backgrounds."[47] This suburb was a melting pot, at least for whites.

It should be underscored that, despite some residential discrimination (for example, some covenants that excluded the sales of homes to Jews), whites did not by this period face insurmountable hurdles when it came to geographic moves to improve their residential situations; and in this respect their experience has been very different from that of African Americans, who, much research shows, have been very constrained in their residential options regardless of their economic status.[48] This residential mobility was critical to the assimilation process, because it brought second- and third-generation ethnics into contact in schools, at work, and in neighborhoods with a variety of others, some of them ethnics from other groups and some of them native white Protestants. The consequence was a thoroughgoing integration of ethnics into the mainstream, as indicated by the rising rates of intermarriage among whites of diverse ethnic backgrounds. Socioeconomic mobility that does not translate into greater proximity to mainstream whites does not have the same impact on social boundaries, as the record of African-American segregation demonstrates. Greater proximity without the social mobility to raise members of disadvantaged minorities to parity also lacks a boundary-changing character. On the social-structural plane, it is in the combination of these two that the synergy to change boundaries is generated.

Perhaps these forms of mobility would have been far more difficult for white ethnics had there not been an accompanying change on the ideological plane that elevated their perceived moral worth. Perceiving them as worthy of the opportunities that many Protestant whites took for granted as part of the American Way (however much these same opportunities were simultaneously denied to nonwhite American citizens) made it much easier to accept the growing presence of upwardly mobile white ethnics, who were now turning up in greater numbers in jobs and in places where they had been rare before. Of course, because this mobility was very much concentrated in the cohorts coming of age and left behind many older individuals or those who were not sufficiently acculturated, Protestant whites could console themselves with the thought that these *nouveaux arrivés* were a select group and hence especially worthy of inclusion.

In any event, the perceived moral worth of the white ethnics was very much changed by the war. Given the ethnic divisions of American society and the potential for many Americans of recent European origins to feel some residual attachment to countries that were now the enemies of the United States, it was critical for the war effort to recognize the contributions that ethnics were making.[49] These were highlighted by wartime reporting—by the famous reporter, Ernie Pyle, for example—and subsequently by a very prominent postwar literature and cinema. In

sharp contrast to the xenophobia unleashed by World War I, World War
II, occurring when the floodtide of immigration had receded and the
young men of recent immigrant origins reporting for military service belonged overwhelmingly to U.S.-born generations, brought about a self-
conscious wartime unity that transcended ethnic lines among whites.
The wartime reporting and films made for domestic consumption more
or less deliberately portrayed the American military as a national cross-
section of the white population. For instance, *Time* magazine, reporting
on a raid in France, claimed that its participants,

> sounded like the roster of an all-American eleven . . . There were Ed-
> ward Czeklauski of Brooklyn, George Pucilowski of Detroit, Theo-
> dore Hakenstod of Providence, Zane Gemmill of St. Clair, Pa., Frank
> Christensen of Racine, Wisconsin, Abraham Dreiscus of Kansas City.
> There were the older, but not better, American names like Ray and
> Thacker, Walsh and Eaton and Tyler. The war . . . was getting Ameri-
> canized.[50]

A 1943 episode in which four chaplains, two Protestant, one Catholic
and one Jewish, chose to go down with the torpedoed ship on which
they served after giving up their life jackets to sailors who needed them
was seized on to exemplify multifaith sacrifice for the American cause.
This carefully cultivated wartime unity presaged a different vision of
America, which for the first time included white ethnics as potential
members of the charmed circle of full-fledged Americans. Nonwhite
Americans, however, remained outside it; their men fought in segregated
military units, their accomplishments little noted by mainstream media,
with the exception of the Japanese-American 442nd Brigade, which became the most decorated unit of the American army.

World War II and the decade or so immediately following it could be
said to represent the zenith of the melting pot ideal, at least for Americans of European origin, and the basis for subsequent conceptions of
it. The ideal permeates the popular novels about the war, published dur-

ing it and afterward, such as Norman Mailer's *The Naked and the Dead*, James Jones's *From Here to Eternity*, Harry Brown's *A Walk in the Sun*, and John Hersey's *A Bell for Adano*, all of which were also made into successful films and served to interpret the war experience for a large segment of the American population.[51] The novels portrayed military groups that represented the white-ethnic diversity of American society in miniature. At the same time, they openly acknowledged the prejudice present in American society. Indeed, that was one of their major themes, as they showed ethnic soldiers in the lower ranks subordinated to non-ethnic white officers. But where their vision was triumphant was in their portrayal of ethnic Americans, who were lifted out from behind a curtain of stereotypes and presented as the moral equals of other Americans and as men who were contributing to ultimate victory with everyday heroism and sacrifice.

The Story Is More Complex

The three conditions in concert are sufficient, I argue, to explain the profound boundary changes of the decades following World War II. That does not make them necessary to all boundary change: that is, they can be understood as one route to change, which can also be attained in other ways, for example, by mass movements that arise from below and successfully challenge the boundaries protecting an established group. The civil-rights and women's movements offer cases in point. Yet to fully understand the story of boundary change in the middle of the last century, we also need to inquire how these conditions themselves came about.

To be sure, the white ethnics made strenuous efforts in the postwar period to advance, and they probably didn't perceive at all that the way had been smoothed for them by structural changes. This point invokes the perennial debate over the relative weight of agency and structure: in a nutshell, how much do the efforts of individuals and groups matter?

Those efforts mattered in this case—I have already cited the postwar legal and political efforts of Jewish groups as especially effective—but the theory just sketched implies that they may be more consequential at some historical moments than at others. During the several decades following World War II, American society was unusually open to the agency of the white ethnics because non-zero-sum mobility, combined with the ideological affirmations of their moral worth, decreased resistance to their efforts; indeed, a vanguard of "enlightened" white Protestants assisted these efforts, believing their success to be morally blessed and in the best interests of American society.[52] The suddenness with which resistance to the ethnics could give way could be startling. Leonard Dinnerstein, who asserts that colleges and universities "were being influenced by the changing tone in society," notes that "in 1948 Jewish undergraduates at Yale protested being automatically assigned other Jews as roommates. As soon as they raised the issue, the practice ceased."[53]

For at least two of the conditions I have cited, the inclusion of the white-ethnic groups in the U.S. political system was a precondition. This inclusion was a by-product of their legal status as whites, which gave them access to citizenship and the ballot box. And their votes, though perhaps not initially, were courted by the urban political machines of the Democratic Party. By the middle of the century, the white ethnics were represented in electoral bodies at municipal, state, and national levels. The Italians serve as a good index because they were initially slow to take U.S. citizenship since so many of the immigrants envisioned returning home. Their political breakthrough came immediately after World War II. The first Italian-American governor was elected in 1946 in Rhode Island; then, in the congressional elections of 1948 eight Italian Americans were elected to the House, double the number in any previous year. By the early 1950s, more than twice as many Italian Americans served in the legislatures of states with large Italian populations (Connecticut, Massachusetts, New Jersey, New York, Pennsylvania, and Rhode Island) as had done so in the mid-1930s.[54]

The political power of the ethnics can be glimpsed in both the creation of non-zero-sum mobility and the reconfiguration of residential space in a way that promoted social integration among whites of various ethnic backgrounds. That is, government policies, at national and state levels, were fundamental to generating these conditions, which in turn were conducive to boundary change. The influence of white-ethnic politicians, or of others who had the interests of white-ethnic constituents in mind, was critical to ensuring that these policies were devised in ways that benefited the members of these groups. For example, the expansion of the postsecondary education system, which occurred at a robust clip in the 1945–1970 period and made educational opportunity much more widely available to whites from modest family backgrounds, depended mainly on changes in public systems of higher education and hence on the willingness of state legislatures to fund the expansion of existing public colleges and universities and the construction of new ones. Just after the war—when the first enrollment data are available separately for the public and private sectors of higher education—approximately equal numbers of students were enrolled in the two. But the number enrolled in public colleges and universities soared during the 1950s and 1960s, exceeding by 1965 the number in private higher education by a margin of two to one.[55]

The critical role of public higher education in non-zero-sum educational mobility speaks to the power of politicians representing white ethnics to see that the interests of their constituents were met in any expansion of opportunity. For example, in New York State, where a large system of private colleges and universities along with a public one, in New York City, already existed, the state government nevertheless formed the State University of New York in 1948. At its birth, the public system brought under its aegis thirty existing colleges with a total enrollment of fewer than 30,000 students. But these institutions provided the foundation for a rapid expansion of public higher education's offerings. By the early 1970s the system comprised seventy-two campuses educating 350,000 students. The placement of some of these campuses near large white-ethnic population concentrations—for example, one of the system's premier campuses, Stony Brook, was placed on Long Island, home to many recently suburbanized families—opened the pathway to educational opportunity for many first-generation white-ethnic college students.

The power of white-ethnic political representatives is implicit also in the changes in the residential landscape after World War II, which allowed the upwardly mobile ethnics to leave urban enclaves and integrate into the suburban melting pot. The federal government played a major role in the development of the modern mortgage instrument: the creation of the Federal Housing Authority home mortgage insurance program in 1934, followed by a similar Veterans Administration program aimed at returning GIs, enabled banks to offer mortgages on much more favorable terms to home buyers. Consequently, in just three decades, between 1940 and 1970, the proportion of American households owning their homes shot up from 44 to 63 percent. The emphasis in these programs was on new single-family home construction in socioeconomically and "racially stable" communities. The plans were formulated within government agencies in ways that made it very difficult for African Americans and other nonwhites to benefit from them, while the way to new opportunities was being opened for white ethnics. The FHA approval process was, at the outset, explicitly biased against neighborhoods that contained African Americans or were likely to undergo any racial shift; even after the FHA was forced away from overt consideration of race, it did little to challenge the institutionalized discrimination in the real-estate industry. The potent role of government policy in forging new avenues to better residential situations for white ethnics, while excluding nonwhites, underscores the political power of white-ethnic representatives, who were in a position to look after the interests of these groups. That matters could have turned out differently is suggested by the low desirability rankings assigned by some realtors to neighborhoods in which many southern Italian families resided. According to Thomas Guglielmo, on one important evaluation of the influence of "races and nationalities" on neighborhoods, southern Italians came in "just above African Americans and Mexican Americans." In a different political context, the red line that excluded some groups from participation in the massive expansion of homeownership and the exodus to the suburbs during the postwar decades might have been drawn above the Italians rather than, as happened, below them.[56]

The unique economic conditions under which this non-zero-sum mobility occurred might seem to limit its generalizability. For the United States had emerged victorious and relatively unscathed from the war, and for several decades it was a colossus dominating the global economy. According to the estimates of Angus Maddison, the United States accounted for about 19 percent of world GDP in 1913, falling just barely in second place behind the British Empire, but by 1950 it was responsible for 27 percent and no other country came anywhere close.[57] Given this hegemony, it was easier for the United States to open up the sluices of mobility without washing established Protestant groups off their privileged perches.

These political and economic factors point to the forces that created, and shaped the access to, non-zero-sum mobility in the decades after 1945. They do not qualify the claim that I have made about the role of such mobility in ethno-racial boundary change. Mobility of this type can arise under other circumstances, and the argument of ensuing chapters will be that a predictable demographic process, the departure of the massive and heavily white cohorts of baby boomers from the labor market during the first three decades of the current century, will also engender non-zero-sum mobility on a large scale. The question of who will benefit most from future non-zero-sum mobility is one that cannot be answered in advance, however. The answer will depend on decisions that we will make as a national political community.

One unresolved issue about the changes of the post–World War II period concerns the extent to which the arrival in urban America of groups below the white ethnics in the queue of employer preference facilitated white ethnics' upward mobility. This in-migration crested in the decades after World War II, the period when the strides of the children and grandchildren of the immigrants were at their greatest. The availability of African Americans, Puerto Ricans, and Mexicans to take the jobs at the bottom must have made it easier for some second-generation Irish and Italians to escape the socioeconomic fate of their parents. Moreover, many working-class white ethnics made strenuous efforts to keep blacks in particular from gaining parity with them in the labor market—for example, many unions, by virtue of their constitutions or practices, prevented blacks from joining and stayed as all-white preserves. This exclusion, along with a great deal of informal discrimination, pinned blacks to the bottom strata of jobs, which were redefined as jobs not suitable for the groups now being accepted as "white."[58]

The efforts white ethnics made to separate themselves from African Americans and to keep them out of labor-market niches and residential areas that they controlled have led some scholars, such as those working from the "whiteness" perspective, to suggest that the continued exclusion of African Americans and some other nonwhite groups was necessary to white-ethnic advance. While the leapfrogging of white ethnics past racial minorities was accomplished with maneuvers to prevent African Americans and others from sharing the same avenues to mobility that ethnic whites enjoyed in the postwar period, the story is more complex than the simple formula of "white-ethnic advance = minority exclusion." For one thing, much upward mobility would have happened in any event. One suggestive clue is that patterns of white-ethnic advance seem to have been very similar in many cities, some of which received large numbers of black and Hispanic migrants after World War II and some of which did not.[59]

But more important is that African-American advance was also a prominent feature of the postwar period. Some of the earliest fair-employment laws that barred ethno-racial discrimination were passed in states like Massachusetts and New York that had large white-ethnic populations; and black workers counted among the beneficiaries of these laws.[60] Moreover, at the same time that white ethnics were advancing in the North, the civil-rights movement was gaining moral momentum in the South and heading toward its greatest successes. These came from legislation at the national level during the 1960s that depended on the support of northern congressmen, many of whom had many white-ethnic constituents but were enthusiastic backers. In this sense, there appears to have been no ultimate contradiction between two types of boundary change, one affecting the boundaries between white-ethnic populations and the mainstream and the other between racial minorities and whites.

Conclusion

The immigrant ancestors of the so-called white ethnics, the Catholics, Orthodox Christians, and Jews coming from Ireland and southern and eastern Europe, landed in the United States mostly as low-wage laborers or petty entrepreneurs. Even after the immigrant generation, the white ethnics were widely viewed as inferior to native-stock white Americans, partly on grounds that were racial in nature and partly on grounds that were ethno-cultural (including, most notably, their attachment to suspect religions). While white ethnics rather quickly pushed themselves ahead of African Americans, some of them seemed destined at the middle of the twentieth century for an intermediate position in the racial and ethnic hierarchy, as sociological studies of the Italians in particular seemed to show. Yet by the final quarter of the century, it was apparent that the boundaries that separated them from white Protestant Americans had largely disintegrated. The mass assimilation of white-ethnic groups into the mainstream took place within a very short period, the few decades after World War II. By 1970, the process had been largely accomplished—that is to say, the cohorts of young people reaching maturity after that point no longer exhibited the large differences, such as those in education, that had previously helped to mark off one group from another. The result was a social world during the final decades of the twentieth century in which the boundaries based on the countries in Europe from which white Americans were descended and the religions to which they were attached were so diminished in salience that they became a part of the "background" rather than the foreground for many Americans. Apart from a fairly exclusive social and political elite, those who continued to cling to the ethnic affiliations, as for example the denizens of urban ethnic communities, were generally seen as having made choices rather than as having suffered exclusion. Ethnicity, in the trenchant formulation of sociologist Mary Waters, became an "option" rather than a constraint.[61] U.S. history offers no comparable example of such a wholesale dismantling of major ethno-racial boundaries.

Ethno-racial change—that is, change to the boundaries that distinguish groups as opposed to the crossing of these boundaries by individuals—appears to require special conditions to occur. Most of the time, more privileged groups are on guard to protect boundaries and the social distinctions that inhere in them, which form the foundation for their privilege. It is therefore easy to cite instances where the more privileged act to create new mechanisms or strengthen existing ones in order to restore and reinforce social distance and unequal life chances when a boundary seems to be weakening. The well-known imposition of anti-Semitic quotas by Harvard and other elite colleges during the 1920s is but one such case. It is more difficult to identify instances where a major ethno-racial boundary has faded in salience and the less privileged have been able to attain parity with their former superiors.

Three conditions in combination seem sufficient in theoretical and empirical terms to account for the boundary changes associated with the mass assimilation of the white ethnics. To begin with, the phenomenon of non-zero-sum mobility appears central to this process. Non-zero-sum mobility occurs when individuals can move up in a social system without the need for compensating downward movements by others. The explosive expansion of opportunity because of economic growth in the immediate post–World War II period made non-zero-sum mobility possible in the white-ethnic case. Non-zero-sum mobility is a key condition, because socioeconomic ascent can occur without the members of more privileged groups perceiving that their life chances and those of their children have diminished; hence, in such a situation, they should be less likely to strive to fortify the boundary that distinguishes them from upwardly striving groups.

Although non-zero-sum mobility may be a key condition, as well as one that occurs only under special circumstances, it is not the only factor needed to explain white-ethnic assimilation. In addition, it was necessary for mobile ethnics to be able to translate their improved socioeconomic position into greater social proximity to other whites, a process that was enhanced by the enormous residential shifts associated with the suburbanization of the postwar decades. And a cultural shift is implicated, too: as a consequence of the war, the moral position of the white ethnics was upgraded, through reportage, cinema, and literature that portrayed white-ethnic soldiers as the equals of other whites. After the war, discrimination on the basis of religion and ethnicity came under suspicion in a way that was not true during the first forty-five years of the twentieth century; the relenting of overt anti-Semitism during the 1950s and the 1960 election of Kennedy as the first (and, so far, only) Catholic president are but the most salient indicators.

Based on this analysis, an obvious question is: will the three conditions that brought about the assimilation of the white ethnics occur in the future in a way that affects the prospects for the second and third generations issuing from contemporary immigration? Might they also affect African Americans? The ensuing chapters explore the possibilities for such profound changes to the current ethno-racial contours of American society.

4

Contemporary Dynamics of Minority Mobility

The profound ethno-racial boundary changes that reshaped American society in the decades following World War II depended on a combination of forces that included large-scale non-zero-sum mobility as a critical ingredient. Its key role makes theoretical sense: ethno-racial boundaries are most likely to fade in relevance for those on the disadvantaged side when the perceived threat to the privileges of those on the advantaged side is reduced, and the latter are consequently less tempted to resort to the devices of ethno-racial exclusion. In the middle of the twentieth century, non-zero-sum mobility was largely the consequence of the economic preeminence of the United States, which produced massive economic changes of a type that increased the places available in higher institutions of learning and in the occupational strata to which their credentials are linked.

At first sight, the mid-twentieth-century formula for boundary change would seem impossible to replicate in the early twenty-first century. For one thing, the prospects for upward social mobility by African Americans and the children of immigrants are viewed pessimistically by many social scientists and other Americans.[1] The primary reasons lie in racism and economic structural change: in a common view, the latter is hollowing out the broad middle of the occupational structure while expanding its top and bottom. The emerging structure has been described as an "hour-glass" labor market, where the changes at the margins, produced by additions and deletions of positions, are adding to the extremes and reducing the middle. In addition, it is widely believed that many previously good jobs have deteriorated, as wages have stagnated and benefits have been shaved by employers; new forms of employment, such as independent contracting, have introduced precariousness where long-term stability once ruled.[2]

Such changes would seem to imply that in a racially stratified society, the children of nonwhite parents who are on the bottom rungs of the occupational structure—the Mexican-American second generation, say, whose parents are mainly engaged in low-wage labor in agriculture, construction, manufacturing, and service sectors—will have at best limited chances to move significantly upward, given the dearth of footholds in the middle.[3] The force of this implication is strengthened by recent studies of income mobility that indicate that the children of poor parents are more likely to remain poor in the United States than in any other economically advanced society.[4] And abundant research reveals the near-desperate situations of many nonwhite poor children, who are concentrated in distressed, heavily nonwhite communities that lack resources as well as ready access to the mainstream; white poor children on average are by no means as marginally situated.[5] Within immigrant populations, socioeconomic stagnation might be subjectively experienced as "downward" mobility by young adults raised in the United States, who would evaluate their social position exclusively by U.S. standards, unlike their immigrant parents, who could employ a dual frame of reference, one of them derived from their expectations of what would have happened to them had they remained in their homelands. Youngsters faced with limited prospects for success and experiencing blockages due to prejudice and discrimination are likely to react by rejecting mainstream goals and embracing oppositional identities, which carry high risks of dropping out early from school and involvement in criminal activity and other behaviors with negative consequences for their futures.[6]

This pessimistic account, however, overlooks the likelihood of mobility occurring as the number of European Americans available to take good jobs declines, relatively and even absolutely. The demography of young Americans is changing rapidly, with the birth cohorts coming to maturity and entering the labor market containing much larger shares of nonwhites and Hispanics than do the cohorts that are exiting. This demographic dynamic is likely to increase ethno-racial diversity throughout the labor force, including on its higher rungs. Moreover, during the next quarter century, some of the dominant demographic, economic, and social phenomena are certain to involve the retirement of the baby boomers, the cohorts of individuals born in the two decades following the end of World War II, specifically in the years 1946–1964.[7] This huge group, born before the current era of immigration was initiated by 1965 changes to U.S. immigration law and made up disproportionately of non-Hispanic whites, occupies a massive portion of the U.S. labor market—more than 50 percent of prime-age, full-time workers as of 2005. Their retirement will open up a huge swath of positions, running from the bottom to the top of the workforce. Because of the disproportionate concentration of white baby boomers in the middle and upper ranges of the occupational structure, the potential for racial and ethnic shifts will be especially large there. The implications of their retirement for the non-zero-sum mobility of disadvantaged nonwhite groups, especially Americans of African and Latin-American ancestry, whether they are descended ultimately from slaves or from recent immigrants, calls out for examination.

Contemporary Evidence of Racial/Ethnic Socioeconomic Shifts

Minorities are already penetrating in greater numbers into the higher tiers of the socioeconomic hierarchy largely as a result of demographic shifts—the gradient in the direction of larger proportions of nonwhites and Hispanics among younger birth cohorts—and, to a lesser extent, affirmative action. The demographic gradient is exemplified by the following comparison: in 2000, non-Hispanic whites, the cumbersome demographic term that encompasses the descendants of European immigrants, constituted 62 percent of the age group that was just beginning to enter the labor market, the 15- to 24-year-olds; however, they made up a substantially larger fraction, 78 percent, of the age group on the edge of retirement, the 55- to 64-year-olds. Such differences create a demographic dynamic that, in the absence of countervailing forces such as intensifying discrimination and other reinforcements of ethno-racial privilege, will lead to increased racial and ethnic diversity on the middle and upper rungs of the labor-force ladder.

Whatever the precise roles of simple demographic change and of affirmative action, shifts are increasingly visible in the recruitment of minorities into good jobs in the American economy. But what are "good jobs"? Here I equate jobs with occupations, which classify jobs according to the kind of work their incumbents typically do, and I take the average income that full-time workers[8] earn in various occupations[9] as a measure of the jobs' "goodness." One reason to measure position in the labor market using occupation rather than individual earnings is that the latter can fluctuate from year to year and, even worse, vary systematically with experience and hence age. But, more generally, the key problem in contriving a measure of labor-market position is to combine the systemic economic potential of jobs, including their prospects as careers, with what sociologists view as their social status, as reflected for instance in their "prestige." Both aspects are critical when it comes to studying socioeconomic mobility's link with potential ethno-racial shifts.

Occupations, as "the backbone of the reward structure" and the "elementary building blocks of modern and postmodern labor markets,"[10] provide the best schema for solving the problem. As Kim Weeden and David Grusky have argued, occupations generally represent coherent job slots—they have recognized titles (for example, firefighter, lawyer) by which the individuals who work in them identify themselves; they often have training and credentialing requirements, along with professional associations in some cases; and they mostly possess their own subcultures, into which those who would work in them must be initiated. Workers generally sport what Weeden and Grusky describe as the "social clothing" appropriate to their occupations, a term that refers to the relevant cultural traits and identities.[11] Sometimes, the actual clothing workers wear signals their occupations.

Using average earnings to measure the goodness of an occupation is suitable given the interest here in the ability of minority workers to convert socioeconomic advance into social proximity with the mainstream majority. That proximity is first of all reflected in residence, which is determined through market processes. Using occupations as the base for measurement also taps into the social-status dimension, which is crucial to the likelihood that mobile minorities will be treated as equals by middle-class whites. In social-status terms, a well-paid black electrician is not in the same position as a black financial analyst who has the same earnings; and this difference will be reflected in the social circles where they are welcomed and feel comfortable.[12] Ranking occupations on the basis of their systematic economic potential rather than ranking individuals on the basis of current earnings also does a reasonable job of reflecting this dimension.[13] (To continue the example: financial analysts have median earnings of $60,000, according to 2000 Census data, which places them on the boundary between the fourth and fifth percentiles on the U.S. earnings scale; the median earnings of electricians are just $40,000, and their occupation is located at the seam between the thirty-second and thirty-third percentiles.)

I slice into the hierarchy of ranked occupations in ways that account for different tiers of the full-time labor force: for example, the best-paid occupations that encompass 10 percent of full-time workers constitute the top decile; the top quartile is defined equivalently. These tranches are then applied as a grid to birth cohorts in order to look for shifts in the

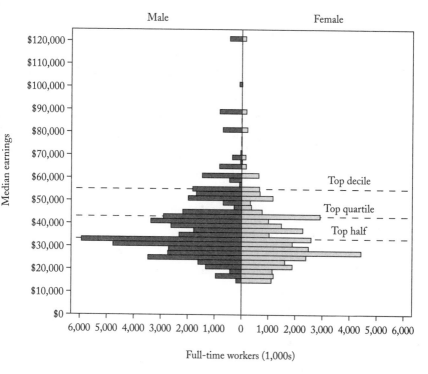

Figure 4.1. Full-time labor force (aged 25–64 in 1999) by median annual earnings of occupation. (2000 Public Use Microdata Sample (5 percent); see note 8 for definition of full-time worker.)

racial and ethnic composition of different tiers of the workforce. Figure 4.1 shows what this view of the workforce looks like on the basis of 1999 earnings (the earnings data collected by the 2000 Census); note that for the sake of visual coherence, the occupational codes have been classified within $2,000-wide bands of earnings. Interestingly, except perhaps for the narrow indentation between $46,000 and $50,000, there is no re-semblance here to an hour glass; rather, the labor force exhibits a large bulge in the lower middle, where the workers of the third quartile are concentrated, and then gradually narrows in numbers with increasing remuneration—an incongruous combination, it would seem, of sliced pear and pyramid.

The division of the labor force into tiers based on the average pay of their occupations sharply stratifies workers according to their educational and ethno-racial and nativity characteristics, as shown in Table 4.1.[14] The top decile includes many professional and highly technical occupations, such as dentists and engineers; some well-paid management and financial jobs are also located there. The median earnings of jobs in this tier were $65,000 in 1999. Almost three-quarters of all its workers possessed a bachelor's degree, and virtually all the rest had at least some postsecondary education. The majority group still dominates this tier, though it increasingly is also occupied by immigrants who arrive with high levels of human capital: nearly 80 percent of the top-decile workers in 2000 were U.S.-born non-Hispanic whites, and foreign-born whites and Asians accounted for an additional 11 percent. While U.S.-born Asians made up only 1.3 percent of workers in this tier, this small percentage was in fact higher than the native-born Asian percentage of the total workforce. The numbers of second and later generations of Asian groups in adult ages were still modest in 2000, though growing; the sizable Asian percentage of the U.S. workforce was dominated by the foreign born who had come since the late 1960s. The representation of disadvantaged native minority populations, U.S.-born blacks and Hispanics, was quite small, at 6 percent, relative to their overall percentage in the full-time workforce, 13 percent.

This racial/ethnic stratification is modestly ameliorated further down the ladder within the top half of jobs. For the jobs in the remainder of the top quartile (the jobs between percentiles 11 and 25), the 1999 median earnings were on average substantially lower, at $48,000, and the percentage of workers holding a baccalaureate degree was down to about half, though most of the remaining workers still had spent some time in college. The jobs in this tier exhibit a wide range in terms of their required training and preparation, from such professions as architect to

Table 4.1 Characteristics of occupational tiers of prime-age, full-time workers in 2000

Tier	N (1000s)	Median earnings	Postsecondary education		Race/ethnicity/nativity composition of tier[a]							
			% with some coll., no BA	% with BA or more	% U.S.-born non-Hispanic whites	% foreign-born non-Hispanic whites	% U.S.-born non-Hispanic blacks	% foreign-born non-Hispanic blacks	% U.S.-born Hispanics	% foreign-born Hispanics	% U.S.-born Asians	% foreign-born Asians
Top decile	8,600	$65,000	20.2	72.7	78.4	4.8	3.8	0.7	2.2	1.7	1.3	6.1
Rest of top quartile	13,051	$48,000	32.5	52.3	78.7	3.4	6.1	0.9	2.9	2.2	0.9	3.7
Second quartile	21,525	$38,000	33.3	37.7	77.0	2.3	8.1	0.8	3.8	3.3	0.8	2.4
Third quartile	22,253	$30,000	35.3	17.0	71.2	2.5	10.4	1.0	4.4	5.9	0.6	2.5
Fourth quartile	20,725	$22,000	29.1	8.0	58.8	2.5	14.0	1.7	4.7	11.9	0.5	4.1

Source: 2000 Public Use Data Sample (5 percent).

a. Percentages of ethno-racial/nativity categories add to less than 100 because two residual (other) categories are not reported.

such unionized, well-paying blue-collar jobs as railroad brake operators and fire fighters. Yet nearly 80 percent of the jobs were still held by native-born non-Hispanic whites as of 2000. U.S.-born blacks and Hispanics had nevertheless increased their share to 9 percent, with most of the increase due to the rising share of jobs held by African Americans. Immigrants play a less prominent role here: the percentage of foreign-born whites and Asians was down to 7 percent. In the second quartile, the median earnings fell to $38,000 in 1999, and only a third of workers had earned a four-year college degree and another third had some post-secondary training. Because the second quartile covers a wider spectrum than the two higher tranches just discussed, the range of job situations is correspondingly broader, from police officer, to clerical supervisor, to machinist, to sociologist. The role of U.S.-born blacks and Hispanics is again greater at this tier than higher up, and in 2000, they held 12 percent of these jobs, with the former outnumbering the latter by a 2-to-1 margin. U.S.-born whites still occupy the lion's share of these jobs— more than three-quarters in 2000—suggesting that the higher portion held by U.S.-born minorities comes mainly at the cost of immigrants. The proportions of foreign-born whites and Asians are indeed lower than in the higher tiers, but that of workers born in Latin America is higher.

The jobs in the bottom half of the labor force are much less desirable. The median wages in 1999 were $30,000 in the third quartile and $22,000 in the fourth (but went as low as $14,000 for full-time workers in the last-ranked occupation, dishwasher). Only a small minority of workers here have earned a baccalaureate degree, although roughly a third attended college and left without that credential. Below the halfway point on the job ladder, the concentration of whites starts to diminish noticeably, and that of minorities, both U.S. and foreign born, increases. Nearly two-thirds of U.S.-born black and Hispanic full-time workers are found in the bottom half of the workforce; in 2000 they made up 15 percent of the full-time workers in the third quartile and almost 20 percent of those in the fourth, where foreign-born Latinos were an additional 12 percent. Still, U.S.-born whites are the majority of these workers, even in the fourth quartile, where they were approximately 60 percent of the workers in 2000.

Some shifting of racial and ethnic groups among these tiers is already under way, as can be observed in Figure 4.2, which introduces the characteristics of birth cohorts and shows the changing ethno-racial and nativity composition of the top quartile. The changes are visible in the increasing representation of minorities, especially blacks and Hispanics, among younger workers. In looking for shifts, it is sensible to focus on the top strata because these are the locations where the advantages of whites are most evident; if changes are taking place there, they are also taking place at lower levels, where there is greater minority representation, in any event.[15] The causes of the shifts lie, as we will shortly see,

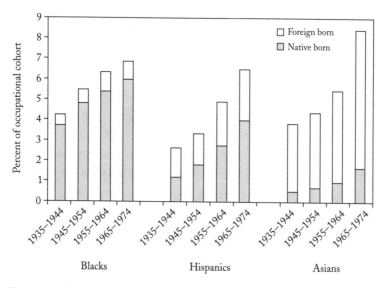

Figure 4.2. Full-time employment in top-quartile occupations for minorities by nativity and birth cohort, 2000. (2000 Public Use Microdata Sample (5 percent).)

mainly in demographic dynamics, that is, changes in ethno-racial composition across cohorts in the population, though it is plausible that affirmative action also plays a modest part.

The growing diversity in the top quartile implies that the majority group holds a decreasing share of the best jobs. (The figure does not show this because the bars for whites have been omitted; given their incommensurate size, they would dwarf those for the other groups and make the shifts for them difficult to see.) In the oldest birth cohort, that is, individuals born in the period 1935–1944 (who were aged 56–65 in 2000),[16] 83 percent of the incumbents of the top quartile are native-born non-Hispanic whites. This fraction barely decreases in the next oldest birth cohort, 1945–1954 (aged 46–55 in 2000), but is lowered more noticeably with each younger group. Among those in the youngest cohort as of 2000, born in the period 1965–1974, the fraction of native-born white workers has slipped to 73 percent.

African Americans[17] and U.S.-born Hispanics have been steadily expanding their representation in this occupational tier, but even in the youngest group of workers their share of good jobs falls well below their proportions among all workers or in the population of these ages. In the oldest group, they constitute 5 percent of full-time workers holding top-quartile jobs; in the youngest, their share has doubled, to 10 percent. The rise has been especially steep for U.S.-born Hispanics, who held just 1 percent of the jobs in this tier in the cohort born in 1935–1944 but 4 percent in the 1965–1974 cohort. The nonwhite and Hispanic foreign born are also contributing to the rise in the diversity in top jobs. The immigrants have gone from 5 percent of the oldest cohort to 10 percent of the youngest (white immigrants, mainly from Canada and Europe, add another 4–5 percent to these figures). The increasing immigrant presence is, above all, a story about Asians, who have taken nearly 7 percent of the top-quartile jobs in the youngest cohort. By a considerable margin, they outnumber U.S.-born Asians, whose share among the youngest workers falls out at almost 2 percent, though as low as this figure seems,

it represents a jump from the tiny fraction of jobs the American born
hold in the oldest cohort, just 0.5 percent.

In the most elite sphere of the labor market, the top decile of jobs,
U.S.-born minorities are also playing a substantially larger role. (See
Figure 4.3.) The growth in their share has been steep across different
cohorts of workers; however, it started from a lower base and has not
achieved the same height as their representation in the rest of the top
quartile. U.S.-born blacks and Hispanics held only 3 percent of these
jobs in the oldest cohort of workers of 2000, but among the 26- to
35-year-olds, their fraction of these jobs had risen to 8 percent. In this
tier, where many of the jobs are professional or technical and postsecondary educational credentials are often a requirement, the importance
of Asian immigrants is remarkable. Even in the oldest cohort, they provide nearly 5 percent of the workers, and in the youngest cohort, this

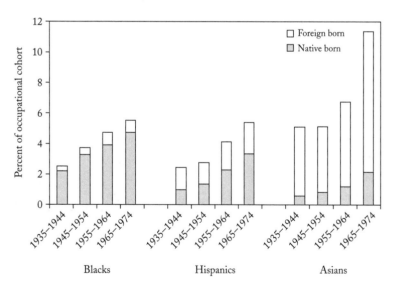

Figure 4.3. Full-time employment in top-decile occupations for minorities by
nativity and birth cohort, 2000. (2000 Public Use Microdata Sample (5 percent).)

figure has shot up to 9 percent, far above their percentage of the working-age population.

Native-born minorities, African Americans and Latinos, are making some remarkable gains as they are penetrate more and more into unexpected occupations, contradicting stereotypes about minority achievements. Table 4.2 shows a selection of well-paid occupations where, on the left-hand side, the share of African or Hispanic Americans is rising and, on the right-hand side, it is stagnating. The increases are notable in engineering fields, for example: among the ranks of electrical and electronics engineers, an occupational category that ranks in the top 5 percent of the labor force according to the median earnings of its incumbents, African Americans tripled their representation between the oldest and youngest cohorts; and Hispanics are now much more numerous among engineering managers. Large increases have occurred in most other engineering occupations and in computer-related occupational titles (for example, computer hardware engineers and computer programmers). U.S.-born minorities are also progressing in a number of financial fields: for instance, among financial analysts, a job that is ranked at the fifth percentile on the basis of remuneration, African Americans were 7 percent of the youngest workers in 2000, more than triple their representation among the oldest ones.

Yet blacks and Hispanics are not advancing uniformly throughout the tiers of the labor force: there are some occupations in which they remain rare. For example, in 2000 African Americans and U.S.-born Hispanics combined were just 4 percent of the chief executives who were 45 or younger (it doesn't seem appropriate to consider only the very youngest group of chief executives, aged 26 to 35 at the time, because there is an almost inherent contradiction between such youthfulness and authority in an organization). This still represents an improvement over their representation among older chief executives, which was just 3 percent. But it indicates that minorities are rare in some positions that offer the potential for very high economic rewards. They are also infrequent in some

Table 4.2 Minority advance and stagnation in selected top-quartile occupations

	Greater-than-average advance				Lower-than-average advance or decline			
	Occup. title	Percentile rank (0 is top)	% of incumbents 1965–74 cohort	% of incumbents 1935–44 cohort	Occup. title	Percentile rank (0 is top)	% of incumbents 1965–74 cohort	% of incumbents 1935–44 cohort
African Americans	Lawyers	2.4	4.9	1.5	Chief executives	1.4	2.3	1.7
	Electrical engineers	4.8	5.7	1.8	Optometrists	2.9	0.6	1.7
	Financial analysts	5.0	7.4	2.1	Physical therapists	16.2	2.9	5.4
U.S.-born Latinos	Engineering managers	3.0	3.6	0.4	Optometrists	2.9	1.3	2.6
	Judges and judicial workers	3.8	9.2	1.9	Mathematicians	10.7	1.7	1.6
	Psychologists	13.8	4.2	0.5	Tool and die makers	22.3	1.4	1.6

Source: 2000 Public Use Microdata Sample (5 percent).

professional and technical occupations requiring prolonged training—in 2000, for example, together they made up 3 percent of the young chiropractors, 4 percent of the young actuaries, and 5 percent of the young astronomers, physicists, and aircraft pilots and flight engineers. In some cases, the absence of appropriate qualifications does not seem a possible explanation for the severity of minority underrepresentation: it is striking, for instance, that U.S.-born blacks and Hispanics made up less than 6 percent of young construction managers, a large and well-paid occupational category (located at the sixteenth percentile in average remuneration); the history of African-American exclusion from the construction trades must be taken into account here.[18]

Also true is that minority representation in well-paid occupations comes about partly through their incumbency in specific blue-collar jobs whose wages have been protected by unions. For example, locomotive engineers, railroad conductors, and yardmasters are categories with relatively high minority representation—U.S.-born blacks and Hispanics, the former especially, accounted together for about a quarter of the members of these categories at or under the age of 45 in 2000—and the relatively high earnings of their full-time workers place them near the boundary between the top decile and the rest of the top quartile. Nevertheless, these occupations are not growing, and they do not provide a base for future increases in well-paid minority employment. By the same token, they cannot account for the *increasing* numbers of blacks, Hispanics, and other minorities to be found on the higher rungs of the occupational ladder.

The diversification of the ethno-racial origins of the incumbents in the top tiers of the labor force has continued since 2000, as shown by the data in Table 4.3, which were compiled from the 2005 and 2006 American Community Surveys.[19] The increasing penetration of nonwhites and Hispanics into these tiers is potentially consequential for boundaries as it brings middle-class whites and minorities into more frequent interaction as status equals, perhaps not only at work but also in less formal settings.[20] The table presents, this time in numerical rather than in graphic form, the updated ethno-racial data for the same birth cohorts used before; to them I add the data for relatively new entrants to the labor force, who were born in 1975–1980 and were aged 26 to 31 in 2006. The data for the second quartile are also shown for the first time.

The table strongly emphasizes the split between the older cohorts and the younger ones. While a shift in the direction of greater minority representation begins with the cohort born in 1955–1964, it becomes very pronounced in the two youngest cohorts, born in the 1965–1980 period. An unmistakable signal is being sent by the rapidly falling fraction of good jobs held by the ethno-racial majority, native-born non-Hispanic whites: while they are more than 80 percent of the occupants of top-decile and other top-quartile jobs in the two oldest cohorts, their grip on the best jobs loosens noticeably in the middle-aged cohort and then even more in the two youngest ones. Among the youngest workers, native whites hold less than two-thirds of the top-decile jobs and about 70 percent of those in the remainder of the top half of the workforce.

The representation of U.S.-born blacks and Hispanics in these tiers of good jobs is increasing in two ways. The first is the one already noted: the youngest cohort, whose members have generally entered the full-time labor market within the preceding decade and mostly since 2000, has an even higher share of minorities than do older ones. In the youngest cohort in 2005–2006, African and Hispanic Americans held almost 10 percent of the top-decile jobs, an improvement—it should be remembered—over the 8 percent held by them in the youngest cohort as of 2000. And they occupy 13 percent of the other top-quartile jobs in the youngest cohort, again a significant step beyond their position in 2000. Much of this improvement (but not all of it) is due to the rapidly rising share of good jobs held by U.S.-born Hispanics. For instance, they represented 3.3 percent of the top decile and 4.4 percent of other top-quartile jobs in the youngest cohort of 2000, but among the new labor-market entrants of 2005–2006, their shares are now 4.5 and 6.1 percent,

Table 4.3 The shifting race/ethnicity/nativity composition (%) of the best-paid occupations, 2005–2006

Birth cohort (age in 2006)	U.S.-born non-Hispanic whites	Foreign-born non-Hispanic whites	U.S.-born non-Hispanic blacks	Foreign-born non-Hispanic blacks	U.S.-born Hispanics	Foreign-born Hispanics	U.S.-born Asians	Foreign-born Asians
Top decile								
1975–80 (26–31)	64.9	4.3	5.0	0.8	4.5	2.5	4.2	12.6
1965–74 (32–41)	68.1	5.7	4.9	0.9	3.5	2.5	2.1	11.3
1955–64 (42–51)	77.3	5.3	4.0	0.8	2.5	1.9	1.3	6.1
1945–54 (52–61)	82.1	5.1	3.0	0.6	1.5	1.6	0.8	4.5
1935–44 (62–71)	81.7	5.6	2.2	0.5	1.1	1.9	0.8	5.5
Rest of top quartile								
1975–80 (26–31)	69.4	3.1	7.3	1.0	6.1	3.3	2.6	6.2
1965–74 (32–41)	70.5	3.9	7.3	1.1	4.8	3.5	1.4	6.5
1955–64 (42–51)	76.9	3.5	6.4	1.3	3.2	2.5	0.9	4.2

1945–54 (52–61)	81.8	3.5	5.2	0.8	2.2	1.7	0.7	3.1
1935–44 (62–71)	82.0	5.0	4.4	0.8	1.7	1.7	0.5	3.1
Second quartile								
1975–80 (26–31)	69.9	1.9	8.0	0.9	8.0	5.5	1.8	2.8
1965–74 (32–41)	69.8	2.3	9.0	1.0	6.2	5.7	1.1	3.6
1955–64 (42–51)	75.5	2.4	8.1	1.0	4.1	4.0	0.8	2.8
1945–54 (52–61)	79.4	2.8	7.1	0.7	2.9	2.7	0.7	2.6
1935–44 (62–71)	79.9	3.8	5.4	0.6	2.5	3.2	0.7	2.8

Source: 2005 and 2006 American Community Surveys.

Note: Rows total less than 100% because small categories containing workers of other races are not shown.

respectively. The second way that minority representation is increasing occurs over time for the same cohorts of workers. Comparing the 1965–1974 birth cohort in 2000, when it was the youngest group, with 2005–2006 shows, for instance, that the African-American share has climbed from 4.7 and 6.9 percent in the top decile and the rest of the top quartile, respectively, to 4.9 and 7.3 percent, respectively. The changes are not very large, granted, but they demonstrate a dynamic that is consistent in direction and favors growing diversity in the top tiers.[21]

The post-2000 data also indicate the increasingly powerful role of immigrants, especially from Asia, in these tiers, particularly in the top decile. Among the youngest workers, the Asian-immigrant share of top-decile jobs has soared to 13 percent. However, it falls to half this level in the remainder of the top quartile and is quite small in the second quartile (where, however, Latino immigrants hold a non-negligible fraction of jobs). Apparently, the labor-market role of immigrants from Asia is quite specialized, a fact that has implications for an immigration-based strategy to meet U.S. needs for workers in the near future. U.S.-born Asians, a group whose adult portion is now expanding rapidly a generation or so after the renewal of large-scale immigration from Asia in the late 1960s, are also increasing their share of top-tier jobs. They hold 4 percent of the top-decile jobs in the youngest cohort as of 2005–2006, a leap beyond the 2 percent held by their youngest cohort in 2000. Because they often possess high postsecondary educational credentials, Asian Americans achieve their greatest level of labor-market concentration in the top decile.

Limits to the Ethno-Racial Labor-Market Shifts

Impressive as the shifts in the ethno-racial composition of the higher tiers of the labor market are, they are largely due to underlying demographic change in the population rather than to an amelioration of structures of ethno-racial inequality. In other words, the potent role of demography as the driver of these ethno-racial changes implies that at least so far, we have not moved much toward equality of opportunity for Americans of different racial and ethnic backgrounds in the labor market. We can observe this with hyperclarity if we focus specifically on U.S.-born blacks and Hispanics. By separating out the foreign born, we eliminate the possibility that any disadvantage we find is due to immigrant status. The key question then is whether the population-based probabilities for different groups to enter the ranks of good jobs have changed. Because these probabilities are based on a group's population size rather than on its number of workers, they take into account the extra risks to which members of ethno-racial minorities are exposed—under- or unemployment or even incarceration—that prevent them from appearing in the full-time workforce.[22]

Figure 4.4 shows these probabilities in graphic terms. (The oldest cohort, born in 1935–1944, has been omitted because its probability of full-time employment has already dipped considerably as a result of retirements.) The inequalities between whites and Asians, on the one hand, and blacks and Hispanics, on the other, are marked. For instance, in the cohort born in 1945–1954 (aged 46–55 in 2000), the leading edge of the baby boom, just 2.1 percent of African Americans held down full-time top-decile jobs and 6.1 percent had jobs located elsewhere in the top quartile. By comparison, the equivalent probabilities for non-Hispanic whites were 7.2 percent and 11.8 percent, respectively. Stated in other terms, whites were more than three times as likely as African Americans to land a top-decile job and about twice as likely to obtain one in the rest of the top quartile. Their advantages over older native-born Hispanics were almost as large—the probability for the latter to enter the top decile was 2.9 percent, and for moving into the rest of the top quartile, 7.1 percent. Asians were slightly more advantaged than whites in these terms, so the comparisons are even more unfavorable for blacks and Hispanics when Asians are the reference point. Moreover, these inequalities are not counterbalanced by bringing in the second

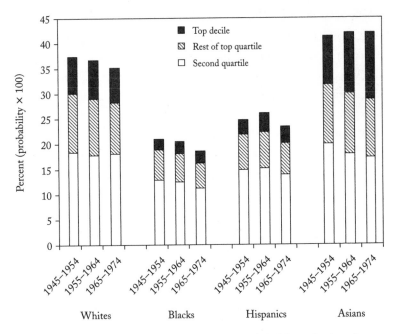

Figure 4.4. Probability of full-time job by tier, race/ethnicity and cohort for U.S. born, 2000.(2000 Public Use Microdata Sample (5 percent).)

quartile, where in the 1945–1954 cohort 18.4 percent of all whites had full-time jobs, but only 12.8 percent of African Americans and 14.8 percent of Hispanics did. These highly unequal chances, it should be underscored, are found in a cohort whose members came to maturity after the major legislative and moral victories of the civil-rights movement in the mid-1960s.

Inequality has improved—but only a bit—in the youngest cohort. The probability for African Americans to enter the top decile has risen to 2.4 percent; that for Hispanics, to 3.3 percent. Since the equivalent probability for whites has dropped slightly to 6.9 percent—the youthful ages of this cohort may limit its occupational attainments and, correspondingly, the white advantage—the relative inequality among these groups has clearly been reduced with respect to the top tier. However, it remains just as powerful as before below the top decile. Minority probabilities of occupying other top-quartile positions are lower in the youngest cohort than in the middle-aged ones—4.9 percent for African Americans and 6.2 percent for Hispanics. The probability for whites is also somewhat smaller, at 10.1 percent, but the relative inequality among the groups is not any different. The one sharp change concerns U.S.-born Asians, whose probability of holding a job in the top tier has shot upward—to 13.2 percent in the youngest cohort, almost twice as large as that for whites.

If the underlying probabilities for different groups of entering the tiers of good jobs have not fundamentally changed, then the ethno-racial shifts we have observed in the composition of these tiers are a consequence of demographic changes taking place in the population—as more and more minorities appear in the cohorts entering the labor market, their greater numbers are also reflected in those hired to become attorneys, engineers, and computer programmers. Stating the dynamic that is driving change in this way does not deprive the compositional shifts of all significance—for they are still affecting the occupational worlds inhabited by whites and thereby having an impact on boundaries—but it does affect our understanding of them. It also implies that the shifts are likely to continue, for the cohorts still too young to enter the labor market contain even higher proportions of nonwhites and Hispanics. For example, among the children born in the United States in the late 1990s, the 0- to 5-year-olds of 2000, the fraction of non-Hispanic whites was down to 60 percent; among the U.S. born who had just entered the labor market, the 26- to 35-year-olds of that year, it was 75 percent; and among those on the edge of retirement, the 56- to 65-year-olds, it was 85 percent. Immigration will only increase the proportion of minorities in the youngest cohort by the time it reaches prime working age.

The demographic dynamic also implies, however, that the bottom half of the workforce will see even greater concentrations of minori-

ties in the future than today, unless the ethno-racial inequalities in the
chances to escape into the realm of better jobs improve. Here, as well,
the probabilities have not changed very much across U.S.-born cohorts,
though the degree of ethno-racial inequality is not as marked as it is for
entrance to the higher tiers. The probability for whites to take jobs in the
bottom half varies between 28 and 31 percent for different cohorts, that
for Hispanics between 32 and 34 percent, and that for blacks between
34 and 36 percent. Only Asians stand apart from the others: their probabilities of winding up in the bottom half of the workforce vary between
23 and 27 percent, with the lower figure characterizing the youngest
cohort.

There are other important ways in which the occupational gains of
African and Hispanic Americans are more limited than they seem at
first sight. One is that minorities depend more than whites on government employment to advance into good jobs. (See the data in Figure
4.5.) This reliance has long been known for African Americans and explained on the grounds that affirmative action is more effective in government. Because, in addition, many government jobs are filled through
civil-service rules and depend on examination scores, the scope for racial
discrimination is reduced.[23] However, native-born Hispanics also depend more on government employment for access to good jobs than do
whites. This dependency is evident when we look at minority representation in specific occupations: combined, blacks and Hispanics represented 9 percent of the young attorneys of 2000 (more than tripling their
share of the profession by comparison with the oldest group), but they
were almost a quarter of the young judges and magistrates. They also
made up nearly a fifth of the young air traffic controllers, 15 percent of
the young urban and regional planners, 19 percent of the young education administrators, 20 percent of the young detectives, and 23 percent
of the young budget analysts (according to the Bureau of Labor Statistics, more than half of all budget analysts work for government).

As Figure 4.5 reveals, the divergence in type of employment is consis-

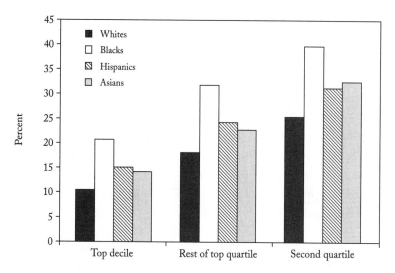

Figure 4.5. Government employment by tier for U.S.-born, full-time workers, aged 26–65, 2000. (2000 Public Use Microdata Sample (5 percent).)

tent throughout the top half of the labor force, even though the overall level of government employment dips higher up on the occupational ladder. Whites are always the most likely to be employed in the private sector, blacks the least; Hispanics and Asians are in between. Where overall the level of government employment is lowest, in the top decile, the ethno-racial differences are particularly striking and consequential, since many professional and management occupations allow workers in the private sector to earn very high salaries. Only 11 percent of the native whites with full-time jobs there are employed by government. The comparable figure for African Americans, 21 percent, is nearly twice as high, and that for Hispanics, 15 percent, nearly 50 percent higher. However, in the top decile, as elsewhere in the labor market, the dependence on government employment is lower in general in younger cohorts, where minority advance is greater. Apparently, the penetration of young blacks and Hispanics into higher labor-market tiers is less dependent on government employment than one would expect from the historical record. Yet it is also possible that, as these cohorts age, they will move more into government employment, which seems overall to increase in likelihood with age.

Further, African Americans and U.S.-born Hispanics exhibit gender-inflected patterns of social ascent: that is to say, women play a critical role in their penetration into top tiers of the labor market. The salience of minority women has largely to do with their superior postsecondary educational record, or, perhaps better put, with the greater obstacles faced by minority men, beginning with those in the educational system. It implies that the advance of minorities in the labor market depends on affirmative action not only for minority groups but also for women. At the same time, the dependence of minority mobility on the attainments of women potentially imposes limitations on its significance for the economic well-being of minority families and communities: since women still average less pay in the labor market than do men, even when they perform the same work, the economic benefits of minority mobility may be less than they would be if minorities were represented in top-tier occupations in the same gender proportions as whites are.

The gender-inflected pattern is most pronounced among African Americans and at the highest levels of the labor market. (Figure 4.6 shows the pattern in terms of sex ratios by cohort and tier; by definition, a sex ratio is the number of men per 100 women, and thus gender parity is indicated by the horizontal line at 100 in the graph.) The changes occurring in the top decile bring the prominent role of women in minority occupational ascent into sharp relief. While this tier has been dominated by men, that dominance is gradually weakening. Overall, three-quarters of the full-time occupants of top-decile positions were men in 2000, but the hold of men on the best jobs was loosening with each new cohort. In the oldest cohort, the one born in 1935–1944, 86 percent of the incumbents were men, but in the youngest, born in 1965–1974, the percentage had fallen to 70 percent. Among African Americans, the gender imbalance in these jobs was never as lop-sided as it was among whites, and, in

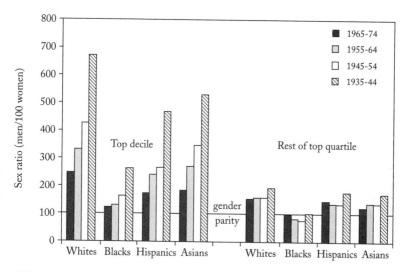

Figure 4.6. Sex-ratio changes in top tiers across U.S.-born cohorts, 2000. (2000 Public Use Microdata Sample (5 percent).)

the youngest cohort, there is near parity, as men make up 55 percent of the black contingent. (By comparison, among the native-born whites of this cohort, men are 72 percent.) Elsewhere in the top quartile, in contrast to the continuing dominance of men among whites, women outnumber men among black holders of these good jobs.

Women are also critical to Hispanic advance, but not to the same degree. Indeed, Hispanic men outnumber Hispanic women in the top tiers of the labor market, but not as much as is the case for native-born whites. In the youngest cohort of top-quartile workers, men are 61 percent of the Hispanics found there. This is, however, a reduction from the male dominance in the oldest cohort, where men outnumbered women among Hispanics by a more than 2-to-1 ratio.

These patterns—the more prominent role of women in occupational mobility and the dependence on government employment—suggest limits to the economic benefits of the socioeconomic advance of youthful minorities, since women typically earn less than men and, at higher levels, government jobs pay less than their equivalents in the private sector. But the limits on minority advance are deeper and more systemic than just these two patterns. They are evident in two additional respects. One is in the relationship of occupational placement to educational credentials, for at the same level of educational attainment, whites enjoy a more favorable occupational placement than minorities generally do. The advantages of native-born whites are revealed by the results of regression analyses that rely on post-2000 data from the Census Bureau, the American Community Survey of 2005.[24] The dependent variable is the median earnings (logged) of an individual's occupation, and the independent variables include his or her educational attainment in years, plus the highest degree, along with other key control variables, such as whether employment is in government or private industry. Because of changes in occupational placement across birth cohorts and possibly different patterns of recruitment of men and women into occupations, the regressions are estimated separately by gender in different ten-year cohorts.

The numbers in Table 4.4 are informative about the occupational placement of minority and foreign-born categories relative to that of U.S.-born whites. Specifically, these numbers express the expected percentage differences in the median earnings of occupations between categories with other variables held constant.[25] The predominance of negative values indicates that native-born whites are generally the best placed, while African Americans and U.S.-born Hispanics are placed in jobs that pay distinctly less than one would predict from their educational credentials. Disadvantages of this sort are greater for African Americans: in most cohorts, the net disadvantage of African-American men is 10–12 percent in the median salary of their occupation. The gap is moderately reduced in the youngest cohort to about 7 percent. African-American women are also disadvantaged by comparison with native-born white women, but not to the same extent: in the older cohorts, they are 8–9 percent behind in occupational placement, and in the youngest, 6 percent. The Hispanic disadvantage, though lower, is still statistically mean-

(numbers express percentage differences in median earnings of expected occupations relative to those of non-Hispanic whites)

Birth cohort (age)	U.S.-born non-Hispanic whites	Foreign-born non-Hispanic whites	U.S.-born non-Hispanic blacks	Foreign-born non-Hispanic blacks	U.S.-born Hispanics	Foreign-born Hispanics	U.S.-born Asians	Foreign-born Asians
Men								
1970–79 (26–35)	—	−3.1	−7.3	−12.6	−4.0	−15.4	+2.6	+3.7
1960–69 (36–45)	—	−2.5	−10.7	−15.0	−4.4	−16.0	+0.5	−5.4
1950–59 (46–55)	—	−1.9	−11.7	−16.3	−4.3	−14.3	−3.5	−10.0
1940–49 (56–65)	—	−0.5	−11.0	−15.8	−5.2	−12.3	−4.1	−9.8
Women								
1970–79 (26–35)	—	−3.9	−5.9	−8.8	−1.2	−13.7	+2.2	+0.9
1960–69 (36–45)	—	−5.0	−7.7	−9.3	−2.3	−16.6	−0.4	−6.3
1950–59 (46–55)	—	−8.0	−9.4	−12.7	−3.9	−15.0	−2.3	−10.1
1940–49 (56–65)	—	−5.8	−8.7	−12.7	−6.6	−12.9	−3.4	−8.6

Source: 2005 American Community Survey.

Note: Nonsignificant coefficients are indicated by shading.

a. The independent variables include education (in years of attainment) plus dummy variables to indicate highest postsecondary degree, employment in government (vs. private) sector and region, along with ethno-racial/nativity dummy variables. Percentage differences are calculated by the formula $100(e^{b} - 1)$, where b is the coefficient of an ethno-racial/nativity dummy variable in an equation with a logged dependent variable.

ingful. Among men, it is consistently on the order of 4–5 percent, while among women, it is very low in the youngest cohort, just 1 percent, but rises with age to attain 7 percent in the oldest group. The occupational placement of U.S.-born Asians is also worth noting in this context, because it can be helpful in deciphering how ethno-racial disadvantages arise. Among both men and women, native-born Asians are at least as well placed, net of education and degrees, as their white peers in the two youngest cohorts; however, in older cohorts, some degree of disadvantage, in the 2–4 percent range, is evident.

The difficult interpretive issues that arise from these findings concern how much of the ethno-racial disadvantage to attribute to discrimination and whether the reduction of disadvantage in the youngest cohort indicates the start of a possible trend of improvement in the occupational placement of minorities. An explanatory alternative to labor-market discrimination would hold that the disadvantages of blacks and Hispanics have to do with the quality of the educational institutions they have attended (unmeasured in Census data). A recent study of young people in New York City found that blacks and Hispanics attend lower-ranked colleges than do whites; there, they attend the less prestigious institutions of the City University of New York.[26] Presumably, the credentials they earn do not have the same labor-market value as those earned at more highly regarded institutions. Moreover, William Bowen and Derek Bok's examination of the black graduates of elite colleges reveals the sizable earnings premium that they obtain because of the imprimatur of an elite education.[27] The quality of credentials clearly matters at the top of the job ladder. However, it is hard to believe that this alternative is sufficient to explain the less favorable placement of blacks and Hispanics entirely. Asian Americans have a much higher rate of attendance at top-ranked colleges and universities than whites do, but their labor-market placement is only slightly better than that of whites in the youngest cohort and not at all better in the next oldest. Discrimination of one sort or another—perhaps, for example, a failure to promote qualified Asian

Americans at the same rate as whites are promoted—seems involved. The same conclusion carries over to the other ethno-racial differences, especially since abundant research on ethno-racial differentials in the labor market establishes that they cannot be fully explained by any plausible set of intervening variables.[28]

The other issue, whether there is evidence of an improved labor-market position in the smaller disadvantages for blacks and Hispanics in the youngest cohort, is equally thorny to resolve. The differences across cohorts can be understood in two ways: in one, they express historical changes in life chances, which are reflected in the attainments of different birth cohorts because they reach maturity under varying conditions; in the other, they express variations across the life cycle, which each cohort experiences as its members age. These interpretations are not mutually exclusive, and it is quite possible that both apply here, though the mix of their influences remains unknown. It is certainly possible that the less disadvantaged position of the younger cohorts of nonwhites reflects true improvements in life chances, as might happen from a decline in labor-market discrimination (perhaps due to the rising numbers of nonwhites in positions to make employment decisions or to counsel nonwhite newcomers about career options and strategies). But it is just as plausible that the more disadvantaged positions of older cohorts reveal an accumulation of disadvantages over the life course, as the careers of minorities develop more slowly or stall because of discrimination that occurs after hiring. Indeed, much labor-market research demonstrates the cumulative nature of white advantage over the course of work lives.[29] Nevertheless, one should be cautious about inferring from the experiences of older cohorts as they age that the smaller ethno-racial differentials at young ages will necessarily grow as workers become older (the life-cycle interpretation). One cannot rule out the possibility that the experiences of currently younger cohorts will be different, that genuine improvements in life chances are now manifesting themselves as more and more minorities climb into the top tiers of the labor market.

But it is not just a matter of whether African Americans and U.S.-born Hispanics lose out to their white peers in terms of occupational placement: for even when that placement is held constant, it appears that minorities are paid less. The inequalities, which are shown in Table 4.5, are striking among men. Typically, black and Hispanic men earn about 10 percent less than whites, when all are U.S.-born and when occupational placement (in the form of median earnings per occupation), education, and private versus public sector employment are statistically controlled.[30] The analytic scheme is the same as in Table 4.4—in other words, the estimates of earnings disadvantages are for different birth cohorts (or age groups) in 2005 data and are expressed as net percentage differences from native-born non-Hispanic whites. By contrast with the previous findings, however, there is little patterned variation across the cohorts in the disadvantages of minority men. U.S.-born Asian men, too, appear to be disadvantaged by comparison with white men, though the disadvantage is less than for other nonwhites and in some cases is not statistically significant. The combination of ethno-racial minority status and being foreign born, that is, an immigrant, produces even larger earnings disadvantages, which rise to the level of 15–20 for black and Hispanic men.

These disparities can mount up and loom large at their peaks. The gross earnings discrepancies in the top tier are in fact quite large: if we restrict ourselves to the 46- to 55-year-olds of 2000, on the grounds that the earnings trajectory associated with age and experience has likely reached its zenith for the members of this age group, then the annual median earnings of European-American males holding top-decile jobs exceeded those of their African-American peers by 32 percent ($103,994 versus $78,648 in 1999 earnings) and those of U.S.-born Hispanic peers ($81,906) by 27 percent. The discrepancy is almost as large for the remainder of the top-quartile occupations, though the earnings are of course lower on average. The discrepancy is reduced in the second quartile, where the annual median of the middle-aged white males in differences in expected individual earnings relative to those of similar U.S.-born non-Hispanic whites)

Birth cohort (age)	U.S.-born non-Hispanic whites	Foreign-born non-Hispanic whites	U.S.-born non-Hispanic blacks	Foreign-born non-Hispanic blacks	U.S.-born Hispanics	Foreign-born Hispanics	U.S.-born Asians	Foreign-born Asians
Men								
1970–79 (26–35)	—	-4.2	-10.4	-16.5	-7.7	-18.0	-3.1	-6.1
1960–69 (36–45)	—	+1.4	-12.4	-20.2	-10.6	-17.9	-2.6	-13.9
1950–59 (46–55)	—	-0.9	-13.3	-18.3	-9.5	-19.7	-4.1	-18.0
1940–49 (56–64)	—	+1.2	-8.2	-10.3	-12.2	-15.5	-2.9	-14.4
Women								
1970–79 (26–35)	—	+0.3	-3.1	-0.2	+0.3	-11.6	+10.7	+3.1
1960–69 (36–45)	—	-0.4	-0.9	-1.1	-3.3	-13.4	+2.3	-3.8
1950–59 (46–55)	—	+0.3	-1.5	+3.0	-4.2	-10.1	+4.6	-3.5
1940–49 (56–64)	—	+1.5	+0.8	+5.5	-8.4	-4.0	+8.9	-1.9

Source: 2005 American Community Survey.

Note: Nonsignificant coefficients are indicated by shading.

a. Regression analyses are estimated separately by gender and birth cohort (age); the independent variables include median earnings of occupation, education (in years of attainment) plus dummy variables to indicate highest postsecondary degree, employment in government (vs. private) sector and region, along with ethno-racial/nativity dummy variables. Percentage differences are calculated by the formula $100(e^{b} - 1)$, where b is the coefficient of an ethno-racial/nativity dummy variable in an equation with a logged dependent variable.

these jobs was greater than that of black males by 20 percent ($52,137 versus $43,475) and that of Hispanic males ($44,406) by 17 percent. That ethno-racial earnings inequalities are greatest at the top of the occupational hierarchy has been shown in other research, and the paradoxical consequences of this pattern have been pointed out: namely, that improvements in the occupational placement of minority workers risk exacerbating earnings disparities.[31]

There is considerably less earnings inequality along ethno-racial lines among women, but of course women are paid less on average than men in the first place. White women are generally advantaged in comparison with black and Hispanic women, but their edge is small in percentage terms. In the four comparisons between U.S.-born white and black women in Table 4.5, two differences are not statistically significant; and in the others, black women trail by between 1 and 3 percent. U.S.-born Hispanic women are somewhat further behind—apart from the insignificant difference in the youngest cohort, their earnings lag 3–8 percent behind those of their white peers. In three cases, U.S.-born Asian women enjoy significant earnings advantages over their white counterparts. In the youngest cohort, this advantage rises to more than 10 percent.

One possible explanation of minority earnings disadvantages fails: it would be possible in principle that, through a combination of choice and selective recruitment, minorities might end up with jobs in lower-paying sectors of the economy. This could be true even for highly qualified minorities if they disproportionately took jobs in sectors like social services (in fact, African Americans do), since even the best jobs there do not pay as well as the best jobs in other sectors. However, the distribution of minorities across the major industrial sectors is too varied to support this explanation. Minorities are entering some well-paying sectors in substantial numbers, too. For example, in the youngest cohort of workers in 2000, U.S.-born blacks and Hispanics held 9 percent of top-decile jobs and 15 percent of those elsewhere in the top quartile in the well-paying communications industries. Consequently, when the analyses in Table 4.5 are repeated with the industrial sector taken into account, the earnings disadvantages of U.S.-born minorities are not reduced, because differential entry into specific industries does not explain them.

The overall conclusion from these analyses has to be that white men remain the most advantaged group, profiting not just from more favorable occupational placement given their educational credentials but also from higher earnings than other workers in the same occupational category. While the ethno-racial order of inequality may be shifting somewhat, by this evidence the shifts have not eroded the privileged position of white men very much.

What Role for Equal-Opportunity Efforts?

Although the increasing penetration of disadvantaged minorities, African and Hispanic Americans, into the higher tiers of the labor market tracks closely the underlying changes in the population, that is, the growing ethno-racial diversity of youthful birth cohorts, it probably should not be regarded as simply a mechanical transmission of advancing demographic gears. That is to say, efforts by government and civil-society actors to promote equal opportunity, by pressuring educational institutions and employers to open their doors to underrepresented groups, including racial minorities, also seem implicated in these changes, even if their impacts are difficult to identify and measure.

Broadly, we can think of these efforts as divided into two overlapping classes: antidiscrimination and affirmative action. Antidiscrimination efforts have a basis in law, epitomized by Title VII of the Civil Rights Act of 1964, which prohibited all employers with more than a small number of employees from discriminating on the basis of race, color, religion, national origin, or sex. The act also created specific mechanisms for reporting, investigating, and remedying discrimination. At the state level, antidiscrimination laws in fact predate the civil-rights period in much of the United States, so their impacts date back in some places to the period just after World War II. Affirmative action originated in the early 1960s, in executive orders issued by presidents Kennedy and Johnson requiring federal contractors to take "affirmative action" to overcome the disadvantages faced by racial minorities because of past discrimination.[32] The executive orders did not define "affirmative action," which remains hard to bound precisely. Barbara Reskin's expansive definition provides a good starting point: according to her, the term refers to "policies and procedures designed to combat ongoing job discrimination." She explains that affirmative action "represents a break with the strategy of ending discrimination by outlawing it." Because "much discrimination results from employers doing business as usual," affirmative action "requires employers to do more than refrain from actively discriminating—it entails proactive efforts to promote equal employment opportunities for groups traditionally subject to employment discrimination."[33] By crossing out such words as "employment" and "job," this definition can easily be extended to the sphere of education, where affirmative action has also played a potent role.

In the domain of education, both types of equal-opportunity efforts have been important, but in recent decades the role of affirmative action has loomed much larger, controversially so for some Americans. Studies indicate that admissions procedures at many selective colleges and universities effectively give preference to students coming from minority families, especially blacks and Hispanics, making entering classes more diverse than they would be if race were excluded from consideration. This form of affirmative action is relevant mainly to selective institutions, because less selective colleges and universities admit large portions of their applicants. A recent analysis by Sigal Alon and Marta Tienda shows that during the 1980s and 1990s affirmative action was coupled with the growing selectivity of admission to the top ranks of colleges and universities, which gave increasing weight to test scores in their admission decisions; without also increasing attention to the racial backgrounds of their students, according to this analysis, the selective institutions would have failed to maintain the ethno-racial diversity of their student bodies. William Bowen and Derek Bok's study of minority students at some of the most highly selective colleges and universities appears to demonstrate that attendance at these schools has for the most part had a durable, positive influence on students' lives, revealed in subsequent professional success and civic participation.[34]

The impacts of equal-opportunity efforts have also been demonstrated in the labor market, though direct effects on a broad scale (as opposed to those in specific cases) appear more tenuous there than in higher education. (The indirect effects resulting from race preferences in higher education, which lead to more diversity in the pool of highly qualified job applicants, have not been investigated, though they are clearly implied by Bowen and Bok's study.) In a systematic examination of workplace integration since the mid-1960s, Kevin Stainback, Corre Robinson, and Donald Tomaskovic-Devey find an unsteady trajectory, affected by the political shifts in the federal government, which reflect to some degree the level of support in the population at large for equal opportunity but also color the entire atmosphere surrounding it, from rhetoric to enforcement intensity. These sociologists show that the workplace integration of African Americans advanced most during the fifteen years following the major enactments of civil-rights legislation and then more or less stalled, though there has been a weak drift in the direction of increased integration since 1980.[35] In a comprehensive review of the state of research on affirmative action as of 2000, Harry Holzer and David Neumark also note its modest effects.[36] They observe that detecting the effects depends on the distinction between federal contractors subject to affirmative-action requirements and other employers, who are not. Research generally reveals that the employment of minorities and women has outpaced that of white males among federal contractors; however, the impact is generally not large. A recent analysis of municipal police hiring that compares cities whose hiring practices were litigated with other cities whose practices were not estimates the effect of court-ordered affirmative action as roughly a 14-point gain in the percentage of blacks among new recruits. Perhaps this formulation understates the impact, for as Barbara Reskin observes, "between 1970 and 1990, the numbers of minority and female police officers in the U.S. increased tenfold: from less than 10,000 to 97,000 minorities and from less than 2,000 to more than 20,000 women."[37]

In the preceding analysis of shifts in the top tiers of the labor market, equal-opportunity efforts seem implicated in two respects. Affirmative action in higher education has expanded the pool of African and Hispanic Americans with the educational qualifications to take top-tier jobs, the great majority of which require some degree of postsecondary education. In addition, antidiscrimination pressures and affirmative action in employment likely play a role in the rising share of good jobs held by minorities, although in toto the impacts may not be great. At any rate, their influence is suggested by the increasing probabilities for young African and Hispanic Americans to land top-decile jobs, which were noted earlier. Since these probabilities have risen in the youngest cohort, whose occupational attainment is to some extent constrained by its youth, perhaps there is a signal here of a modest shift in the direction of greater parity between whites and minorities in the chances to obtain the best-paying jobs.

Yet one can doubt the future potential for equal-opportunity efforts to play a significant role. Stainback and his colleagues argue that workplace integration comes about through a "politically mediated process" that requires government to apply consistent pressure on employers. That consistency has been absent since the early 1980s, when political support for equal opportunity declined precipitously during the Reagan administration; hence, integration of blacks (but not of women) has stalled.[38] To be sure, antidiscrimination law is not going to disappear, but the regulatory environment in which claims of employer discrimination are made, investigated, and adjudicated is shaped by the larger political atmosphere, and consequently the outcomes of antidiscrimination efforts are variable over time. Affirmative action has faced significant challenges in the recent past—the anti–affirmative action initiatives passed in several states, for example, Proposition 209 in California, which was approved by voters in 1996 and bars public institutions in the state from utilizing affirmative action on behalf of women or minorities; and Supreme Court decisions, for example, Gratz v. Bollinger (2003), in which the Court struck down the University of Michigan's use of a point system to increase minority admissions to its undergraduate programs. (However, in a simultaneous decision, Grutter v. Bollinger, the Court left in place the university's use of affirmative action in admissions to its law school. Michigan voters subsequently approved via a referendum a ban on affirmative action in university admissions.) But as Holzer and Neumark argue, affirmative action as currently implemented includes some policies and procedures that are likely to pass the strictest legal scrutiny, such as actions taken to encourage job applications from minority-group members (for example, advertising openings in media with large minority audiences). Even some stronger measures, such as the requirement imposed on federal contractors of a certain size (fifty or more employees) to file regular reports on any "underutilization" of women and minorities on their workforce and to take corrective steps if underrepresentation exists, are likely to continue.[39]

In admissions decisions, it is possible to craft policies that pass legal muster while promoting more diverse student bodies. Race preferences in admissions decisions were legally challenged as early as the *Bakke* case of the 1970s, when the Supreme Court's decision ruled out preferences that take the form of quotas but at the same time, in Justice Lewis Powell's famous opinion, gave sanction to the use of race as one among multiple considerations in the admissions process. More recent court decisions and referenda have curbed the role of affirmative action in public higher education, but not so far in private colleges and universities. Since this is to some degree an artificial distinction, in the sense that virtually all colleges and universities receive federal and state monies in some form, in principle the race preferences in the private sector could probably also be challenged. The analysis by Alon and Tienda suggests that alternative performance-based criteria, such as class rank, now implemented at the University of Texas in the form of a "top 10 percent" rule, could be used in place of racial preferences to achieve diversity.[40] Whether other selective colleges and universities would find such a rule an acceptable way to maintain the quality of its student body, given the high variability of academic achievements across U.S. high schools, is open to question.

The Geography of the Labor-Market Shift and Its Implications

The penetration of U.S.-born minorities into top labor-market tiers is not occurring to the same extent everywhere in the nation: it is in fact much further along in those regions where their population densities are highest. For African Americans, that means the South; for Hispanics, the West. (Figure 4.7 shows the regional variations in ethno-racial representation in top-quartile jobs for the youngest cohort of workers in 2000.) In the 1965–1974 birth cohort, the 26- to 35-year-olds of 2000, U.S.-born Hispanics account for 7 percent of the top-quartile jobs in the West, but nowhere else does their share exceed 4 percent. African Americans occupy nearly 10 percent of the top-quartile positions held by young people in the South, a fraction double that found in other regions. In the case of African Americans, the advance into the top quartile appears to be occurring predominantly in their region of concentration: between the oldest and youngest cohorts, the proportion they make up of this occupational tier has approximately doubled there; it has not increased as much anywhere else. The gains of U.S.-born Hispanics are somewhat more evenly spread, but the greater penetration into top jobs

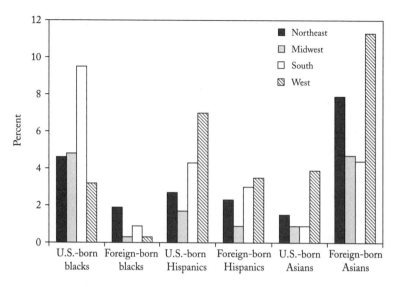

Figure 4.7. Percentage shares of top-quartile jobs by region for 26- to 35-year-old nonwhites and Hispanics, by nativity, 2000. (2000 Public Use Microdata Sample (5 percent).)

in the West builds upon the greater share of good jobs there that Hispanics hold even in older cohorts.

These regional variations bear on two opposing sociological principles. On the one hand, the socioeconomic advance of some minority workers could be expected to be erected upon a foundation of demographic concentration. This principle has already been borne out in the growing ethno-racial diversity evident among younger cohorts in the top labor-market tiers. Where groups are large in number, they are likely to dominate in some labor-market niches and therefore are able to give assistance to their younger members as they seek jobs.[41] Moreover, where there are many workers from the same minority group, there will also be a demand for supervisors and managers of that background. Recent research establishes that black and Hispanic managers are mainly placed in positions where they supervise workers with the same ethno-racial origins; rarely are they placed over white workers.[42] Quite apparent, then, is that the demographic principle of minority advance is nevertheless consistent with disadvantage even for its beneficiaries. If black and Hispanic managers are largely confined to supervising minority employees, then their opportunities for advancement are blatantly constrained by race/ethnicity and they are losing out to whites in the competition for the places that are the best remunerated and carry the greatest authority, that is, those where white employees are under a manager's control.

On the other hand, another long-running strand of sociological theorizing posits that majorities respond to minority demographic concentrations with greater discrimination—reinforcement of ethno-racial boundaries, in other words—because increased minority numbers translate into greater threats to majority status and privileges.[43] This principle implies that there should be barriers raised to minority advance in those areas where their numbers are greatest, and considerable research backs this hypothesis up. For instance, racial segregation in residence is typically highest in cities with a high minority concentration, like Chicago.[44] This hypothesis is also borne out here, for the probabilities of minority workers climbing high up the occupational ladder are lowest in regions of minority concentration. Just 12 percent of young African-American workers in the South occupied top-quartile positions in 2000, a fraction lower than in any other region (in the West, where the African-American population concentration is the lowest, the equivalent percentage is 17 percent). The regional variation in this probability is much lower for U.S.-born Hispanics. In the West, their region of greatest concentration, 16 percent of their young workers are found in the top quartile, and this fraction is only slightly higher in other regions. In the Northeast, where young U.S.-born Hispanics fare best, 18 percent have entered the top quartile.

Another kind of geography, namely, metropolitan region, seems less consequential than region. One could expect that the best opportunities for the advance of U.S.-born minorities would come in the largest metropolitan regions, where many big firms are found, since they are more likely to pay attention to affirmative-action principles (and also to fear antidiscrimination lawsuits and government scrutiny). To be sure, there is a potential counterargument here, too, for the globalism theorist Saskia Sassen has argued that ethno-racially segmented labor markets emerge strongly in a country's global cities—in this case, the United States' largest cities and their surrounding suburbs—which constitute key nodes in the intricate international web of finance and commerce.[45] Immigrant and minority workers are drawn to these places, according to her argument, by a labor market that requires many services for the huge numbers of professional and technical workers needed to keep globally plugged-in firms humming. Yet this ethno-racial dualism may not prove as rigid as the argument seems to suggest, because of the opportunities for mobility available in such places. A recent study of the second generation in the New York region, a global metropolis par excellence, has found that in general the children of immigrants are doing quite well, in part because they are able to take advantage of institutions and opportunities created in prior generations to assist minorities.[46]

In any event, the highest African-American representation in the top quartile is found in the South, no matter what the size of the metropolitan region. I have grouped the regions for convenience according to three population sizes: 2 million or more; 500,000 to 1.99 million; and less than 500,000. In the largest southern metropolitan regions, African Americans are 12 percent of the young incumbents of top-quartile jobs, the highest penetration anywhere; this percentage is consistent with the view that middle-class prosperity is most concentrated among African Americans in places like Atlanta. In the mid-size and smaller regions of the South, African Americans occupy 9 percent of these good jobs in the youngest cohort, a percentage that is higher than can be found in metropolitan areas of any size outside the south. In the west, Hispanic representation in the top quartile exhibits less of a gradient across metropolitan areas by size than is the case for African Americans. In the largest metropolitan regions, Hispanics hold nearly 8 percent of top-quartile jobs in the youngest cohort, and the equivalent figure is 6 percent in other parts of the west.

The regional variations in minority penetration into top labor-market tiers throw a revealing light on common suspicions that the benefits of minority advance are going mainly to select subgroups. For example, the disproportionate recruitment of second-generation Afro-Caribbeans by top Ivy League colleges could suggest that the children of black immigrants rather than the African Americans descended from slaves are largely the ones who are forging ahead.[47] But there are few Afro-Caribbeans in the South, yet that is where the largest group by far of U.S.-born blacks in good jobs is to be found: more than half of all African-American incumbents of top-quartile jobs live there. In the case of Hispanics, similar suspicions, through not quite to the same degree, could be expressed about Cubans and South Americans versus Mexicans, Central Americans, and Puerto Ricans. However, the Hispanic population of the West is dominated by individuals of Mexican ancestry, by far the largest nationality group among Hispanics, and one whose immigrant stratum is overwhelmingly constituted by low-wage workers with low levels of education compared with U.S. natives.

Conclusion

Greater ethno-racial diversity in the top tiers of the U.S. labor market is one of the safest bets for the future. Increasing penetration of America's most disadvantaged minority populations, namely, African and Hispanic Americans, into these tiers is already evident when we look across cohorts; and the representation there of Asian Americans and Asian immigrants is already so far advanced that, relative to their population base, it exceeds that of whites. The cohorts just now entering the labor market in full force show considerably higher percentages of U.S.-born blacks and Hispanics in top-decile and top-quartile positions than do older ones. While equal-opportunity efforts are probably playing some role in effecting the entry of more minorities into good jobs, the driving force appears to be demographic: the changes in the labor market more or less track underlying demographic changes, that is, the changing racial and ethnic composition of youthful birth cohorts.

The role of demography does not necessarily detract from the significance of the changes. Privileged whites are not able to exclude minorities from the higher tiers of the labor market, though they are still able to monopolize the best-paying positions within them. Clearly diversity is increasing throughout the labor force, including near and at its pinnacle, and many whites located in high positions now interact with minorities who are their status equals, at least in the workplace. Diversity is certain to continue to increase as long as the recruitment into good jobs continues to reflect the racial and ethnic demography of birth cohorts, for the percentage of minorities is increasing. This is particularly true for immigrant-origin minorities, for given the resumption of large-scale immigration in the late 1960s, the numbers in the second (and third) generation entering adulthood are rising rapidly and will continue to do so for the foreseeable future. This point holds especially for U.S.-born Asians, given their record of strong educational achievement.

But it also holds for Hispanic Americans. In most of the higher-tier occupations, the representation of African Americans among youthful job holders was substantially higher in 2000 than was that of U.S.-born Hispanics. Overall, among the youngest workers located in the top quartile in 2000, African Americans outnumbered U.S.-born Hispanics by 50 percent. This is in large part a straightforward matter of demography: because of immigration history, the number of U.S.-born Latinos is small in older cohorts, but rises steeply among younger ones. Even among the individuals born in the United States in the 1965–1974 period, the group that was between the ages of 26 and 35 in 2000, the population of African Americans was nearly two times as great as that of

Hispanics. In this age group, the numerical preponderance of African Americans in good jobs is less than is true for the population as a whole. Not only is the penetration of Hispanics into the top ranks of jobs increasing robustly, but as shown earlier the probability that a U.S.-born Hispanic worker can make it high up the ladder is somewhat greater than is true for an African American. One reason may be that Hispanics are able to enter some well-paying occupations where African Americans are rare (whether because of continuing exclusion or other reasons, it is hard to say). In the youngest cohort of 2000, U.S.-born Hispanics were at least as numerous as African Americans among pilots and construction managers, for instance. If these patterns continue, then Hispanics will outnumber African Americans among the new entrants to top jobs in a few decades because of their rapidly rising proportions in younger age groups.

The increasing penetration of minorities into the ranks of the most highly paid occupations is not a harbinger of full-fledged equality of life chances anytime soon. The potent role that demography is playing in these shifts is not altering fundamental ethno-racial inequalities. Thus the chances that young blacks and Hispanics will scale the heights of the labor market are hardly different from those of their elders. Moreover, the earnings of the minorities who enter these occupations are lower than those of their European-American counterparts. To some extent, this gap is a matter of differences in educational attainment and recruitment to the less remunerative occupations in the higher tiers. But it is more than this, since black and Hispanic men earn less than white men when these factors are taken into account. In addition, minority advance depends crucially on the educational and labor-market achievements of women, and of course women of all races earn less than white men as well. While there could be uncontrolled factors, such as the quality of educational credentials, which would reduce the gap further, given the history of minority exclusion from the best jobs some degree of "discrimination"—taking this term in its broadest sense, as the unequal treatment of equals—is almost certainly involved. Whites, especially white men, remain very privileged: to be sure, the absence of a substantial dent in white privilege could be argued to be a feature of a non-zero-sum mobility situation, which entails little or no change to the perceptions whites have of the opportunities open to them and to their children.

Yet despite all these qualifications, the rising percentage of good jobs held by minorities is, quite possibly, a portentous change. Rises in the minority representation in the top tiers of the labor market are highly likely to continue as younger cohorts mature and enter the labor market. Among the 16- to 25-year-olds of 2000, the age group preparing to enter the labor market en masse during the first decade of the new century, the ratio among the U.S. born of non-Hispanic whites to blacks and Hispanics had dropped to 2.7 to 1. In the next youngest group, aged 6 to 15 in 2000, it was down again, to 2.1 to 1. By contrast, in the oldest working-age group, the 56- to 65-year-olds, who were mostly on the point of leaving the labor force in the 2000–2010 period, it was 6.5 to 1. The almost certain expansion of the minority penetration into the best-paying jobs virtually guarantees the increasing exposure of highly placed whites to racial and ethnic diversity at work and, potentially, in their living spaces, that is, in their neighborhoods. This scenario holds the promise of some change to the major ethno-racial boundaries as a consequence.

But, granted, this change is incremental in character and, so far at least, has not touched the foundations of ethno-racial inequality in life chances. The question that must be asked is whether more profound change is possible.

5

An Extraordinary Opportunity: The Exit of the Baby Boomers

Incremental changes in favor of diversity seem virtually assured for the United States in the near future. Each new cohort reaching adulthood contains a larger proportion of nonwhites and Hispanics than the one before it, and this demographic shift is reflected throughout the labor market, including at its highest levels. This phenomenon does bring about ethno-racial change, as worlds of work and socializing that were previously all white or nearly so become more integrated, and more and more whites interact with minorities who are their peers. Yet because white males in particular remain very privileged, the change involved seems limited; and fundamental ethno-racial inequalities, such as the chance to land a good job in the first place, remain untouched. The question that must be addressed is whether the system can open up in a more profound way, to allow for a more thoroughgoing form of non-zero-sum mobility. The answer, in a word, is "yes," and the reason lies in what is sure to be one of the dominant phenomena of the next quarter century: the retirement of the baby boomers.

The baby boom refers to the huge group of Americans born in the two decades following World War II, in the years 1946 through 1964.

Simply by virtue of their numbers, the baby-boom cohorts have formed a socially and culturally dominant group in American life since the 1950s: indeed, the decade of the sixties is defined by their youthful experiences of it—the Vietnam War and the antiwar movement, rock music and Woodstock, and sexual liberation and experimentation with drugs. The metaphor often used to describe this outsized impact has been one of a large animal swallowed by a snake, resulting in a bulge that with time moves along the length of the snake's body. The bulge has now proceeded past the midway point. Economic forecasts for the future have been concerned with the financial impact of the retirement of the baby boom, which might tilt out of balance the ratio between those at work and those who depend on the work of others to survive. Crises have been envisioned for the Social Security and health-care systems. It will surely be the case that the treatment of diseases associated with old age will be of much greater urgency in coming decades because of the aging of the baby boomers. But our concerns—with the possibilities for ethno-racial change—are different. From this perspective, the salient fact about the baby boom during the next quarter century is that it will exit from the labor market—by the early 2030s, the youngest baby boomers will be in their late sixties. The retirement of this massive group will open up the labor market in a way that has not been true since the middle of the twentieth century.

Who Will Replace the Baby Boomers?

The baby boom accounts for a large share of American workers, numbering 48 million full-time workers in 2005, out of a full-time workforce in the prime ages between 26 and 65 that totaled 88 million. Combined with the workers who were born just before the baby boom, those who were in 2005 age 60 and older, this group accounted for nearly 60 percent of the prime-age workforce. Some members of the baby boom's leading edge retired soon thereafter, in their early sixties; but the retirement of this huge population stratum is likely to stretch across three decades at least, as some workers delay retirement for the sake of income and health insurance. Nevertheless, by the early 2030s, when the youngest members of the baby boom are in their late sixties, the vast majority will have left the labor market. Since most of the jobs they will be leaving will have to be refilled, their departure plus that of workers born before the end of World War II could create, in gross numbers, 50 million or more openings.[1] To these jobs can be added those that will be created as a result of population growth. Projected at more than 30 percent between 2000 and 2030, population growth could add 15 million or more full-time jobs needing to be filled.[2]

The retirement of the baby boomers will have a disproportionate impact on the top tiers of the workforce, since this group is among the best educated in U.S. history—this is especially true for the young men who came of age during the 1960s, who often delayed leaving the educational system in order to avoid the Vietnam-era draft.[3] Their sisters also attained an unusually high level of education for the time and made a large leap beyond the postsecondary record of their mothers and aunts. Consequently, the baby boomers account for very large fractions of some occupations, especially those where high remuneration is associated with prolonged training and experience and thus young workers are less likely to be found. For instance, in 2000, baby boomers were 70 percent or more of the chief executives, dentists, engineering managers, and supervisors of police. (See Table 5.1.) And they were 60 percent or more of a slew of other occupations, ranging from physicians and surgeons, to information systems managers, to judges, to electrical and electronics engineers, to veterinarians. The occupations in the bottom half of the labor force were less dependent on the baby boomers, but even there they typically made up at least half of the workers.

Some degree of ethno-racial change is virtually inevitable in the wake of the baby boomers' departure. In the ranks of the incumbents of well-paying jobs, the baby boomers are heavily white: almost 80 percent of

Table 5.1 The baby boom's share of selected occupations, 2000

	Baby boom %	Occupation N
Top decile		
Dentists	69.9	104,930
Chief executives	69.5	997,905
Engineering managers	70.9	153,684
Rest of top quartile		
Police supervisors	74.6	103,807
Construction managers	67.2	549,381
Education administrators	68.9	547,472
Registered nurses	67.2	1,485,208
Second quartile		
Supervisors of mechanics, installers, repairers	67.3	791,874
Stationary engineers/boiler operators	68.2	89,333
Mail carriers	73.8	303,748
Construction, building inspectors	68.5	63,913
Waste treatment plant operators	69.3	64,996

Source: 2000 Public Use Microdata Sample (5 percent).

them in the top decile and elsewhere in the top quartile were native-born non-Hispanic whites in 2005, and the figure would go over 80 percent if foreign-born non-Hispanic whites were included. In the second quartile, the fraction is just a bit lower, but native-born whites account for more than three-quarters of the baby-boom job holders.

Who will replace them during the next quarter century? Unless the already broad access of whites to the highest occupational tiers expands markedly, there will not be enough of them to fill the places vacated by their elders. While it is impossible to say with certainty what the ethno-racial composition of younger cohorts will look like in 2030 because of the uncertainties associated with large-scale immigration from Africa, Asia, Latin America, and the Caribbean, one can be reasonably sure of the size of the non-Hispanic white working-age population (counted here as individuals aged 26–65 for the sake of consistency with other tables) at that date. Apart from a small immigrant component, all of the

Table 5.2   Projection of non-Hispanic white working-age population (aged 26–65), 2000–2030

Age	2000 N	2010 N	2010 % change from 2000	2020 N	2020 % change from 2000	2030 N	2030 % change from 2000
26–35	26,110	24,633	−5.7	26,130	+0.1	23,753	−9.0
36–45	32,060	26,154	−18.4	24,793	−22.7	26,347	−17.8
46–55	27,744	31,319	+12.9	25,678	−7.5	24,456	−11.9
56–65	18,605	26,114	+40.4	29,630	+59.3	24,445	+31.4

Source: U.S. Census Bureau, *2008 National Population Projections,* http://www.census.gov/population/www/projections/2008projections.html (extracted 8/15/08).
Note: Both U.S.-born and foreign-born whites are included.
Population numbers are in 1,000s.

individuals who will be part of this population have already been born in the United States and thus counted in data; the primary uncertainty about its size is associated with future mortality rates, which are very unlikely to make a large difference in this age range. (For convenience, I take advantage of the Census Bureau's 2008 projections of the non-Hispanic white population, and these include immigrants, who however make up only a small proportion of these whites.)[4]

Table 5.2 shows a projection of white working-age groups for the next decades, at 2010, 2020, and 2030. The decline in the number of working-age whites is particularly noticeable in the cohort that will take the place of the 36- to 45-year-olds of 2000. The white incumbents of top jobs in that age group were recruited from a population that, despite the mortality by early middle age, still numbered 32 million individuals. As the projection shows, by 2010 the white population in that age range will decline by nearly 20 percent, and it will remain at about that size through the next two decades. This decline is a consequence of the relatively small sizes of the birth cohorts that will mature and replace this middle-aged group during the coming decades. For instance, the 6- to

15-year-olds of 2000, who will replace it in 2030, amounted to 25.5 million (the projections envision this group growing slightly because of immigration, which is seen as sufficient to offset the mortality over three decades).

The only age group of non-Hispanic whites that is expected to grow in size by the beginning of the fourth decade of the twenty-first century is the 56- to 65-year-olds. This does not represent a gain for the pool of white workers, however, because this group, made up of the 26- to 35-year-olds of 2000, has already been counted in the working-age population and attained a high rate of labor-force participation (in 2000, 66 percent of its members worked full time, a figure only one-half of a percentage point lower than is found in the next higher age group). By 2030, all of the white workers in younger age groups will come from groups that were under the age of 26 in 2000, that is, born in 1975 or later, only a small proportion of whom (among the 16- to 25-year-olds) were already employed full time in 2000. Put a bit differently, those whites who will replace the retiring baby-boom workers will come mainly from these younger cohorts, which can be expected to have 13 percent fewer whites in 2030 than the cohorts from which the white workers they are replacing have issued.

Some back-of-the-envelope calculations demonstrate the opening up of the system this demographic mismatch could engender. I begin with a simple scenario. For this purpose, I will take the jobs represented by occupations ranked in the top half of the full-time workforce according to their average remuneration as "good" jobs. Let us assume that, by 2030, almost all of the workers in these jobs older than age 35 in 2000 will have exited the full-time workforce, for they will then be older than 65 (based on current patterns of mortality and retirement, a small portion of the 36- to 45-year-olds of 2000 is assumed to still hold full-time jobs in 2030). In addition, many of the workers who in 2000 were between the ages of 26 and 35 will also have left the labor market because of retirement or mortality (more than half, according to current patterns).[5] All told, that would mean a departure from the workforce of 35.2 million occupants of full-time good jobs, of whom 28.8 million (81.8 percent) are non-Hispanic whites. (Key numbers are reproduced in Table 5.3.) Another way of thinking about the problem is that, over the period 2000–2030, the departures from the top half of the workforce would average 1.17 million per year, of whom about 960,000 would be white workers. If we assume further that all of the job vacancies these departures create must be filled (in other words, no jobs disappear) and that the recruitment probabilities of whites into full-time positions remain as they were in 2000, then there would be about 900,000 new white workers available per year; in other words, there would not be enough whites to replace the retiring white workers, let alone the other retirees.

However, this estimate understates the magnitude of the problem, for the labor force, whose size tracks, if somewhat imperfectly, population size, is certain to expand during the next few decades.[6] (For this reason, the assumption made a moment ago that jobs continue to exist after the retirement of their occupants is simply a convenience, not a necessity. The overall growth in the number of jobs in different tiers implies that any jobs that disappear are replaced somewhere else in the same tier and that the creation of jobs exceeds the number required to replace those that go out of existence.) The Census Bureau projections envision a 32.7 percent increase in the population between 2000 and 2030. It is, to be sure, just a projection, not a forecast; and projections, which are but the numerical consequences of their assumptions, are often off the mark. But it is consistent with the rate of growth in the population during the early years of the new century. According to Census Bureau population estimates, the population grew by 8.0 percent in the eight years after 2000—1 percent per year, in short.[7]

The growth in the labor force is expected to lag well behind that in the population. The Bureau of Labor Statistics forecasts that labor-force growth will be slow for the foreseeable future and much lower than the growth experienced in the later decades of the twentieth century. But

Table 5.3 A back-of-the-envelope calculation of the deficit of white workers, 2000–2030

| | Stock of jobs, 2030 | | Assumed departures by 2030 | | | | | | | |
	Full-time workers, 2000	New jobs (18.0% of 2000 base)	1935–44 birth cohort	1945–54 cohort	1955–64 cohort (92% depleted)	1965–74 cohort (55% depleted)	Jobs to fill by 2030	Jobs to fill/yr	White recruits/yr	Deficit/yr
First decile	8,600.1	1,548.0	886.4	2,275.2	2,798.5	1,047.7	8,555.8	285.2	184.7	100.5
Rest of first quartile	13,051.4	2,349.3	1,436.2	3,759.5	4,085.6	1,381.5	13,012.1	433.7	274.7	159.0
Second quartile	21,525.1	3,874.5	2,159.1	5,989.9	6,630.2	2,765.0	21,418.7	714.0	443.4	270.6
TOTALS	43,176.6	7,771.8	4,481.7	12,024.6	13,514.3	5,194.2	42,986.6	1,432.9	902.8	530.1

Note: All figures are in 1000s.

Assumptions: Full-time employment growth in each tier = 18.0% of the 2000 employment base (growth rate inferred from BLS projections of labor-force growth; see text and note 8).

All members of the two oldest cohorts are out of the full-time labor force by 2030; the departures from the full-time workforce of the two youngest cohorts reflect current patterns of mortality and retirement (see note 5).

The population-based probabilities for whites (U.S.- and foreign-born combined) to enter various tiers remain as they were in 2000.

growth in employment, closely associated with that of the number of workers, is still likely to add substantially to the number of positions to be filled. This is true even if we adopt a conservative projection of labor-force growth. The projection that I use here envisions 18 percent growth between 2000 and 2030. It follows from a Bureau of Labor Statistics scenario for the future in which labor-force growth is expected to slow in the early decades of this century, averaging 1 percent per year in the 2000–2015 period and 0.2 percent per year from 2015 to 2025 (and, I assume, afterward).[8] Given the economic uncertainties that loom large because of the deep recession at the end of the first decade of the new century, this growth projection is appropriately conservative in a historical sense: in the thirty-year period leading up to 2000, employment grew by almost 75 percent, in other words, four times as much as the growth I assume.[9] If we assume, again for the sake of simplicity, that this labor-force growth rate applies to the number of full-time jobs in the top half of the labor force, then another 7.8 million jobs might be added over the period, for an additional 260,000 positions per year to be filled. According to this calculation, then, the number of good jobs to be filled would average 1.4 million per year, but the number of whites, who have historically dominated such jobs, available to take them would average 900,000, enough to fill about 63 percent of the jobs, well below their current near monopoly of more than 80 percent.

The mismatch appears to be just as acute high up the job ladder. Applying the same accounting to the jobs in the top decile in 2000 indicates that 7 million full-time workers could depart from this sector between 2000 and 2030, for an average of almost 235,000 per year; and labor-force growth could add another 50,000 new jobs per year. Eighty-four percent of the retiring workers, almost 200,000 per year, will be non-Hispanic whites, but if whites enjoy the same probabilities of entering this tier as they have in the recent past, only 185,000 whites per year are expected to be available to fill their shoes. By this calculation, whites could fill 65 percent of the top-decile positions, a figure that suggests a considerable relaxation of their current stranglehold.

While the numbers in such highly simplified projections must not be taken as anything like forecasts, they are sufficient to demonstrate that the declining size of the white working-age population, combined with the huge number of good jobs that will open up as a consequence of the retirement of the baby boomers, will create the prospect of a large-scale non-zero-sum mobility, even under conditions of slow employment growth. This mobility, an ascent into higher tiers of the workforce by individuals whose family origins are situated further down the social ladder, is non-zero-sum in the sense that the labor-force needs that produce it cannot be fully satisfied by the individuals whose family histories would lead them to "expect" to be able to take such good jobs in the absence of some personal failure. Such non-zero-sum mobility in turn could allow a massive penetration of currently disadvantaged minorities into social arenas where their presence has been unusual, though other groups, such as working-class whites and new immigrants, could also benefit.

A "What If" Scenario

The potential ramifications of this non-zero-sum mobility for African Americans and U.S.-born Hispanics are suggested by a "what if" scenario—in particular, what if nearly all of this mobility was enjoyed by these groups? Such a scenario is not intended to be realistic, a prediction of what is likely to happen; rather, it establishes the outer limit of the possible, an outcome that might be approached under favorable circumstances, if, say, as a society we were willing to invest resources to maximize the degree of minority mobility. To implement the "what if" assumption, I assume that the availability of whites to take good jobs remains as it has been recently (some of the numbers are identified above) and that the number of new nonwhite immigrants who can fill them stays at the level it was during the 1990s, when the volume of legal immigration was at an all-time high.[10] (The number of legal immigrants has increased slightly during the first decade of the twenty-first century; undocumented immigrants do not need to be considered here since they are very unlikely to be able to fill good jobs in the U.S. economy.) For U.S.-born Asians, I assume that their availability triples in coming years compared with what it was among the 26- to 35-year-olds of 2000, a factor of increase that closely approximates the rapid growth of second and later generations in cohorts younger than prime working age at that time.

Consider what these assumptions imply for the supply of workers filling the jobs in the top decile during 2000–2030. The numbers of whites, Asians, and immigrants who would enter this tier would average 232,000 per year, but the number of jobs coming available in that tier would average 285,000. If all of the remaining jobs were taken by U.S.-born blacks and Hispanics, their share, 54,000, would represent just under a fifth of the jobs being filled. (Table 5.4 shows the calculations.) In 2000, these minorities accounted for only 6 percent of these jobs. Non-zero-sum mobility has the potential, in other words, to more than triple that fraction in the next few decades.

A very similar story holds for the other jobs in the top half of the labor force. Under the assumptions already sketched, the average number of jobs available per year in the remainder of the top quartile is 434,000, but the numbers of whites, Asians, and immigrants available to take them is 323,000 in an average year. If all of the remaining jobs go to U.S.-born blacks and Hispanics, then they will take 111,000 per year, or more than a quarter of them. Since they held down only 9 percent of them in 2000, non-zero-sum mobility could come close to tripling their share. In the second quartile, where African and Hispanic Americans were better established as workers in 2000—they occupied 12 percent of the jobs at that point—the gain is almost as large. During the coming

Table 5.4   A simple "what if" scenario: What if the open good jobs went disproportionately to U.S.-born blacks and Hispanics?

	First decile	Rest of first quartile	Second quartile	Total
Jobs to fill by 2030/yr (from Table 5.3)	285.2	433.7	714.0	1,432.9
White recruits/yr (from Table 5.3)	184.7	274.7	443.4	902.8
Foreign born/yr	31.3	34.4	56.9	122.6
U.S.-born Asians/yr	15.6	13.6	20.3	49.5
Remainder: U.S.-born blacks and Hispanics	53.6	111.0	193.4	358.0
% to U.S.-born blacks and Hispanics	18.8	25.6	27.1	25.0

Note: Population numbers are in 1000s.

Assumptions: The foreign-born line does not count foreign-born non-Hispanic whites (who are counted here among whites) but does include a small number of non-Hispanics of "other" races (that is, not white, black, or Asian), regardless of birthplace.

The foreign-born representation in tiers is assumed to remain at the level found for the youngest full-time workers (ages 26–35) in 2000.

U.S.-born Asians are assumed to attain three times their 2000 representation among the youngest full-time workers because of the rapid growth of this group during coming decades. All jobs that are not filled by whites, immigrants, or U.S.-born Asians are taken by U.S.-born blacks and Hispanics.

decades, they could take about 27 percent of the jobs coming free, more than double their 2000 share.[11] (See Figure 5.1.)

The "what if" scenario amounts to a sketch, not an in-depth analysis, which is not feasible when we are discussing an uncertain future, in any event. As such, it doesn't give us any insight into how the inequalities within tiers, in occupational positioning and earnings, would be altered if the advance of U.S.-born blacks and Hispanics were of this magnitude. It seems plausible to think that these inequalities, which we saw in the last chapter are substantial, would be reduced, if only because more minorities would be moving into positions of authority; but we cannot be certain. Nevertheless, in one respect, it is clear that a transformation of the ethno-racial order of life chances would be unleashed: younger African Americans and U.S.-born Hispanics would come much closer to parity with whites in the opportunities to enter the top tiers of the labor market.

This closing of the gap is most striking below the top decile of jobs. For instance, among the 26- to 55-year-olds of 2000, minority individuals had a 5.9 percent chance of gaining a full-time job elsewhere in the top quartile, while whites had a chance of 11.1. (These figures, it should be recalled, compare the numbers of full-time workers in the occupational tier to total population counts, and thus they indirectly take account of various ethno-racial disparities affecting participation in the full-time workforce, such as those arising from the underutilization of minority workers and their disproportionate confinement in penal institutions.) If the "what if" scenario held, then the chance of minority entry to this tier would shoot up to 9.8 percent, a little shy of the white probability (held constant, by assumption); for entry to the second quartile, the minority and white chances would be nearly identical. While the disparity in minority and white probabilities to enter the top decile does not narrow to the same degree, it is substantially reduced under the "what if" scenario. In 2000, the overall chance that a member of the minority populations would reach this elite tier of occupations was just 2.6 percent, compared with 7.4 percent among non-Hispanic whites. The white chance was almost three times better than that of native-born minorities. In the "what if" scenario, the chance that U.S.-born minorities will occupy full-time top-decile jobs rises to 4.8 percent, still lower than the equivalent figure for whites, but not by nearly as much as before.

Of course, the "what if" assumption that African Americans and U.S.-born Latinos enjoy almost all of the benefits brought about by non-zero-sum mobility is unrealistic. To begin with, one has to ask whether in the near future there will be a large enough pool of minority workers with the levels of education needed to take so many highly placed jobs. Nevertheless, the scenario drives home a critical point: there is an un-

Top Quartile

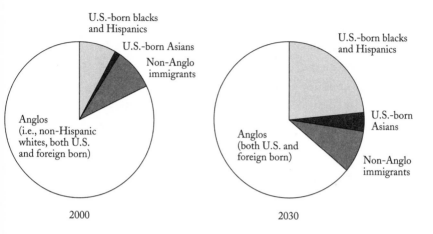

2000   2030

Second Quartile

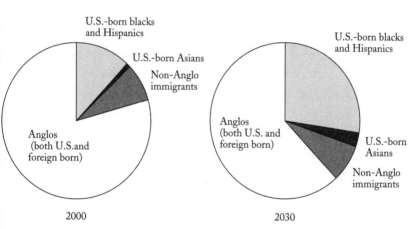

2000   2030

Figure 5.1. Changes between 2000 and 2030 in the composition of the 26- to 55-year-old workforce holding good jobs under the "what if" scenario.

usual opportunity to address ethno-racial inequalities that is beginning to unfold before our eyes. We should be asking what actions we can take to maximize the potential for change, not just what realistically is likely to happen if the "rules of the game" continue as they have been. I will consider both questions in greater depth in the next chapter, but now I want to consider some factors that might complicate the employment side of the scenario I have just sketched—factors, in other words, that might alter the availability of good jobs during the next quarter century.

Some Complications

How Many Good Jobs in the Future?

Complications arise, for one thing, because future economic structural change could impede the growth of, if not even reduce, the number of good jobs. The hour-glass metaphor for the workforce anticipates change of this sort because it envisions a hollowing out of the middle by a contraction, or at best a stagnation, in middle tiers of the labor market. The metaphor suggests that what expansion there is will take place mainly at the bottom and the top; and some analysts who employ it suggest that the job growth at the top will be out of the reach of many minority Americans because of high educational requirements. The metaphor has been lent empirical substance by the research of economists and sociologists. For example, Randy Ilg and Steven Haugen, reviewing labor-force changes during the 1990s, find patterns consistent with the metaphor. Their analysis views the labor force in terms of a grid defined by 10 broad industry groupings crossed by 9 occupational ones, or 90 categories in all. Clustering these categories into three roughly equal-sized sectors based on average earnings—top, middle, and bottom, in other words—Ilg and Haugen find that employment growth was concentrated at the top and bottom of the workforce, especially at the top.[12] The middle sector, by contrast, grew little during the 1990s, despite the relatively prosperous period of economic expansion that occurred during most years of the Clinton administration.

Although the polarization featured in the hourglass metaphor has been the dominant characterization of changes in the U.S. labor market in recent years to emerge from careful research, a pessimist might go so far as to argue that there is no guarantee that the top tiers of the work-force will continue to expand at the same rate as the bottom ones. So far, though, there is no support for such pessimism. A comparison of the oc-cupations of full-time workers in the 2000 Census with those found in the 2005 and 2006 American Community Surveys shows stability in the distribution of jobs across major tiers.[13] Because of the uneven breaks created by discrete occupational categories, the bottom half of the work-force accounted for 49.9 percent of the full-time workers in 2000 (not 50.0 percent), and this is identical to its fraction in 2005–2006. A small amount of change appears to have taken place in the distribution of oc-cupations in the top half, but it is not one that is consistent with a pessi-mistic view. The occupations in the eleventh through the twenty-fifth percentiles—in other words, the top quartile with the top decile re-moved—account for a slightly larger percentage of full-time workers in 2005–2006 than they did in 2000: the difference is 16.2 percent versus 15.2 percent, and this slight expansion comes at the expense of both the top-decile occupations and those in the second quartile.

Nevertheless, the pessimist might reply that the continuing migration of jobs outside the United States, to less-developed countries where la-bor is cheaper, could sap the potential of even the highest tiers of the la-bor market to provide good jobs. Alan Blinder, an economist at Prince-ton University and, under President Clinton, a member of the Council of Economic Advisers and vice chairman of the Board of Governors of the Federal Reserve System, has attempted to measure the potential for occupations to be relocated off-shore.[14] He estimates that about a quar-ter of all U.S. jobs are potentially mobile in this way, meaning that the work can be performed from a distance without degradation. This figure, he stresses, is not a forecast but an estimate of vulnerability. His estimates are based on subjectively applied criteria of the degree to which work requires physical proximity to people or places in the United States (as do, for example, child care and agriculture) and reveal that skill level, or education, is minimally related to "offshorability," as are earnings. In other words, the vulnerability of jobs to be moved to other countries is not confined to those in manufacturing and those service-sector jobs involving low skills and modest pay, such as most of those in call centers. Occupations well up in the hierarchy of remuneration, such as accountants and computer programmers, could be affected.

However, the carefully constructed labor-market forecasts of the Bureau of Labor Statistics do not square with the hourglass metaphor, nor with the idea that the top tiers of the labor market will stagnate.[15] These forecasts have been carried through 2016, and Figure 5.2 depicts them in terms of the occupational ranking scheme by median earnings that I have used since the last chapter (see Figure 4.1). The portions of occupational tiers that will grow rapidly are portrayed in darker shades, those that will grow more slowly if at all, in lighter ones, and decline is indicated by blank space. Because of the concern about decline or stagnation in some tiers, the portions of the bars that indicate such forecasts are grouped toward the middle, so that the eye can easily detect their regions of concentration. At all levels, according to the graph, there are occupations that are expected to contract in relative or absolute terms, but the occupations in the bottom half of the labor force are more affected in this way. Through 2016, the largest job contractions (in absolute numbers) are expected to occur for stock clerks, cashiers, packers, and file clerks, all jobs in the bottom quartile of the workforce. The occupations anticipated to experience rapid growth are spread more evenly through labor-market tiers, and this implies that the top tiers are expected to receive a proportionate share of this growth. Of the four occupations with the largest proportional increases, two are in computing and rank in the top quartile—network and systems administrators and software pro-

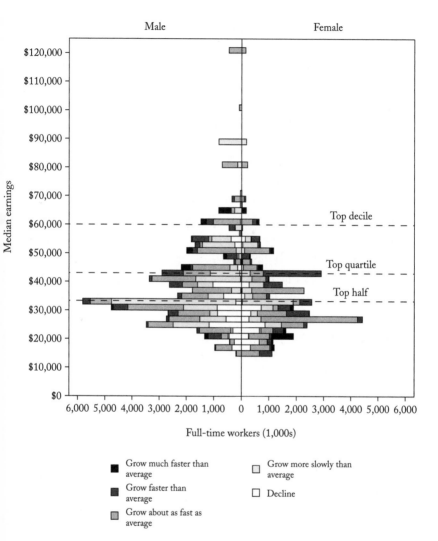

Figure 5.2. Occupational forecast (through 2016) of the Bureau of Labor Statistics, by median earnings of occupation and number of full-time workers.

grammers—and two are in health and rank in the bottom half—personal and home care aides and home health aides (the former provide the housekeeping and personal services that help the elderly and the chronically ill at home, while the latter minister to their health needs, dispensing medications, for example). The largest absolute increases are projected, first, for registered nurses, an occupation on the border between the first and second quartiles, and, second, for retail sales clerks, who are located in the third quartile. There is little hint here of an emerging hourglass.

When these forecasts for detailed occupations are aggregated by tiers, they suggest that the future expansion of employment will be greater in higher tiers than in lower ones, hinting at greater opportunity for non-zero-sum mobility than the "what if" scenario suggests. The occupations in the highest quartile are expected to grow on average at nearly twice the rate of jobs lower down in the rankings, while the lowest growth is anticipated for the occupations in the bottom quartile. Overall, the occupations in the top quartile are forecast to expand in numbers by an average of nearly 14 percent (the average is weighted to take into account the varied sizes of the occupational categories). By contrast, the growth forecast for the jobs in the bottom quartile averages only 7 percent. The second quartile—a region that is often seen as critical to the chances for intergenerational upward mobility of minorities—has the second-highest projected rate of growth, although, at 9 percent, it is well below that for the highest one. In any event, the picture is clear: the top half of the workforce is expected to enjoy substantially more growth than the bottom half. In sum, the most reasonable conclusion from the detailed BLS forecasts, which are based on a detailed consideration of the impact of general economic conditions on industries and occupations, is for growth that favors the good jobs in the top half of the workforce.

One objection to these forecasts could be that they fail to take into account the potential for even good jobs to be relocated outside the United States. Blinder observes that his estimates of "offshorability" do not correlate with the BLS forecasts for growth, implying that the forecasts have not taken account of the potential impact of this factor. Yet Blinder's somewhat subjective estimates are not forecasts. As he would admit, neither he nor we have any way of guessing precisely which jobs are going to move to other countries. Moreover, a recent analysis of the aggregate effects of offshore outsourcing and of its reverse, the inshoring of jobs previously done elsewhere, finds overall a small positive effect for U.S. workers, with modest negative effects concentrated among less-educated workers.[16]

Blinder's estimates do not take into account the power of the incumbents of an occupational category to resist attempts to move some of their numbers abroad. This power is likely to be greater when jobs are organized as professions and represented by associations. Interestingly, his subjective rating places "economist" high up on the hit list of vulnerable occupations (a sign of humility on his part?), but it is difficult to imagine that U.S.-based economists (counted as 23,100 in the 2000 Census) would not find subtle as well as blatant means to resist a migration of their jobs and to argue for the superiority of the work done in the United States. The same could be true for statisticians, accountants, and survey researchers, among others.

Some of the work that Blinder believes could move offshore would require considerable alteration in customary modes of operation and/or reorganization in the division of labor and responsibility for that migration to occur, and changes of these sorts would take time. Consider the job of "financial analyst," which Blinder places in the highest category of vulnerability. Not only is this job well paid (in the top decile), but the Bureau of Labor Statistics forecasts sharp growth, 34 percent, in the number of financial analysts between 2006 and 2016—so Blinder's vulnerability estimate is potentially consequential for this occupation's contribution to future non-zero-sum mobility. According to the BLS description of this work, it does seem on the surface that it is not tied to a U.S. location, for financial analysts "gather financial information, analyze it, and make recommendations."[17] From this cursory description, it would seem as if the work could be done as well from India as from the United States.[18] However, as the BLS describes the way that many financial analysts perform this work, the picture changes, for in evaluating the worthiness of companies for additional investment, analysts "often meet with company officials to gain a better insight into the firm's prospects and to determine its managerial effectiveness." Perhaps some of these data could be gathered through teleconferencing, but there is often no substitute for on-site visits and face-to-face encounters. (Of course, insofar as companies are located outside the United States, the analysts who undertake these visits could be located there also.) Likewise, the investors who depend upon the work of financial analysts, described by the BLS as "institutional investors, includ[ing] mutual funds, hedge funds, insurance companies, independent money managers, and charitable organizations, such as universities and hospitals, with large endowments" as well as "investment banks and securities firms," are also not likely to be satisfied simply with electronically submitted reports, teleconferencing, and other communications at a distance. There is an unavoidable dimension of trust in the relationship between financial analysts and their clients, and, to borrow a phrase, trust cannot "be phoned in." It is partly for this reason that U.S. financial workers continue to be concentrated disproportionately in and around New York City well into the era of electronic communications, in spite of the fact that information can be gathered via the Internet and e-mail and teleconferences can be carried out in real time among people who are in distant places.

Delayed retirement by the members of the baby boom could also affect the employment side of the non-zero-sum scenario. Fewer young workers will be needed in coming years if current workers retire at later ages, thus holding on to their positions for a longer period of time. This development has been anticipated by observers of labor-force trends, who foresee that many workers will be induced to keep working by the drying up of good (that is, defined-benefit) retirement plans in the pri-

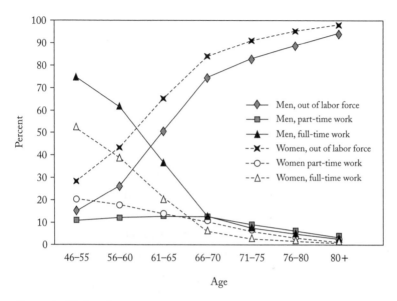

Figure 5.3. Labor-force participation, ages 46 and older by gender, 2000. (2000 Public Use Microdata Sample (5 percent).)

vate sector, the growing expense of health insurance and health care, and the expectation of lengthening post-65 life spans.[19] The meltdown of the stock market at the end of 2008 and the resulting evaporation of the assets in many retirement accounts have given additional force to this expectation. How much could postponed retirement alter the basic thrust of the back-of-the-envelope calculations above? It should be remembered in this context that workers in higher-tier occupations are likely to have better retirement plans and, in any event, more financial resources than other workers, and thus the impact of the factors inducing postponed retirement could for that reason be less. To be sure, they are also likely to be in better health in their sixties, and this fact could lead many of them to choose to work longer.

A look at the data presented in Figure 5.3 serves as a reminder of how many Americans retire early—presumably because many of them want to enjoy more leisure while they are still healthy—and this may in fact be the most important phenomenon to keep in mind with respect to the retirement of the baby boomers. In 2000, 75 percent of men aged 46–55 still worked full time, and another 11 percent worked part time on a regular basis.[20] In the 56- to 60-year-old group, the percentage working full time fell off to 62 percent, and among the 61- to 65-year-olds, it was down to 37 percent. After the age of 65, the percentage plummeted: to 13 percent among the 66- to 70-year-olds and then to 7.5 percent among the 71- to 75-year-olds. As the percentage working full time declines, that working part time does increase in the pre-retirement age groups, but only slightly, reaching a maximum of 13 percent in the 66- to 70-year-old age group before falling off with advancing age.

The trend toward early retirement appears to have leveled off among men during the 1990s, according to some analysts. Even greater changes appear to have occurred among women, especially middle-aged women, who since 1990 have exhibited a substantially higher level of labor-force participation than before.[21] Nevertheless, as of 2000, women were still highly likely to display the same rapid decline in labor-force participation after age 55 as men. In the 46- to 55-year-old group, 52 percent worked full time in 2000, while 20 percent regularly worked part time. Both of these percentages declined monotonically with advancing age, but the full-time percentage did so more rapidly. Hence, among the 66- to 70-year-olds, only 6 percent still worked full time and another 10 percent worked part time.

The proper conclusion to draw from these data is probably that retirement before the age of 65 is a deeply entrenched expectation for many American workers, one that may prove stubborn even in the face of economic disincentives. Advocates of later retirement argue for its postponement by several years, a nontrivial delay: according to a recent book, from the current average age of 63 to one of 66.[22] Let us assume that some postponement does in fact occur in the near future, since, for one thing, the age at which workers can receive their full Social Security benefits will be rising to 67 (for those born in 1960, toward the end of the baby boom). Yet the retirement patterns so evident in 2000 leave no doubt that many workers stop working full time well before they reach the age that entitles them to full benefits in the Social Security system. It seems unlikely that this will change so dramatically in the coming decades as to offset entirely the downward plunge in the percentage working full time between the 46- to 55-year-old group and the 61- to 65-year-old one.

Yet even a substantial postponement of average retirement would not reduce greatly the large number of jobs coming open by 2030. Suppose, for the sake of argument, that the average age at retirement from the full-time labor force does increase by three years by 2030. If the number of jobs to fill each year (in Table 5.3) is recomputed under this assumption, the reduction is about 5 percent.[23] For such a substantial change in retirement age, this is a modest impact.

How "Good" Will the Jobs of the Future Be?

Other major concerns about the labor-market opportunities of the future have been raised because of the rising inequality of earnings among workers and the stagnation in average real wages, indicating that the average worker is not getting ahead—even, it appears, in prosperous times. The deterioration in the "goodness" of many jobs is not limited to earnings: the increasing hiring of workers as "consultants," or "independent contractors," which limits the responsibilities of a firm toward them, is another sign of the erosion of workers' position. Paid typically based on an hourly rate, consultants can easily be dismissed, and they frequently receive few or no benefits. Likewise, the reductions in the responsibilities of firms for employee pension plans—symbolized by the replacement of "defined-benefit" plans with "defined-contribution" ones—indicate the deterioration affecting even good jobs. Political scientist Jacob Hacker has written of the "great risk shift," the increasing vulnerability experienced by average Americans, as their jobs and incomes become more unstable and they increasingly must depend on their own resources for health care and pension investment.[24]

One rigorous empirical analysis, by Annette Bernhardt and others, that examined workers' careers during the latter part of the twentieth century found diminishing chances for upward earnings trajectories and other signs of a fundamentally changed marketplace for labor from that which characterized the middle of the century. The earlier labor market produced the predictable earnings trajectories over the life course associated with postwar prosperity and the assimilation of the white ethnics.[25] The new marketplace is one of heightened inequality in earnings among workers in their mid-thirties, when their careers should be well established. This inequality characterizes even workers with postsecondary education, whose investments in their human capital should, but apparently do not always, lead to steady earnings growth over their careers. It is also a marketplace of considerable job churning, with more employment precariousness for experienced workers than was true in the past. As a consequence of both of these trends, a larger proportion of workers are trapped in low-wage careers.

Much other research supports this picture of growing inequality in the labor market and the deterioration of many formerly good jobs but leaves us, nevertheless, uncertain about the implications for the future linkage of non-zero-sum mobility with ethno-racial boundary change. One reason for the uncertainty is the absence of a satisfactory theory to explain the changes, for without such a theory we are left unsure what to expect in the future. The attempt at explanation that has probably gotten the most attention is often described by the phrase "skill-based technological change." Focusing on earnings inequalities, it sees them as spurred by the technological changes of the late twentieth century, computerization above all, that separate workers from one another on the basis of their abilities at skillfully using the new technologies. However, as a number of analysts have pointed out, there are some notable inconsistencies between the patterns of growing inequality and the implications of this theory.[26] For example, much of the earnings inequality developed in the early 1980s, before the widespread introduction of desktop computers; and earnings inequality grew less during the 1990s, when computers were infiltrating workplaces more and more and the development of the Internet transformed the computer's role.

Without a good theory, we are left with essentially descriptive analyses of how inequalities among jobs have developed; and they have not yet yielded a consistent picture. According to one analysis, much of the growth of earnings inequality has occurred within occupations rather than between them.[27] If individuals performing nominally the same job are being paid increasingly different amounts, the implications are potentially serious for my argument that the exit of the baby boomers from the labor market opens up space throughout the occupational hierarchy for minorities and other disadvantaged groups to advance. If it turns out that the earnings inequalities within occupations correspond with ethno-racial divisions, minorities could move up occupationally and yet remain economically well behind whites. However, other analyses appear to show that most of the growth in earnings inequality has occurred between occupations, in effect widening the distances between jobs located in different labor-market tiers.[28] If this is the case, then the potential of non-zero-sum mobility to provide new opportunities to minorities becomes even more consequential, allowing them to climb a labor-market ladder whose rungs are growing farther apart.

The existing analyses are persuasive about the growth of inequality in the labor market and the deterioration of many formerly good jobs, but the question is: do they force us to change our view of the potential for the retirement of the baby boomers to create non-zero-sum mobility and, with it, the opportunity for ethno-racial change? I think that they do not. Granted, the qualities that made many jobs good are under threat, but this condition applies very broadly across the labor market and hence strikes at jobs held by whites and minorities alike.[29] The changes under way, however, are not a form of extreme leveling, but in some respects its opposite. Hence, even if inequalities of earnings and other important job properties continue to grow, there will still be a hierarchy of job "goodness." Almost certainly it will continue for the next several decades to correlate strongly with the rankings I have used, based on earnings by occupation in 1999. Some of the good jobs may not be quite as good as before (but then some of the not-so-good jobs could be even worse than they are now). To the degree, then, that non-zero-sum mobility will allow minorities to ascend within the occupational hierarchy, this will still represent real change. The suspicion arises, of course, that the best jobs will still be largely reserved for white Americans, and this could turn out to be true. But there will be many more whites below this elite level, and if the promise of non-zero-sum mobility is realized, they will be interacting more and more with nonwhites and Hispanics who have climbed at least a few rungs up the social ladder.

In sum, while the changes under way may have negative impacts on many U.S. workers, engendering increasing levels of inequality in pay and working conditions, they do not of themselves negate the possibilities for ethno-racial change inherent in the non-zero-sum mobility induced by the retirement of the baby boomers. The changes may be deplorable, but there will still be plenty of "good" jobs. Applied to jobs, "good" is a relative concept, in any event. In a relative sense, the goodness of many jobs may even increase if inequality in wages and job conditions continues to grow. If that occurs, then the significance of the opportunities for minority advance afforded by non-zero-sum mobility will be enhanced.

Conclusion

The next decades offer an extraordinary opportunity for minority mobility and for some relaxation of the major ethno-racial boundaries of U.S. society. In a now famous phrase, the historian David Hollinger has described these divisions as the "racial/ethnic pentagon."[30] The metaphor drawn from two-dimensional geometry suggests the historical rigidity of these fundamental social configurations. But a new fluidity could wash over and erode that solidity in the next quarter century.

The massive retirement of the baby-boom cohorts will open up the system in a way that has not been true for decades. The baby boomers, who were by the time they reached adulthood the most highly educated birth cohorts in U.S. history, have dominated the top tiers of the labor market, holding disproportionate numbers of the best jobs. Those baby boomers who do so are overwhelmingly white, of course; and it is quite unlikely that the substantially smaller cohorts of whites that follow can provide enough highly educated workers to replace them, let alone to occupy the additional good jobs that will be created through economic expansion, however slow this may prove to be.

As I finish this book, the world has been plunged into deep recession, and gloom about the economy in the foreseeable future is all pervasive. Does the state of the U.S. economy at the end of the century's first decade vitiate my conclusions? I don't think so. The exit of the baby boomers from the labor market will extend over a quarter century, through the early 2030s, at least. The economy will recover long before this period ends, even if the better part of a decade is required for it to do so. (Nobel Prize-winning economist Paul Krugman has recently written, "No doubt this, too, shall pass—but how, and when? . . . In fact, the seeds of eventual recovery are already planted. . . . But recovery may be a long time coming.")[31] Recovery is likely to bring a period of catch-up economic growth. It is worth remembering that the United States suffered three recessions in rather close succession between the mid-1970s and early 1980s; in the first one, unemployment rose to near 10 percent, and in the last one, above it.[32] Yet the last three decades of the twentieth century were, overall, a period of substantial job growth, as the labor force expanded by about 75 percent over the period.

Hence, it is reasonable to conclude that a period of non-zero-sum mobility stands before us, even if there is considerable uncertainty about when it will fully take hold. It will allow some individuals to move upward without threatening the position of those who take for granted that good jobs will be available to themselves and their children. Greater penetration of America's most disadvantaged minority populations, namely, African and Hispanic Americans, into top tiers of the labor market is already evident when we look across cohorts. The cohorts now entering the labor market in full force show considerably higher percentages of U.S.-born blacks and Hispanics in top-decile and other top-quartile positions than do older cohorts. These shifts more or less track underlying demographic changes, that is, the changing racial and ethnic composition of youthful birth cohorts, but that does not eliminate their significance. That is, privileged whites are no longer able to exclude minorities from the higher tiers of the labor market, though they are still able to monopolize the best-paying positions within these tiers. Clearly, ethnoracial diversity is increasing near the top, and many whites located there now interact with minorities who are their peers. Diversity is certain to continue to increase as long as the recruitment into good jobs continues to reflect the racial and ethnic demography of birth cohorts, for the percentage of minorities is increasing. This is particularly true for immigrant-origin minorities, for given the resumption of large-scale immigration in the late 1960s, the numbers in the second (and third) generation entering adulthood are rising rapidly and will continue to do so for the foreseeable future. This point holds especially for U.S.-born Asians, given their record of strong educational achievement.

In light of past history—specifically, the rapid and full incorporation of disadvantaged white ethnics into the mainstream during the middle decades of the last century—non-zero-sum mobility holds a special significance for ethno-racial change. Because this kind of mobility by minorities is less threatening to the majority, it can occur without strenuous efforts by the majority to reinforce ethno-racial boundaries in order to preserve its privileged position. When socioeconomic advance can be translated by minorities into social proximity to the majority and when the majority perceives the upwardly rising minorities as its moral equals, then the conditions are in place for change to occur to racial and ethnic boundaries themselves.

This is a possible scenario for the near future, but it is not the only one. Demography is of course not destiny, or at least it is not so in such a simple-minded fashion. Whatever future changes occur will not be dictated solely by demographic and socioeconomic structures, which are to a great degree predictable, but forged by human agents. This fact makes them less predictable and more contingent. We need thus to consider some of the contingencies that could alter the scenario of ethno-racial boundary change.

6

The Contingencies of Change

Although the next quarter century seems to offer an extraordinary opportunity for minority mobility and for some degree of alteration to the major ethno-racial boundaries of U.S. society, there can be no guarantees. Non-zero-sum mobility creates opportunities for advance that are not exclusive to African and Hispanic Americans, but can benefit other parts of the American population, such as new immigrants and white women. The degree to which U.S.-born minority-group members can make use of these opportunities is likely depend upon policy choices that Americans make—say, to admit more highly skilled immigrants or to invest more in the education of currently disadvantaged groups.

The mid-twentieth-century ethno-racial transformation that fully incorporated the Irish and the southern and eastern Europeans into the white mainstream pivoted on three main factors that came together to produce it. In addition to massive non-zero-sum mobility, which these groups were best positioned to take advantage of, these factors included the conversion of socioeconomic gain into social proximity to mainstream whites and an ideological shift that emphasized the moral worthiness of the new groups. The threats to fundamental ethno-racial change during the next quarter century will be most likely to arise from complications and contingencies involving these three factors.

Threats to the Mobility of Minorities

The employment side of the formula that implies large-scale non-zero sum mobility—that is, the need for highly trained workers to replace the retiring baby boomers and their elders—seems well established. It could be altered by a very prolonged and deep economic slump or by structural economic changes that radically alter the shape of the occupational distribution, which still exhibits a large bulge in the middle, but these seem unlikely, though not impossible. Current occupational forecasts suggest that the long-term prospects for the expansion of jobs in the top half of the workforce are good. Inequality certainly could intensify between elite jobs, those in the top few percentiles, and other good jobs, if further deterioration in the quality of many good jobs continues; such deterioration is indicated in the increasing use of contract rather than permanent employees and in overall reductions in the benefits employees can expect. But the impact of these trends on the opportunities for ethno-racial change afforded by a period of non-zero-sum mobility is unclear: one could argue for the increasing importance of non-zero-sum mobility at a time of growing inequality as a means of reducing the risk and gravity of an exacerbation of overall ethno-racial inequalities. The prospects for a period of substantial non-zero-sum mobility could also be affected by large-scale postponement of retirement by members of the baby boom, though that, too, seems unlikely to be on a scale that would substantially reduce the need for new workers.

The main threats to minority mobility are located elsewhere, in the supply of workers, and come, first, from alternative sources of recruitment into the highly placed occupations that will experience large numbers of vacancies during the next twenty-five years and, second, from the realistic possibility that the pool of trained minority workers will not be deep enough to take up a larger-than-ordinary share of the openings.

One alternative source of highly qualified workers lies in immigration—in the potential for the United States to resort to the recruitment of immigrants trained partly or wholly in their home countries to fill jobs requiring high levels of qualification. Such a strategy is already under consideration at the highest levels of policymakers in Washington. In 2007, in the waning years of the George W. Bush administration, the U.S. Congress considered an immigration bill that proposed precisely this strategy, as it contained provisions that would have altered the primary basis for immigration from family ties to a point system giving priority to educational credentials, occupational qualifications, and English-language proficiency. Analyses at the time demonstrated that this scheme would likely have produced a geographical reorientation of the sources of the immigration stream, away from Latin America and toward Asia, presumably reinforcing the tendency, already evident, to recruit many technical and professional workers from the ranks of Asian immigrants (see Chapter 4).[1] Relying on immigrants is an alternative to the training of minority and immigrant-origin youth already in the United States, and a cheap one at that since much of the cost of educating highly qualified workers is wholly or partly borne by other countries. The economist George Borjas has argued forcefully for years that U.S. immigration policy should favor the highly skilled.[2] Despite the defeat of the 2007 bill in the Senate, largely because of its provisions to chart a path to legality for the millions of currently unauthorized immigrants, there remains a possibility that immigration law will be changed in this direction in the near future.

To a substantial degree, the United States is already drawing on immigrants to fill the need for highly skilled workers. One of the two main portals in current immigration law grants immigrant status—permanent residence and the right to work—to individuals who are admitted through their qualifications for employment, such as so-called priority workers, who are described as "persons with extraordinary ability in sciences, arts, education, business, or athletics," "outstanding professors and researchers," and "managers and executives subject to international transfer." The annual quota of visas granted on the basis of employment is set at 140,000.[3] In addition, the United States admits highly trained foreigners to work for extended periods under the controversial H-1B visa program.[4] This program targets so-called specialty workers, who are individuals in occupations for which a minimum of baccalaureate training is required, and under the law they are generally allowed to work in the United States for up to six years, although under some circumstances this period can be extended. The numerical extent of the program is hard to grasp with precision, because the annual cap on new admissions under the program has fluctuated. The cap is currently set at 85,000, a figure that includes a special quota of 20,000 workers with advanced degrees earned at American universities; and in some recent years it has been set substantially higher. (In fiscal years 2001–2003, for instance, the United States allowed as many as 195,000 annual H-1B admissions.) In addition, some visas of this type are exempt from the cap—for example, colleges and universities and some nonprofit organizations can hire H-1B workers above the cap. Also, the educated citizens of some countries—the NAFTA countries (Canada, Mexico) but also Australia—can be hired under visa programs like that of H-1B but outside of its numerical limit. The recipients of H-1B visas have been shown to come much more from Asian countries than is true of permanent immigrants—India alone accounts for a substantial share of these visas, on a par with the proportion of Mexicans among permanent immigrants.

It is apparent that the foreign born already play an important role on the highest tiers of the occupational hierarchy, and this could increase as a result of future decisions by the federal government, which could—without changing the basic provisions of immigration law—simply raise the cap on the number of H-1B visas granted per year or extend the period for which they are valid. In certain professions, for example, advanced levels of engineering, the foreign born play a much larger role than they do elsewhere in the workforce, and the number of the U.S. born receiving the required training is stagnant, if not shrinking.[5] Thus the United States is certain to require highly trained foreign-born workers in the future, but the question is how to balance their intake with the prospects for the mobility of U.S.-born minorities. To be sure, no matter what strategy the United States adopts with respect to this balance, the racial and ethnic diversity on the higher rungs of the occupational ladder will increase. However, that diversity will be much greater, as well as more reflective of the entire population, if it includes African and Hispanic Americans, for the immigrant workers who can fill the need for highly educated workers come disproportionately from Asia. We have already seen that foreign-born Asians make up the leading nonwhite category among the young adults holding top-decile occupations.

Nevertheless, the ability of the United States to recruit highly trained immigrants is not unlimited, and the strategy of replacing the retiring baby-boom workers in top occupational tiers with immigrants may not be entirely successful, if it is ever implemented. Inevitably, the United States will face increasing competition from other countries in attracting immigrants with advanced levels of education and training. The need for most European Union countries to recruit workers from abroad has been clear for a while, and that need is growing. Countries like Germany, Italy and Spain, whose fertility levels have been well below replacement level for some time, must either bring in immigrants or face steep declines in their working-age populations at a time when the numbers of their citizens at elderly ages are climbing sharply.[6] This need will be not just for lower-level manual and service workers but for highly skilled ones, too, as was recognized in the German green-card program, instituted in 2000 to bring in more IT workers.[7] The program was not terribly successful—the numbers recruited from abroad fell well short of the targets, which were not set very high to begin with—but this does not mean that a program with a similar goal could not be successful in the future. Moreover, China and India, which now supply many highly skilled immigrants to the United States and other countries, could reach a point of economic development and demographic shift where they try to hold on to their highly skilled nationals, though whether such a point would be reached in the next quarter century is open to question.

In the nearer term, an indicator of possible trouble ahead for the United States in this domain is the stagnating number of foreign students at U.S. universities, since much of the recruitment of highly educated immigrants takes place in fact through the higher-educational system; once foreign-born youth have invested in educational credentials earned in a specific national system and in mastery of its language, they are likely to remain there, thus becoming immigrants, if they do not return home. After steadily climbing for decades, the number of the foreign born studying in the United States has leveled off since 2001, with the entry of some foreign students impeded by post-9/11 restrictions and limits imposed on their access to some technologies by the Patriot Act. In the academic year 2006–2007, the total number of foreign students at U.S. colleges and universities, 583,000, was almost identical to what it had been in 2001–2002, though the figure represented a recuperation after several years of decline and presumably could continue to increase.[8] In any event, the position of the United States within the worldwide market for international students has been affected not only by the uncertainties of student visas in the post-9/11 era but also by the growing attractiveness of, and aggressive recruitment by, universities outside the United States. Some European countries such as Germany, the Netherlands, and the Scandinavian countries have established university programs in English in order to bring in more international students. Since the costs of attending European universities are typically much lower than those in the United States, these schools are competing with increasing success against U.S. higher-educational institutions for this valuable segment of students. In addition, countries such as Australia, Canada, and France now see a valuable source for highly trained workers in foreign-student populations and are adjusting their immigration policies accordingly.[9]

Another potential threat to the scenario of ethno-racial change lies in the possibility that the non-zero-sum mobility of the next quarter century will produce enhanced opportunities for whites, especially those of working-class origins, rather than for minorities. One challenge to the notion, then, that a new fluidity will soften major ethno-racial boundaries in the near future is the prospect that white privilege will continue to exert a powerful hold on channels of mobility, allowing whites of lower socioeconomic origins to rise and occupy the positions coming open. In this respect, one could argue from the past record, which reveals critical moments in which apparently universalistic regimes of opportunity (for example, the GI Bill) allowed whites to forge ahead at the expense of minorities.[10] To be sure, some degree of ethno-racial change is already visible in the shifts across cohorts within the highest occupational tiers, but future change will be constrained to the extent that whites can exploit new opportunities.

But while an expansion of opportunity for working-class whites is possible and perhaps even likely, it seems unlikely that it could be on a scale that could drastically reduce the opportunities for the mobility of others. The cohorts of whites that will come of age during the next twenty-five years are notably smaller than are those of the white baby boomers they will replace. Since, in addition, the jobs on the higher rungs of the labor market, where many vacancies will occur, typically require advanced education and the white baby boomers are highly educated, it would take a substantial rise in the educational attainments of young whites to create enough replacements, let alone the workers who will be required for the jobs that will be generated by the growth of the population. Such a rise seems implausible, and in fact the evidence is one of stagnating college attendance among recent cohorts of whites, especially white men. (More precisely, these statements are true so long as we assume that, net of education, the probabilities for whites to enter different tiers of the labor market as full-time workers remain as they are. One way these probabilities could change is if white women, many of whom already possess the requisite levels of postsecondary education, were to gain from the exit of the baby boomers. We will get to this possibility in a moment.)

The analysis by Claude Fischer and Michael Hout of educational changes over the course of the twentieth century indicates that the college graduation rate of U.S.-born whites reached an initial apogee of nearly 30 percent for the cohort that attained its twenty-first birthday in 1971: born in 1950, this group represents the first half of the baby boom, and its high rate of college attendance is partly due to student deferments during the Vietnam War.[11] In the next cohort, whose members came of age in 1981, the college graduation rate fell off by a few percentage points to about 25 percent. It has since recovered, climbing to about 30 percent in the next cohort, which celebrated its twenty-first birthday in 1991. In that group, however, the position of the sexes reversed, with women for the first time earning baccalaureates at higher rates than men.

Recent Census data (in Figure 6.1) reveal a stable rate of college graduation for native-born white men: 25–30 percent of each cohort has garnered at least a baccalaureate since the Vietnam-era cohort (born in 1945–1954), when the college-graduation rate attained its zenith, at approximately 35 percent. These figures are somewhat higher than those referred to in the previous paragraph because the Census data for older cohorts indicate cumulative graduation rates, which include degrees earned when some men are past the usual college-going ages. (The increase of education with age, even after the mid-twenties, is especially visible in postbaccalaureate education.) There has been a continuing rise across cohorts in the college attainments of white women, however. If we take the pre-Vietnam-era cohort (women born in 1935–1944) as a reference point, the college-graduation rate of women experienced a

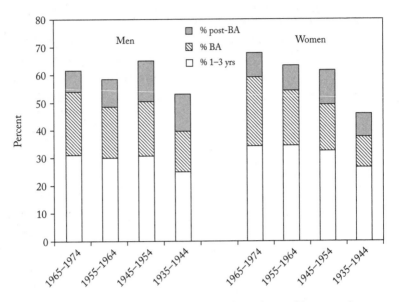

Figure 6.1. Rates of postsecondary education by gender, working-age cohorts of native-born non-Hispanic whites, 2000. (2000 Public Use Microdata Sample (5 percent).)

fairly steep climb—going from nearly 20 percent in this cohort to almost 30 percent in the two baby-boom cohorts (born in 1945–1964), to just under 35 percent in the youngest working-age cohort (born in 1965–1974) as of 2000. To be sure, the women of the Vietnam era, when this spurt began, were not using the educational system as some men were—to avoid the military draft. For both men and women, then, more was involved in the spurt than a response to wartime conditions. This is demonstrated also by the subsequent, continuing rise in the postsecondary attainments of white women, whoses college attendance and graduation rates are now higher than those of white (and nonwhite) men.

This brief analysis suggests the limited potential of a recruitment of whites that reaches further down the socioeconomic ladder to occupy very much of the empty space in the system created by the retirement of the baby boomers and the growth of the economy. The departing baby-boom cohorts have high levels of educational attainment. The cohorts of white men recently entering the labor market (for example, the 1965–1974 cohort, the 26- to 35-year-olds of 2000) have, if anything, slightly lower levels of education, while the youthful cohorts of women have modestly more education on average than the baby boomers. It is impossible to say whether the college graduation rate of white women can rise further, but it seems doubtful that it could rise by much. Not everyone is going to go to college, let alone graduate. White men may be another story. While the reasons for the decline of college-going among young men are disputed, it seems quite reasonable to take the Vietnam-era rates of white men's college-going and graduation as high-water marks that could be reached again in the near future. To simplify, let us assume that there is, overall, a 5-percentage-point increase in the rate of college education for whites, partly as a result of a modest rise in the rate for white men and partly because we project that future cohorts of women will attain the very high rate of the most recent cohort in Figure 6.1 (born in the 1965–1974 period). For white women, this rate would be higher than those of the cohorts they will replace in the workforce during the coming quarter century. For our purposes, it is not worth worrying too much about how this rise is distributed among the categories of postsecondary education—how much of it, in other words, occurs in the baccalaureate category versus that containing individuals with one to three years of college.

A simple order-of-magnitude calculation suggests that such a rise, consistent with an expansion of mobility opportunities for working-class whites, will make a dent in the need for highly qualified workers, but will by no means prove enough to shut down the engines of non-zero-sum mobility. If we assume that the pool of workers with postsecondary education in some form is the one from which the great majority of workers in the top half of the workforce will be recruited, then a 5-percentage-point increase in the college-going of whites will expand this pool for whites by only 8–9 percent at best. This is true because 60 percent or more of whites in young cohorts now receive some education beyond high school, and an increment of 5 points to this figure is an increase of just 1/12. In terms of the top-quartile "what if" calculations shown in Chapter 5, this would mean that 38,300 more white workers would be available per year, and consequently the number of African and Hispanic Americans annually entering the tier would fall from 164,600 to 126,300. These minorities would still fill 18 percent of the top-quartile jobs coming open, a share that is well above their share in 2000, 8 percent. In short, the potential for the mobility of minorities would remain robust.

Women constitute an alternative group who could provide many recruits to fill the need for highly skilled workers during the next quarter century. Just as the foreseeable openings could bring many minorities into the higher ranks of the labor market, they could do so for women as well. Indeed, women seem highly likely to make substantial advances in the near future as a result of the baby boom's retirement. They can be expected to be more numerous than men among the highly educated young people coming of age during the next quarter century.[12]

Ironically, the potential for women to plug a large portion of the holes in the upper tiers of the workforce opened up by the retirement of the baby boomers is a consequence of the continuing gross inequality between the positions of male and female workers; women, in short, are not used to their potential. Consider the data in Table 6.1, which shows the numbers of women and men by birth cohort/age group in different tiers of full-time workers as of 2000. Only the 26- to 55-year-olds are presented, because older age groups of workers have already been drawn down by retirement, which differentiates by gender.[13] It is noteworthy that gender inequalities seem to have changed only modestly across the cohorts, even though opportunities for women to advance have presumably been improving in recent decades. The principal signs of change appear in top-decile occupations, where, in the youngest cohort, the 26-

Table 6.1 Ratio of men to women among full-time workers by labor-market tier and birth cohort: 2000

Birth cohort		Top decile		Rest of top quartile		Second quartile	
		Ratio	N	Ratio	N	Ratio	N
1965–74	Male		1,680.6		2,033.3		3,735.8
	Female		715.9		1,371.6		2,401.3
		2.3		1.5		1.6	
1955–64	Male		2,305.6		2,668.3		4,547.9
	Female		736.4		1,782.5		2,691.1
		3.1		1.5		1.7	
1945–54	Male		1,821.9		2,247.6		3,619.5
	Female		453.3		1,511.9		2,370.3
		4.0		1.5		1.5	

Source: 2000 Public Use Microdata Sample (5 percent).
Note: Workforce numbers (N) in thousands.

to 35-year-olds, men still outnumbered women in 2000 by a ratio of 2.3 to 1. By comparison, this ratio was 3.1 to 1 among the 36- to 45-year-olds and 4.0 to 1 in the 46-to-55 age group. Further down, however, gender inequality has held steady. In the remainder of the top quartile, the ratio of men to women in the youngest cohort, 1.5 to 1, is exactly the same as it is in either of the two older cohorts; with slightly more numerical variation, the story is the same in the second quartile.

It is unlikely that differentials this large and stable will be erased in the near future, even if the nation desperately needs the talents of women in the workplace. The differentials are rooted to a substantial extent in ways that work and family life fail to mesh harmoniously, especially for women. Many observers have noted that, despite an increase in the amount of housework shouldered by men, the division of labor in the home still places a larger burden of responsibility on women, and this burden increases when children arrive. This is true for women who share parenting duties with their husbands and partners, but the burden is obviously greater for women who are raising children as single parents. For more highly educated, middle-class women, the responsibilities associated with child rearing are especially complex and demanding because of the intensity of the interactions expected to occur between parent and child and the need to manage what has become in many families a highly organized schedule of children's activities. One scholar who has studied the parenting in middle-class and working-class families characterizes the intensive child rearing in the middle class as "concerned cultivation," a phrase that suggests the level of parental effort involved, and contrasts it with the working-class pattern, which leaves children more time to play without direct parental monitoring. Unless more highly educated women gain some relief from their domestic burdens, the time squeeze they experience may limit their further recruitment into higher-tier occupations in the full-time labor force. This is not to deny that many of them do work: one recent study demonstrates that the labor-force participation and full-time employment rates of women with professional occupations increased substantially during the second half of the twentieth century. However, by the beginning of the twenty-first century, the full-time employment rate of professional women, between 50 and 60 percent in most age groups, remained significantly below that of professional men and was reduced quite substantially for women with young children at home.[14]

The greater penetration by women into higher tiers of the workforce is not inherently incompatible with the occupational advance of minorities, since women can obviously belong to minority groups. With respect to women's rise on the occupational ladder as an alternative to minority mobility, the issue thus turns on the degree to which white women, who predominate in the ranks of highly educated women, can occupy the jobs coming open between now and 2030. To examine this issue with another back-of-the-envelope calculation, I will make the simplifying assumption that for the cohorts entering the labor market now and in the next few decades, the recruitment of white women into top tiers increases enough to halve the gap that now separates them from white men—that is to say, the probability for a white woman to enter any tier rises to midway between the white male and female probabilities of 2000. (I further restrict the probability calculations to individuals aged 26 to 55, to avoid the complications created by retirements in the late fifties and early sixties.) For example, in 2000 the probability of a white man's holding a full-time job in the top decile was .114 and the probability of a white woman .035; by assumption, then, the probability for a white woman in the near future would rise to .075, the midpoint between the two prior figures. By applying these gender-specific probabilities to the projections of the white population by gender and age, I arrive at a revised back-of-the-envelope calculation of the expected numbers of white workers by tier. Applying the probabilities in this way gives a rather generous estimate of the potential of women to fill upper-tier positions because, for the calculation, the probabilities are treated as averages over a thirty-year period; since we know that the actual probabilities were lower than these averages at the beginning of the period, we are assuming that at later time points they will be higher than the averages.

This calculation suggests that white women could meet a substantial portion of the expected need for skilled workers, but by no means all of it. The yield of new workers is greatest in the top decile, where the gender imbalance is the most lop-sided. With an influx of highly educated white women into this tier, the number of white workers available per year would rise to 233,600 (see Table 6.2), an increase of about 50,000 per year over the last chapter's "what if" scenario. Such a rise would cut drastically into the room available for U.S.-born black and Hispanic workers to enter the top decile, and their numbers in the tier would fall precipitously (and unrealistically) in this new scenario, from 53,600 entrants per year to 4,700. However, outside of the top decile, the impact would be much smaller. For instance, in the remainder of the top quartile, the increase in the number of white entrants would go up by 30,800 per year under the assumption about the greater recruitment of white women. This scenario would still leave room for about 80,200 U.S.-born

Table 6.2   Revised "what if" scenario: What if white women narrowed the gender gap at the top?

	First decile	Rest of first quartile	Second quartile	Total
Jobs to fill by 2030/yr	285.2	433.7	714.0	1,432.9
White recruits/yr (from earlier scenario)	184.7	274.7	443.4	902.8
Additional recruitment of white women	*48.9*	*30.8*	*53.4*	*133.1*
Foreign born/yr	31.3	34.4	56.9	122.6
U.S.-born Asians/yr	15.6	13.6	20.3	49.5
Remainder: U.S.-born blacks and Hispanics	4.7	80.2	140.0	224.9
% to U.S.-born blacks and Hispanics	1.6	18.5	19.6	15.7

Note: Population numbers are in 1000s.

Assumptions: This table amends Table 5.4. It uses the same assumptions, except that white women are posited to halve the 2000 difference in probability of attaining a higher-tier job separating them from white men.

black and Hispanic workers to enter this tier each year. They would then represent a fifth of the workers filling these desirable jobs during the next several decades. The bottom line is essentially the same for the second quartile.

This analysis implies that the next quarter of the century will offer an opening not just for minorities but for women, too. Young women —more highly educated than their brothers and, by all accounts, more optimistic and ambitious as well—constitute an enormous resource for the U.S. workforce, if we as a society can dismantle the barriers that keep them from rising to their full potential. Their labor will be needed if the United States is to meet the needs for highly skilled workers generated by the retirement of the baby boomers and the growth of the economy as the population expands. The coming quarter century could therefore provide an opportunity for women to renegotiate many of the arrangements that currently constrain their role in the labor force, such as the lower pay they receive for doing what often is essentially the same work as men, and the lack of child care adequate to enable many mothers either to enter the labor force in the first place or to work full time rather than part time.

However, it seems highly unlikely that women can satisfy the demand for highly skilled workers that will arise in coming decades from the retirement of the baby boomers. It would take something close to a revolution in the arrangements currently governing domestic life and the raising of children to unleash fully the working power of women. As long as the burdens of raising children fall disproportionately on women and the expectations about child rearing in the middle class involve an intensive cultivation by parents of children's inner potential, the employment role of many women who could take full-time jobs in higher tiers of the workforce will be constrained. Since revolutions are improbable (and rarely predictable), the nation will need to look to minority populations of women and men in order to recruit new, highly trained workers.

The Educational Challenge

This brings us to the final, and most serious, threat to the potential for ethno-racial change in the next quarter century: the lagging educational attainments of African and Hispanic Americans. Obviously, if minority youth do not possess the educational credentials required for the occupations in the top tiers, they will be unable to fill the places created by retiring baby boomers and the expansion of the economy. The gaps remain large at the upper end of the educational distribution. For instance, among the 26- to 35-year-olds of 2000, an age group whose college-educated members completed their schooling during the 1990s and that reflects, as well as we can easily measure, the recent life chances of minorities, the college-completion rates of U.S.-born African and Hispanic Americans are about half of the equivalents among their white compatriots.[15] (See Table 6.3.) Just 12 percent of African-American men in this cohort possessed baccalaureate degrees; for Hispanic men, the rate

Table 6.3   Rates of postsecondary education by gender for youngest working-
age cohort (aged 26–35) of native-born non-Hispanic whites, non-
Hispanic blacks, and Hispanics: 2000

	% some coll., no degree	% assoc. degree	% BA	% post-BA
Females				
Whites	24.6	9.6	25.0	8.6
Blacks	29.7	7.3	12.8	4.1
Hispanics	27.5	7.7	12.8	4.3
Males				
Whites	23.6	7.6	22.8	7.6
Blacks	25.1	5.2	9.8	2.6
Hispanics	24.2	6.2	10.6	3.4

Source: 2000 Public Use Microdata Sample (5 percent).

was two percentage points higher. As is true among whites, the figures
for U.S.-born minority women are higher, but not greatly so: 17 percent
for both African- and Hispanic-American women, about half the percentage found among white women. Also noteworthy are the low percentages who complete postbaccalaureate training, the prerequisite for
entering into many of the best-paid professional and technical occupations: at 3–4 percent among young U.S.-born minority men and women,
these rates are, once again, only about half of their equivalents among
U.S.-born whites.

Not all of the jobs in the top tiers—in the top quartile, say—will require a baccalaureate degree. The ethno-racial differences in educational
attainment are not nearly so large when it comes to the larger pool of
individuals with some degree of postsecondary training. While two-
thirds of the young white women of working age in 2000 had completed
at least a year of college, this was also true for slightly more than half of
young native-born black and Hispanic women. A similar difference ap-

pears among men, though with lower levels of postsecondary education. The demographic changes ahead could bring many more minorities into jobs in the top half of the workforce. But since within this broad tier considerable sorting will take place according to amount and quality of education, whites (and Asians) will have in the aggregate large advantages over blacks and Hispanics when it comes to the best available jobs. Noteworthy is that blacks and Hispanics even trail whites when it comes to earning an associate degree, though not by nearly as large a margin as is the case for the baccalaureate. The ethno-racial gaps in postsecondary credentials of any sort are quite large, in other words. The inequalities in credentials probably reflect broader differences in preparation and training that could be telling about the racial and ethnic composition of the pools eligible to be hired for these good jobs; at any event, they are likely to be viewed this way by many employers.

If there is no change in the ethno-racial differentials in education, then clearly the mobility of native-born minorities into higher tiers of the workforce will be limited. There will still be some growth of diversity in these tiers as a function of changes in the ethno-racial composition of the cohorts entering the labor market during the next quarter century, but it will fall far short of the level that could otherwise be attained. For instance, if we assume that as a consequence of persisting ethno-racial differentials in postsecondary education there is no change in minority probabilities of entering the top quartile, where jobs are highly likely to require some degree of training beyond high school, then a simple projection suggests that about 96,000 U.S.-born blacks and Hispanics will be available per year to take full-time jobs in this tier. On the basis of the labor-force projections of the last chapter, they would then occupy 13 percent of the 719,000 such jobs open in an average year. This would represent a significant improvement over the percentage they held in 2000 and a nontrivial change in the ethno-racial composition of this tier, especially since the proportion of jobs held by whites is likely to be declining. But it would come up well short of the 23 percent of these posi-

tions that, according to the "what if" scenario in the last chapter, could
be occupied by African and Hispanic Americans. Moreover, this growth
in diversity would be achieved without any change in the probabilities
that different groups enter this tier. In other words, it would leave the
structure of ethno-racial inequality intact.

Reducing or even closing the gaps in educational attainment between
minority and majority youth should be a prominent goal for American society in the near future, especially because it can help the United
States to close the holes in higher tiers of the workforce certain to open
up in coming decades. The focus of this goal should be more concentrated on K–12 education, which prepares students for higher education,
than on postsecondary education. As Claudia Goldin and Lawrence
Katz observe, "In recent years, the quality of the K–12 educational system in the United States has been seriously questioned, but the U.S.
higher educational system has remained the envy of the world."[16] Their
analysis of the stagnation in the overall level of educational attainment
(whites included) leads to the following conclusion:

> Two factors appear to be holding back the educational attainment of
> many American youth. The first is the lack of college readiness of
> youth who drop out of high school and of the substantial numbers
> who obtain a high school diploma but remain academically unpre-
> pared for college. The second is the financial access to higher educa-
> tion for those who are college ready.[17]

Making progress toward the goal of a reduced or closed eduction gap
will require a willingness by majority Americans to invest in the educations of young people from disadvantaged circumstances who do not
look like their own children and grandchildren.[18] The Census Bureau
projected in 2008 that by the early 2020s the majority of American children will come from minority groups. With such a shift in view, Dowell
Myers has called for a new "social contract," a new understanding of in-

dividuals' rights and responsibilities with respect to the larger society; such a new contract, he argues, could be the basis for ensuring, on the one side, greater investment in and therefore improved schooling for minority youth so that they can assume higher-level jobs and, on the other, the labor force that will support the retirement of the largely white baby boomers.[19] Yet logical though it seems in the abstract, achieving a new social contract would be no small feat.

In thinking about the possibility of raising the educational levels of minority youth, Americans need to recall that such an acceleration of educational attainment by a previously disadvantaged group has happened before: in the early twentieth century, no European immigrant group was as far behind the American mainstream as were the southern Italian arrivals of the early twentieth century, the majority of whom were illiterate.[20] Up through the 1950s, their children lagged well behind their peers in American schools, in part because of the low value placed in their homes on getting more than the minimum education and the need of many poor families to send their children into the labor market as soon as possible. The southern Italian second generation, like minority youth today, also had relatively high rates of involvement in juvenile delinquency and adult crime. Yet, in what was admittedly a more favorable climate for education—a national investment in education in the 1950s to meet the perceived challenge of Soviet scientific achievements and the rapid expansion of higher education after World War II—the Italians rapidly caught up to other whites. The Italian-American cohorts born after the war, many of them belonging to the third generation, did not possess on average lower education than other whites; if anything they were slightly ahead.[21]

A similar catch-up with mainstream educational levels would at first sight seem difficult in the contemporary United States. On the positive side of the ledger, it is the case that educational outcomes have been improving over time and that minority students have benefited as a consequence. Jennifer Hochschild and Nathan Scovronick summarize a review of trends in K–12 education and test scores with an upbeat conclusion:

> In short, more people are staying in school, and they are staying in school longer. They are not just attending but learning more, which puts most of them in a better position to attain absolute and relative success than their predecessors. Over the past 30 years, all of this has happened at a slightly faster rate for the most disadvantaged groups. This trajectory—better schooling outcomes across the board and a reduction in the gap between the best-off and the worst-off—is clear evidence that Americans have a real commitment to reforming the public schools to ensure that everyone can pursue the American dream.[22]

However, systemic forces would appear to make an acceleration in minority educational attainments, needed if black and Hispanic students are to catch up with their white counterparts, exceedingly difficult. These forces are rooted in the still pervasive residential segregation among ethno-racial populations and the locally based nature of most public schools. Consequently, the segregation of minority students in primary and secondary schools remains high, and their proportions of the total student population are going up.[23] Large numbers of African Americans and Hispanics attend public schools where there are few, if any, white students: in the school year 2003–2004, nearly 40 percent of African-American students attended schools that were 90 percent or more minority, and nearly three-quarters attended schools where the majority of students belonged to minority groups; for Hispanics, the comparable figures were similar. Observing that predominantly minority schools are also highly likely to serve areas where poverty is concentrated, Gary Orfield and Chungmei Lee note that such schools are typically beset by a variety of problems that impede learning: "less qualified, less experienced teachers, lower levels of peer group competition, more limited curricula taught at less challenging levels, more serious health problems, much more turnover of enrollment," and they could have added more serious levels of threat to the safety of students.[24]

These problems reflect to a large degree the inequalities in funding that correspond to the location of schools, whether they are in cities or suburbs, and the affluence of the populations surrounding them. Among rich nations, the funding of American public schools rests to an unusual degree on locally raised taxes, while the national government plays a limited role. The expenditures of the latter tend to have an equalizing impact—the federal government, for example, spent $12 billion in 2002 on schools serving low-income students—but they account for less than 10 percent of the total K–12 budget for the country. The rest is paid in roughly equal shares by local taxes, mostly the property tax, and by states.[25] This situation contributes greatly to the stark inequalities visible among U.S. primary and secondary schools. According to estimates presented by Hochschild and Scovronick for 2001, the national average in spending per pupil was $7,800, "but some districts spent much more and some much less; between the highest-spending 5 percent of the districts and the lowest-spending 5 percent, there can be a variation of $5,000"— in other words, a 2-to-1 disparity.[26] These spending inequalities do not compensate for the inequalities among students in family and home resources, but broadly speaking reinforce them. That is, the highest spending is frequently found in suburban school districts that serve affluent and heavily white student bodies, while the lowest spending is found typically in inner-city areas serving poor, minority students.

Undoubtedly, this constellation of systemic forces contributes heavily to the substantial gap between the average school skills of white students and those of minorities. According to the 2005 Nation's Report Card for Reading, the reading skills of African-American and Hispanic fourth and eighth graders had improved during the preceding decade but still lagged well behind those of whites and Asians, who also improved their reading skills over the period.[27] The picture for mathematics is a bit more hopeful in that the improvement of all groups in the decade preceding

2005 was greater, and the evidence of a narrowing of group differences seems stronger, but differences remain and are not small.

The inequalities among K–12 schools, if left untouched, will limit the ability of youth from low-income families to rise far above their origins and seize the occupational positions that will be available because of the decline in the number of whites.[28] In addition, recent court decisions and statewide referenda have constrained the ability of the public sector of higher education to open channels of educational mobility through affirmative action in admissions, though private universities are not affected by these decisions and thus retain important affirmative-action initiatives. The experience at the University of California shows that the elimination of affirmative action can drastically reduce the access of minority students to top public colleges and universities. For example, in fall 2006, the number of African Americans entering UCLA reached a thirty-year low, at just 2 percent of the freshman class, a third of what it had been before the 1995 vote that altered the state's constitution to ban the use of racial and ethnic preferences in decisions by state agencies; it has since recovered somewhat, but not to the level of the early 1990s.[29]

What the nation needs is a more intensive investment in the educations of disadvantaged youth: the current system of educational financing creates disparities in favor of largely white and middle-class schools, but even parity in financing between largely white and heavily minority schools would probably not change the picture of educational inequality along racial and ethnic lines sufficiently. Poor minority students need greater support in their educational careers than do middle-class whites, because they generally do not have access through their families and neighborhoods to the cultural attributes that are prized in schools and other institutional settings[30] and because equal funding for their schools will not actually mean equal schools (due to the greater variety of problems from which the schools in poor communities suffer).

A national commitment to greater investment in education, which would have as a side product much greater investment in the schools attended by minority students, is not so out of reach as it might seem. An opening is given by the currently limited role of the federal government in school finances. If this were to increase substantially—if federal spending were, say, to double or triple as a proportion of the total national budget for K–12 schooling—it would create the prospect for much more investment in minority schools, as well as additional investment in the schools attended by middle-class white students.[31] Such an increase may seem out of line with current budgetary realities, but it might be achievable with political leadership committed to the goals of overall improvement in the educations of American children and greater educational parity for minority children. Hochschild and Scovronick observe that in 2001 the total national expenditure on K–12 schooling was just under $400 billion, while the defense budget amounted to $300 billion. However, the federal government's contribution to educational expenditures was less than 10 percent, quite modest when compared with what it spent on defense. Some rearrangement in these priorities could yield many more dollars for education.

The justification for a program of greater investment in schooling lies near at hand. There is of course the obvious and somewhat platitudinous observation that our children are our future. But perhaps more significant as a justification is the relatively weak performance of U.S. students in international comparisons. Goldin and Katz deplore the fact that the United States has lost its previous position of leadership in overall educational attainment; according to OECD data for young adults (aged 25–34 in 2004), the United States ranked eleventh out of thirty countries in the mean years of schooling for men and tenth for women. International tests of school-taught skills and knowledge reveal even more slippage. On the Third International Math and Science Study (TIMSS), characterized by Goldin and Katz as the "gold standard" of such international comparisons, the United States ranked in the bottom half of the twenty nations studied in twelfth-grade mathematics and science. Equally disappointing results were obtained by the 2003 PISA (Program for International Assessment) study, which showed U.S. 15-year-old students achieving well below the OECD average in "mathematics literacy, problem solving, and scientific literacy."[32] The weak performance of U.S. students in scientific and other academic subjects ought to be as great a concern as national defense when it comes to the American future, since the economic performance of the United States in coming decades will depend on the ability of Americans to produce technological innovations and to apply them in workplaces.

A greatly enhanced program of federal investment in education would bypass the primary blockage when it comes to educational reform: the tension between private interests and collective goods. Hochschild and Scovronick incisively summarize this tension as follows:

> Many issues in educational policy have therefore come down to an apparent choice between the individual success of comparatively privileged students and the collective good of all students or the nation as a whole. Efforts to promote the collective goals of the American dream through public schooling have run up against almost insurmountable barriers when enough people believe (rightly or wrongly, with evidence or without) that those efforts will endanger the comparative advantage of their children or children like them.[33]

In a situation that is perceived as zero-sum by powerful actors, the surest path to change lies in an expansion of resources that will transform perceptions and in policies that will engender benefits for all students but bestow them disproportionately on the most disadvantaged.

A program of greater investment could be used, for example, to recruit more teachers with strong academic qualifications and solid preparation for the classroom, who would then strengthen the teacher corps in both good suburban schools and weaker inner-city ones. There is solid evidence in favor of the positive impact of high-quality teaching: that is, the qualifications of teachers, as indicated by their academic strengths (exemplified in their SAT scores) and their training (for example, certification in subject matter) and experience, have a demonstrable and substantial effect on the learning in classrooms. However, the sorting of teachers among schools leaves those schools serving poorer and more minority populations with less qualified teachers. In addition, studies of teacher recruitment in recent decades show that the students who enter the profession disproportionately have below-average SAT and other test scores. There is room for improvement, in other words, especially in the schools attended by youngsters disadvantaged by minority status and poverty.[34]

The recruitment of teachers has changed fundamentally since the period just after World War II when Italian Americans and other white ethnics caught up to other whites in educational attainment, though there can be disagreement on how much the changes have affected the quality of teaching in the classroom.[35] Then as now, teaching was a female-dominated profession. However, in the decades immediately following World War II, the career options for college-educated women were limited, as was their ability to combine work with child rearing. The teaching profession therefore recruited from a pool of women with talents and educational qualifications that would these days allow their daughters, or granddaughters, to pursue professional or other high-flying careers. For women, if not also for men, the option of teaching as a career has slipped down in the list of preferences as other options have opened up. Paying teachers more would improve the standing of teaching for both. Bringing more teachers, and more highly qualified ones, into schools would allow classroom size to fall and improve the caliber of classroom teaching, with demonstrable benefits for the overall quality of education. (Goldin and Katz point to the STAR experiment in Tennessee as evidence that "smaller class size in the early grades improves academic performance particularly for poor and minority children.")[36]

I haven't addressed the second of Goldin and Katz's causes of the stagnation in U.S. educational attainments—namely, the inability of some students to afford a college education—but it should be obvious that a program of greater investment in education can reduce its cost for the neediest students. The potential gain from such a program is substantial: since the educational attainments of African and Latino Americans lag far behind those of whites, the room for improvement is large. This is not true for whites, whose college graduation rates are, in the case of men, not far behind their all-time high and, in the case of women, currently at their high; since not everyone has the aptitude or interest to pursue a college education to a baccalaureate, it is difficult to envision a major leap forward in the postsecondary achievements of whites. However, such a leap is not at all difficult to envision for blacks and Hispanics. During the twentieth century, blacks closed the gap with whites that previously existed in terms of high-school graduation.[37] Were something similar to occur in the early twenty-first century with respect to college attendance and graduation, the yield in terms of highly skilled entrants to the labor market would be considerable.

Even a more modest diminution of the gap would produce an appreciable yield. Suppose for a moment that blacks and Hispanics improved their rate of postsecondary education by just 5 percentage points and that all of this improvement was registered at the high end of attainment, in the numbers earning the baccalaureate or a postbaccalaureate degree; this increase is modest in the sense that it is less than half of the gap separating whites from blacks and Hispanics in the most recent U.S.-born cohorts (in Table 6.3). By the same logic earlier applied to whites, the increase in the pool of U.S.-born minorities holding the baccalaureate or better would be on the order of a third, since only about 15 percent of the most recent cohort of African and Hispanic Americans have graduated from a four-year college or university program (that is, 5/15 = .33). In the larger pool of those with some level of postsecondary education, the increase would also be felt, because this pool would expand by more than 10 percent.

Reducing the educational inequalities that will impair the ability of minorities to take advantage of the massive openings of the next quarter century is not just a moral imperative; it is a commonsense economic strategy that is in the interest of all Americans. Granted, there are alternative sources of highly trained workers, and all of them are likely to be drawn upon in the future. But the ability of the United States to recruit immigrants to take the places of needed workers is likely to be limited by intensifying worldwide competition for the highly skilled workers willing to resettle in a new country and also by the growing attractiveness of their home economies. Highly educated, largely white women are an alternative source. Yet it is highly unlikely that, without fundamental changes in societal arrangements regarding women's responsibilities for child rearing, women could fill the bulk of the labor-market holes that will be opening up. In all likelihood, the United States will need to draw more on native-born minorities than it does now. Because of the inadequacies of the educational institutions serving many black and Hispanic children and young adults, minorities are not represented in the higher tiers of the labor market to the extent that they could be. They form a human resource that the nation cannot afford to squander.

Other Threats to Minority Occupational Advance

Additional impediments to the ability of minority youth to profit from the opening up of the labor market arise from the operation of the legal and criminal justice systems. One lies in the sharp rise in the incarceration rate since the 1980s, which has had a severe impact on minority young men, most especially African Americans but also U.S.-born Mexican Americans and other Latinos. One estimate has it that the lifetime risk of incarceration for a young black man has risen to almost one in three. Once they have prison records, young men—and women—confront great reluctance by many employers to hire them, as the careful audit research of the sociologist Devah Pager has demonstrated.[38] It is apparent that the large number of prisoners and ex-felons among African and Hispanic Americans reduces the pool of young minorities, especially males, who have the potential to climb higher on the occupational ladder.

There is no easy answer to this situation. One could argue that, just as the relatively high rate of criminal involvement in the second generation of the white ethnics declined as opportunities for their mobility became apparent,[39] the involvement in crime might also fall off among young minorities as avenues of social ascent that are open to them become more visible. However, more is involved than simply the oppositional stances of some minority youth who are frustrated by perceived discrimination and lack of opportunity, compounded with the problems associated with poverty, resource-starved communities, and single-parent families. In the current era, government policy has produced much higher rates of incarceration than the United States has previously experienced: since 1980, the number of Americans in prisons and jails has soared fivefold, bringing the country to the position of world leadership in putting citizens behind bars. The correctional apparatus has grown enormously, and the spending of states on penal systems is rising much more rapidly than is spending on public colleges and universities.[40] The punitive treatment of some drug crimes exemplifies this turn to the prison system as a solution to some social problems. Granted, social policy can unmake what social policy has done, but the institutional inertia built into the immense U.S. prison system is considerable and will take major political effort to overcome.

Despite this dismal picture of lives that are stunted in the bloom of youth by imprisonment and by the permanent stigma that results from it, it must be pointed out that the great majority of minority young men and women do not have criminal records. Research demonstrates that the risk of imprisonment falls most heavily on individuals who have not completed high school, a group that has virtually no chance to compete for jobs in the higher tiers of the workforce even in the absence of a criminal record. Thus the ultimate significance of the high rate of incarceration for the ability of minority youth to take advantage of non-zero-sum mobility may be less than it seems at first sight.

Another potential impediment stems from the large numbers of Latin-American immigrants to the United States who have undocumented status. Estimates made in the middle of the first decade of the century indicate that 11.5–12 million undocumented immigrants then resided in the United States, three-quarters of whom originated in Latin America (mostly in Mexico).[41] These estimates imply that, of the 17.7 million Latin-American immigrants in the United States in 2006 (according to the American Community Survey), about half could be undocumented and thus lacking the legal right to live and work here. Adding to this dismaying picture is that perhaps a quarter of the undocumented were brought to the United States as children and raised here. Though their U.S. education is of little use to them in the labor market unless they can find a way to regularize their situation, they cannot go back to a "home" country that they do not know and whose language they probably do not speak adequately.

Not only the Latin-American-born youth brought here as children by undocumented parents are disadvantaged; so too, almost certainly, are the U.S.-born children of these parents, even though their birth on U.S. soil gives them citizenship and frees them from the legal impediments faced by their parents and undocumented brothers and sisters. They are raised in families where parents are condemned to the lowest-wage sectors of the labor force and frequently must live in barrios to protect themselves from the peering eyes of authorities. The ramifications of parental undocumented status for children has not received much research attention yet, but what little there is suggests that the legally impaired status of parents does result in disadvantages for children.[42]

Douglas Massey, Jorge Durand, and Nolan Malone have persuasively made the case that the magnitude of the undocumented-immigrant problem results from ill-conceived policies at the U.S.-Mexican border. In an earlier period, illegal immigration from Mexico was mostly circular in nature: migrants would cross the border into the United States, work for a while, and return home with their saved earnings. The increasing concentration of police forces on the U.S. side and the other tactics used to make crossing more difficult have induced a process of settlement: migrants who now recognize that a reentry into the United States after a return visit to Mexico would be expensive, if not difficult, stay longer and may eventually bring their families to live with them.[43]

There are plenty of proposals that would help to resolve this problem and solve its most pernicious consequences. In 2007, the U.S. Congress considered legislation that would have offered a pathway to legality for many currently undocumented immigrants, but it failed in the Senate. A more narrowly framed proposal is the Dream Act (Development, Relief and Education for Alien Minors Act), which would enable undocumented youngsters who have graduated from high school in the United States to gain a conditionally legal status, attend college or join the military, and, after a period of time, apply for a green card. It, too, has not been able to get through the U.S. Senate so far. Yet I remain hopeful that Americans will recognize the dangers to a democracy that arise when so many residents, one of every 25 persons in the United States (12 million in a country of 300 million residents), lack many basic rights.[44]

Threats to the Conversion of Mobility into Proximity

In the Workplace

Beyond the contingencies that affect the extent to which opportunities for minority socioeconomic mobility will be realized lie others that will affect whether that mobility will translate into social proximity to mainstream Americans in the same way that it did in the past. These contingencies pivot on the extent to which socioeconomically mobile minorities will be able to realize broader social gains from their entry into higher-status occupational spheres. Assimilation in its ultimate sense depends on the ability to integrate into mainstream social settings—to mix with whites and others of the same socioeconomic strata and to provide a favorable starting position for one's children.[45]

One plane on which this issue can be posed concerns the workplace itself—will minority mobility mean that whites work side by side with minorities of the same status? The implications of workplace integration transcend the conventional compartmentalization of adult lives between work and leisure, for many friendships are formed at work, where adults spend, after all, a large portion of their time awake. An intriguing recent finding is that the whites who form their main friendships at work are more likely to have racially diverse social circles.[46] Recent research on workplace integration indicates that racial integration of private-sector workplaces has progressed since the civil-rights legislation of the mid-1960s, but it has slowed if not stalled in recent decades.[47] The greatest progress has been made in virtually eliminating racially homogeneous workplaces, but the introduction of minorities into workplaces that were previously all white (or in a few cases, whites into workplaces that were previously all minority) does not mean that minorities and majority usually interact as equals at work. Within workplaces, the distribution of minorities across broad occupational categories has shifted to come closer to that of whites but at a decelerating pace. For blacks, the index measuring dissimilarity from whites declined most in the two decades following the passage of the Civil Rights Act of 1964, the basis of the attack on discrimination in the workplace, but the decline has just crept along since the mid-1980s. For Hispanics, who were not as segregated from whites at the start of the period, the decline has been more steady but the rate has been very gradual. As of 2003, the endpoint of the research, Hispanics and blacks were equally segregated from whites in America's private workplaces, meaning that they were equally concentrated in tiers of jobs below those in which most whites are found.

The exposure of whites to minority colleagues of roughly equal status is nevertheless very likely to have continued increasing over time as the numbers of minorities at all occupational levels, including those high in status, have risen. Such a rise is indicated by the findings in Chapter 4. It entails what is known as a "compositional change," and the index used to measure segregation in workplace research, the widely used index of dissimilarity, ignores such changes while measuring those in the distribution of one group relative to another.[48] In addition, because of the limitations of the data, the workplace research is not able to examine separately the younger cohorts of workers, where the compositional shift is taking place.

Yet, in some respects, this research may also understate the degree of segregation because it depends on the very broad occupational categories in which the racial and ethnic composition of workplaces is reported to the federal government. One recent study has examined racial stratification for managerial positions and found that white men continue to occupy disproportionately the better-paid positions and the ones vested with more authority.[49] Blacks are more likely to attain management rank in industries that pay less and in workplaces where they manage individuals who are themselves black or members of other minorities. The study concludes that white men have succeeded in holding on to positions of privilege even as workplaces have become more diverse. This important finding is not inconsistent with the argument made here, which envisions that when the mobility of disadvantaged groups does not threaten the position and privileges of the more privileged, it creates favorable conditions for boundary changes. However, if mobility does not ultimately bring minorities into much more equal-status contact with members of the majority population, then the social integration that must serve as a prelude to boundary change—and to essential changes in the majority's perception of minority-group members—will be lacking.

The finding about the continuing privileged position of white men in managerial occupations is also reminiscent of the analysis of occupational placement presented in Chapter 4. It showed that among both men and women, U.S.-born whites are advantaged compared with all other groups. Their advantages are—this is no surprise—quite substantial in comparison with foreign-born blacks and Hispanics, since foreign birth compounds the disadvantages associated with ethno-racial status (because of such factors as lack of recognition of foreign educational credentials in the U.S. labor market, limitations in English-language competence, and discrimination on the basis of accent). However, the advantages of whites are also significant in relation to U.S.-born blacks and Hispanics, even when the educational levels of majority and minority workers are the same. These inequalities are further exacerbated by the lower earnings received by black and Latino Americans when they are in the same occupations as whites. Lower earnings suggest that, within the same occupational category, blacks and Hispanics do not in fact possess the same status as their white colleagues; they may be located in different firms or hold lower job titles. This lack of parity is a significant challenge that must be faced in the future if the replacement of the retiring baby-boom cohorts by a much more diverse group of young Americans is going to fulfill the promise of racial and ethnic change.

In the Neighborhood

The other planes on which the issue can be framed concern the social relations that occur outside the sphere of work. One indirect but powerful perspective comes from residence, a context that configures through propinquity versus distance the possibilities for informal interactions across ethno-racial boundaries. In their review of changes over the course of the twentieth century, Claude Fischer and Michael Hout argue persuasively that, despite the enormity of such advances in communication and transportation as e-mail and the automobile, the social significance of physical distance has not been greatly diminished.[50] Where people live still matters very much for their lives, especially since Americans are apparently becoming more "rooted" over time—that is, more likely to own the home in which they reside and less likely to move. As Fischer and Hout point out, the strength of NIMBY (not in my back yard) movements against developments that neighbors do not want in their vicinity testifies to the importance with which Americans view their residential environs. In any event, these are important if only because they determine access to institutions and resources that are critical for children: the quality of schools, for instance, or the temptations of the street.

The literature on the incorporation of white ethnics documents that they were rapidly able to translate socioeconomic gains into improved residential locations and even integration, a process that Douglas Massey has labeled as "spatial assimilation."[51] By contrast, an enormous wealth of research about African Americans shows that, because of discrimination and institutional racism, they have generally been unable to realize similar gains—for instance, they have usually been confined to largely black residential areas regardless of their economic status. Even when higher-income African Americans enter into largely white residential areas, it appears that they frequently live with whites whose incomes are below their own, a pattern that implies that they pay a premium to live with whites and do not thereby gain access to neighborhoods with qualities commensurate with their own socioeconomic position.[52]

What research there is suggests so far that Asians and light-skinned Hispanics are not as constrained in residential choice as blacks have been. Locational-attainment modeling, which analyzes the kinds of neighborhoods the members of different ethno-racial groups enter according to their personal and household characteristics, shows that middle-class Asians and English-speaking light-skinned Hispanics reside in neighborhoods that are similar to those in which middle-class whites are found; undoubtedly, these are often the same neighborhoods. Without question, many members of minority groups feel more comfortable in neighborhoods where there is some presence of others who are like them; they are not usually eager to become pioneers in integrating heavily white neighborhoods. However, except for African Americans, who because of their experiences with racial discrimination generally look for neighborhoods with a representation of fellow blacks as high as 50 percent, many middle-class minorities choose neighborhoods where their co-ethnics are outnumbered by white residents.[53]

The segregation research based on the 2000 Census is consistent with a picture in which many of the ethno-racial groups originating in contemporary immigration find it easier to enter "good" neighborhoods than do African Americans and others who have visible African ancestry or dark skin.[54] That research reveals a continuing slow decline in levels of segregation between whites and blacks; but the overall level remains quite high, particularly in metropolitan regions with large African-American populations. According to the calculations of John Logan, Reynolds Farley, and Brian Stults, the average index of dissimilarity between blacks and whites across metropolitan regions was 65 in 2000; the index indicates what percentage of either group would have to be moved among neighborhoods (that is, census tracts) in order to bring about complete integration. The 2000 value is still quite high (the threshold value of 60 is typically considered to begin the range of high segregation values). It did not decrease much during the 1990s, because in 1990 the average value of the index for black-white segregation was 69.[55] The segregation of Asians and Hispanics from whites is lower than that of blacks, particularly so in the case of Asians, and these segregation levels changed little during the 1990s, a period of high immigration from Asia and Latin America. In 2000, the average indices of dissimilarity measuring the separation of whites from Latinos and Asians were 52 and 42, respectively. Neither value had budged more than a statistical hair's breadth since 1990. That stability implies some outflow from heavily Asian and Latino neighborhoods, for newly arriving immigrants tend to enter them. Without an outflow, in other words, segregation levels would be increasing rather than stable.

What has been little appreciated so far is how the changing demography of metropolitan regions, driven by immigration as well as by the declining number of whites in youthful cohorts, has changed the residential options for whites. For the fact is that whites have a harder and harder time avoiding some diversity in their neighborhoods. In 1970, at a moment when the new waves of immigration had just begun to beat against American shores, the all-white neighborhood—one, say, whose residents were 95 percent or more white—was quite common, but by 1990 it had become uncommon in larger metropolitan regions, including their suburban portions.[56] Even white-dominated neighborhoods are becoming harder to find. A recent analysis by urban sociologist Samantha Friedman defines such neighborhoods rather broadly, as census tracts in which at least 80 percent of the residents are white.[57] A neighborhood at the lower bound of this category, with up to a fifth of its residents belonging to racial and ethnic minorities, would undoubtedly be judged visually to be diverse, but even by this generous standard, white-dominated neighborhoods have become much less common. Friedman finds that, as recently as 1980, most neighborhoods in the 61 largest metropolitan areas (those with populations of a million or more in 2000) were white-dominated, and about two-thirds of the whites in these regions lived in one of them. By 2000, the residential landscape had changed markedly, for the majority of neighborhoods were no longer white-dominated, and a minority of whites lived in such enclaves.

This rapidly shifting landscape obviously alters the residential options of whites. If they choose to remain in these large metropolitan regions (and some do leave),[58] then they are much more likely to live in diverse neighborhoods than would have been the case only a couple of decades before. For many, this means encountering minority-group members at a minimum on the streets and in stores, but also as parents in their children's schools or fellow rooters for their children's sports teams or even as next-door neighbors. However, the minorities whites encounter in this way are by no means a cross-section of the nonwhite population. The type of diverse neighborhood in which whites most commonly live mixes a white majority (nearly 75 percent on average) with Asians and Hispanics in nearly equal proportions and contains few African Americans. The neighborhoods in which whites live with large numbers of African Americans appear relatively unstable and likely to suffer an exodus of their white residents, though this instability is perhaps less than in the past.[59]

In sum, residing near whites can be viewed as a form of social proximity likely to engender informal, friendly interactions spanning racial and ethnic divisions. It is also one with important ramifications for the circumstances in which the next generation will grow up and thus the opportunities its members will have to work and live in more integrated settings. But it appears that some groups, Asians and light-skinned Hispanics, are better able to translate socioeconomic mobility into this proximity. The social worlds of the most dominant population, namely, whites, are undergoing change, but not of a sort that involves all minority populations in equal measure. Especially African Americans still seem very underrepresented in this integration process.

In the Family: Intermarriage

Another vital indicator of the state of racial and ethnic boundaries is intermarriage, which is generally regarded, with justification, as the litmus test of assimilation. The rate of intermarriage between two groups is informative about the ease with which a particular boundary can be penetrated and the extent to which the social and cultural differences associated with it are perceived to create a barrier to long-term union. For intermarriage to occur, of course, other informal, equal-status contacts between groups must be taking place: in this sense, one could describe intermarriage as the visible tip of a denser mass of interethnic interactions, occurring throughout the social body, but below the surface in the sense that they are not usually measured directly by research instruments. Further, intermarriage carries obvious and profound implications for the familial and, more broadly, the social contexts in which the next generation will be raised. That generation, in both its phenotypic and its social characteristics, can blur a boundary, creating ambiguity over where it is located. (The one-drop rule, according to which individuals with any visible African ancestry were treated as black regardless of how much European lineage they also possessed, would seem to contradict this statement. But the rule could be effective in past eras because black-white marriage, as opposed to sexual liaison, was so rare—indeed, it was outlawed in many states by antimiscegenation laws, which finally disappeared from the books only when the Supreme Court decided Loving v. Virginia in 1967.)[60] The significance of intermarriage in all these respects is not much diminished by a high rate of divorce. For the vast majority of individuals, marriage is still a fateful act and not undertaken lightly.

Intermarriage by minorities takes place primarily with white partners, and thus empirically the typical intermarriage combinations sustain the notion that it functions chiefly as a mechanism of integration into the mainstream. The highest overall level of intermarriage is found among young U.S.-born Asian Americans, more than half of whom marry non-Asians; given the relatively small size of the Asian population, however, this intermarriage rate still implies a high tendency for endogamy, that is, a high likelihood to choose an Asian partner *ceteris paribus*.[61] It is also true that Asian-American intermarriage far more often involves Asian women than men, and this gender disparity may be fueled by stereotypes about the desirability of the exotic.[62] Among young U.S.-born Hispanics, the intermarriage rate is more modest, but far from trivial, at 30 percent. African Americans remain the least likely to intermarry, and here too there is a gender disparity, one that is the reverse of that found among Asian Americans and has a long history that can be interpreted in terms of racial disadvantage: young African-American men have an intermarriage rate of 15 percent, a rate that has risen substantially since the late 1960s, when the last antimiscegenation laws were overturned;

for young African-American women, the intermarriage rate lingers at just 5–6 percent.

In the context of a discussion of minority mobility and the potential for boundary change, it is essential to examine the circumstances under which intermarriage is frequent, and in particular the role of socioeconomic position. If a group is able to convert mobility into proximity to the white mainstream, then intermarriage should increase among those of its members higher up the socioeconomic ladder. The recent research confirms in this respect the different situations of African Americans, on the one hand, and Asians and Hispanics, on the other. In particular, the methodologically sophisticated analysis of Zhenchao Qian and Daniel Lichter reveals that Asian and Hispanic intermarriage with whites is very common among the highly educated; for the U.S.-born members of these groups, the rates hover in the 35–60 percent range depending on the precise category.[63] This finding suggests that the socioeconomic mobility demonstrated earlier is, in many cases, accompanied by social integration. However, for African Americans, the same pattern does not appear: highly educated blacks do not improve their chances of intermarriage above the low frequencies that obtain for the group as a whole.

Intermarriage, it should be noted, directly produces racial change, because the children tend to share physical characteristics of both sets of parents and thus cloud the clarity of the physical distinctions on which any racial classification rests; they also are likely to span two racial populations socially through their connections to relatives on both sides of their families. Qian and Lichter's analysis, while not definitive, appears to indicate in addition that individuals with mixed racial ancestry have elevated rates of marriage to whites, suggesting that they are more integrated into the white mainstream in the first place than are nonwhites of unmixed racial ancestry. Their analysis compares the intermarriage rates calculated with two different classifications of individuals who identify as racially mixed, placing them either in the white category or a minority one. If individuals with a racially mixed heritage have higher rates of intermarriage than do other persons of the same nonwhite racial background, then their inclusion in a minority category will raise its apparent intermarriage rate. This is, indeed, what emerges for all racial categories; the difference is especially large for Asians.[64] Other research demonstrates that a similar tendency toward intermarriage is evident among the children of Hispanic/non-Hispanic marriages: Edward Telles and Vilma Ortiz have found in their intergenerational study of Mexican Americans that the children of intermarriages are themselves five times more likely to intermarry.[65]

The Attitudes of White Americans: Acceptance of Minority Individuals as Moral Equals?

The third condition posited as producing the massive assimilation of white ethnics in the middle of the twentieth century involved what was then an ideological shift that allowed many mainstream whites to see the socially ascending ethnics as their moral equals. Without this acceptance, advantaged whites might have reacted with alarm as more Jewish and Catholic ethnics worked alongside them or moved into their neighborhoods. Perhaps some even did, but not enough to resegregate the neighborhoods that ethnics were entering or to block their rise on the occupational ladder.

In reflecting on whether the present-day attitudes of mainstream white Americans toward ethno-racial minorities allow their members to be perceived as having equal moral worth, one can focus the question on African Americans, as they are the hard case, in any event. In addition, there is a rich record of survey research on the views and feelings whites hold toward blacks, and these have been the subject in recent years of an intense effort to reconceptualize them in the face of some degree of change.[66]

While it is clear that there has been some change in these attitudes over the last half century, what is less clear is how deep these changes have gone and how they should be characterized.[67] For one thing, the stability of important racial inequalities, such as those in residence, combined with the reasonable assumption that attitudes, or prejudice, and behavior, or discrimination, must be linked to some extent have raised doubts about whether the changes are more than cosmetic.

The most systematic analysis of racial attitudes since the middle of the twentieth century, the beginning of the era of scientific polling, found that over time white Americans have become far more willing to embrace abstract principles of racial equality, but they remain reluctant to endorse many government actions to put those principles into action.[68] In the 1950s, many white Americans rejected, for example, the idea that white and black children should go to school together. Rejection was not found only among white southerners, for whom segregated schools were still a tenaciously defended social reality; among white northerners, about a third also repudiated the notion. But by century's end acceptance of integrated schools was nearly universal. This is perhaps the most extreme example of a shift in racial attitudes, but major shifts also took place in other domains—in the acceptance of interracial marriage, in the willingness to vote for African-American politicians, and so forth. Yet it remains true that many whites are uncomfortable with policies intended to bring about greater racial equality. Policies of affirmative action such as the use of racial preferences in college admissions garner the weakest support and are in fact rejected by most whites, as the support for state referenda to end such policies demonstrates (such policies receive less than universal support also from blacks).[69] Even some policies that are seemingly less controversial, such as federal government action to ensure fair treatment in hiring, are supported by a minority of whites.

Such a mixed record of change in racial attitudes has called forth a variety of interpretations, including ones that argue that the changes are no more than cosmetic and that the racism behind white attitudes is simply less crude than it was in the early part of the twentieth century.[70]

This is not the place to try to settle a disagreement that divides scholars who have devoted their careers to understanding racial attitudes. However, it is worth observing that one of the major interpretive strands, often dubbed "group conflict theory," is quite consistent with the social-boundary perspective that informs my main argument. As concisely stated by sociologist Lawrence Bobo, a core notion undergirding this theory is that racial attitudes derive from "a commitment to a relative status positioning of groups in a racialized social order."[71] The attitudes of whites toward blacks are in the main a product, then, of whites' attempts to maintain their sense of superiority in a racially divided society. This sense is linked in their minds to greater rights to the things that matter in society, such as good jobs and living arrangements. There is a moral dimension to whites' racial attitudes, for these must support whites' views that they "deserve" the larger portion of social "goodies" that they possess. Consistent with this idea is the finding that whites frequently invoke a stereotypic explanation, for example, a lack of effort by blacks, when asked about the persistence of racial inequality in the United States.[72]

This record does not induce confidence that most whites are prepared to perceive socioeconomically mobile African Americans as their moral equals in a way that reproduces the shift in perceptions that greeted newly successful white ethnics in the middle of the last century. However, it does not necessarily contradict this possibility, either. The issue remains unresolved, despite the extensive analyses of racial attitudes in recent years. Although white attitudes toward blacks retain aspects derived from a sense of superiority, they also entail a commitment to principles of equality that contradict overtly racist opinions and mandate acceptance, if not a welcoming, of success on the part of some African Americans. Studies of white attitudes toward blacks as neighbors reveal that a majority of whites are quite willing to live with a small number of black neighbors but that reluctance increases sharply as the size of the black population does. These attitudinal data appear consistent with the behavior of whites, moreover, for studies of segregation reveal that the greatest progress toward residential integration has occurred in those metropolitan regions where the black percentage of the overall population is small.[73]

Perhaps this ambiguous situation is characteristic of majority-group attitudes as the possibility of ethno-racial change is growing but before it has destabilized a prevailing ethno-racial order. Many members of the majority are prepared to accept an increasing minority-group presence in their midst—where they live and where they work—as long as they retain a clear numerical preponderance. Although there are also racist whites, who would shun upwardly mobile blacks and occasionally express their hostility openly in words and actions, they are probably outnumbered by the whites who see racial progress as part of the American way or even as a moral imperative. The 2008 election of Barack Obama to the presidency suggests a broader openness among whites to racial change than does the scholarly analysis of survey data. The question that cannot be answered on the basis of these data is whether the attitudes of whites will shift if many African Americans are able to take advantage of non-zero-sum mobility.

Conclusion

This overview of the threats to the potential for major ethno-racial boundary change in the next quarter century indicates the need for extreme caution in drawing any conclusions about the likelihood and extent of such change. Each of the factors that appear to have been important for the mid-twentieth century assimilation en masse of the white ethnics is in question for the near future.

The most serious of the challenges concerns the ability of U.S.-born blacks and Hispanics to take advantage of the opportunities for non-zero-sum mobility, which are a predictable outcome of the baby boomers' retirement and of labor-force growth. The postsecondary educational attainments of these minority populations lag well behind those of whites and Asians, implying that the pool of their members qualified to take jobs in the top tiers of the workforce will remain relatively small unless the educational gaps are addressed. Diversity will still increase throughout the workforce. The white share of jobs in the top tiers seems certain to fall, and the Asian share certain to increase. In the case of blacks and Hispanics, the growth of diversity could be, however, limited to the consequences of underlying demographic change in the ethno-racial composition of cohorts coming to maturity, and thus fall well short of what the opening up of the labor force would make possible under the best of circumstances, as suggested by the "what if" scenarios considered in this and the previous chapters. The educational gaps are addressable; the nation has accomplished something similar for some of the white ethnic groups, such as the southern Italians. But closing them will take national resolve.

The other factors are also not straightforward in their operation. The conversion of socioeconomic mobility into proximity to mainstream whites appears to take place with less friction for Asians and light-skinned Hispanics than for African Americans and others with dark skin or visible African or indigenous ancestry. The strongest research record exists for African Americans, but the same exclusionary mechanisms may be affecting these others. That record shows that African Americans have difficulty translating economic achievements into residence in good neighborhoods or in those with many whites. In addition, African Americans intermarry with much less frequency than do other minority groups, and their intermarriage rates do not change much with educational level, an index of socioeconomic position.

This review raises a question that may come to haunt us like a ghost from the past: will future boundary changes affect African Americans and immigrant-origin groups equally? One of the profoundly rooted patterns in U.S. history is the preference for immigrants over native minorities, especially African Americans.[74] This pattern operated during the twentieth century in the ability of once-despised southern and eastern European groups, such as the southern Italians, to distance themselves from black Americans and rise into the white American main-stream. There is a substantial risk that this pattern will repeat itself in the contemporary era. This risk is visible in several ways, such as: the con-tinuing preference of majority Americans for immigrants, who are seen as unlike African Americans in the degree to which they work hard to improve their lives and to provide opportunities for their children;[75] and the evidence cited earlier that immigrant minorities, especially when they are light-skinned, are more able to convert socioeconomic advance into various forms of integration with mainstream whites.

Finally, one should note the emerging tensions between immigrants and black Americans. In a study that my colleagues Nancy Denton and Jacqueline Villarrubia and I have been conducting of new Latin-Ameri-can immigrants in the smaller cities of the mid-Hudson Valley of New York, we have found that the immigrants perceive their African-American neighbors to be hostile while white Americans are viewed as welcoming or, at worst, neutral.[76] Hence the immigrants, who often live side by side with African Americans in very poor neighborhoods, are motivated to separate themselves from native minorities as soon as they can. This pattern appears to repeat one of the principal mechanisms that, during the nineteenth and early twentieth centuries, led white immi-grants to distance themselves from African Americans and seek entry to the white mainstream while holding blacks down.[77] If immigrants and the second generation from Latin America, who are most likely to live in or near neighborhoods that also have many African Americans and to compete with them for labor-market niches, follow this pathway, blazed originally by groups like the Irish and Italians, the result could be a soci-ety in which the key ethno-racial fault line separates black Americans from everyone else. Some commentators have already envisioned this possibility as a probable outcome of the ethno-racial changes brought about by the current era of immigration.[78] This possibility is worrisome and one that Americans should guard against with wise public policies, as I will discuss in the next chapter.

7

Imagining a More Integrated Future

Suppose that minority mobility takes place on a large scale in coming decades: African Americans and U.S.-born Hispanics, say, double their share of the good jobs—those in the top half of the occupational hierarchy—by taking one of every five of them that are being created by economic and population growth or changing hands as the baby boomers retire. Asian Americans are also certain to occupy a substantially larger fraction of good jobs than they hold now. Clearly, the upper ranks of the American labor force would be far more diverse than they are today, and in all probability many if not most whites would interact with nonwhites and Hispanics of equal status at work. If upwardly mobile minorities can take advantage of their improved socioeconomic position to move into America's better neighborhoods, the vast majority of which are disproportionately white, the equal-status contacts between whites and minorities, as well as between minorities of different backgrounds, would spill out of the workplace and into other social spheres. A more diverse society would result, to be sure, but would it be one in which ethno-racial origins have faded into insignificance? If not, what role would they play and how would it be different from the heavy hand they exert today?

I have to acknowledge the imaginative leap necessary to address these questions. The demographic changes of the next quarter century, such as the exit of the baby boomers from the labor market, can be predicted mostly with reasonable confidence, but as we engage the economic and even more the social changes that may accompany them, we enter increasingly into realms of speculation. Our understanding of past ethno-racial shifts can be helpful, assuming that our analysis has correctly identified its key features and critical causal mechanisms, but the future will not be a replica of the past. How to assess and take into account the differences between past and near future is a task that almost certainly cannot be carried out in a way that will convince everyone, all the more so when the scenarios involve possible racial changes. I cannot help but be aware of numerous threats to the prospect of large-scale minority advance in the near future, and others can, I am sure, envision threats I do not see. Yet if we fail to chart a direction that potentially leads to change, we leave ourselves adrift and without any guidance for the actions we can take to bring about positive movement.

One certainty for the next quarter century is that, even under the most optimistic scenario, the social significance of ethno-racial origins will not disappear. There will still remain important racial and ethnic inequalities, and therein lies a paradox for (and of) American society. Increasing diversity on the higher rungs of the social hierarchy will prove to be compatible with a high degree of ethno-racial disparity. We have become a society of greater and greater inequality, in which wealth and income have become increasingly concentrated at the top.[1] The situation of the poor and near-poor, who are disproportionately nonwhite, has not been improving: in some ways, it could be described as worsening, as the crisis in health care and the lengthening gap between the poor and the affluent in life expectancy, fed by gross discrepancies in access to good health care, reveal.[2] The size of the poverty and near-poverty populations is a function of the income distribution, which is changing not in ways that would alleviate the problems of poverty but, if anything, in ways that could worsen them. The racial composition at the bottom of the economic scale results from the ways that stratification works to impose the greatest risks of social disadvantage on minorities; this is one of the meanings of "white privilege." As much research shows, even when whites are poor, they are not usually as badly off as minority poor. For example, they tend to live in areas that are not poor and that are therefore not burdened with the problems—of crime, drug use, and early dropout rates—that beset poor, heavily minority neighborhoods.[3] The scenario I have posited in previous chapters envisions racial change occurring in part because whites do not feel threatened—they retain their sense of "privilege," even if they do not always recognize it as such. Consequently, the risks of falling to the societal bottom are still likely to be imposed largely on blacks and Hispanics. The growing diversity in the middle and at the top will not be mirrored at the bottom.

Does this make the process of minority uplift that I have argued may occur because of non-zero-sum mobility fundamentally different from that which brought the white ethnics into the mainstream in the middle of the twentieth century? Yes and no. Undoubtedly, if we could go back in time and examine the ethnic changes of the mid-twentieth century in the way that we can do for the prospective ones of the early twenty-first, we would find in the 1950s and 1960s a similar paradox of partially attained parity: that is, the social advance of young, well-educated second- and third-generation southern and eastern European ethnics would be apparent, but so would a large population of those left behind by the new opportunities. Indeed, that group among Italian Americans was large enough to support a conclusion in the early 1960s that the ethnic group as a whole was immobile, stuck in the working class, as two classics of the period, *The Urban Villagers* and *Beyond the Melting Pot*, attest.[4] Granted, stalled in the stable working class is not the same as trapped by poverty, but the point remains that massive mobility and social advance are compatible with overall inequality in life chances across racial and ethnic groups.

However, at least two fundamental differences in context come into play. First, there was much less economic inequality and more economic growth in the mid-twentieth century than there is today. The post–World War II period until the mid-1970s was one of remarkable prosperity that instilled confidence in many parts of the population that the American Dream could be more broadly available to Americans of a variety of ethno-racial origins. The resumption of economic growth after the Depression was fueled by sharply increasing labor productivity, which according to the Harvard economists Claudia Goldin and Lawrence Katz rose by "a whopping 2.77 percent average annually from 1947 to 1973," and then fell to half that level for most of the rest of the century. The income gains produced by economic growth were widely distributed. According, again, to Goldin and Katz, "from 1947 to 1973 family incomes grew; they also grew closer together."[5] That is, low family incomes grew at a faster pace than high ones until the mid-1970s, when growth slowed in the middle and lower income ranges while families with high incomes surged ahead.

The contraction of economic inequality during the 1950s and 1960s pulled almost all of the white ethnics upward, transforming the economic position of groups such as the Italians who entered at the very bottom of the labor force in the early twentieth century and shortening the economic distance that separated them from the middle-class mainstream.[6] It thereby narrowed also the range of life chances within a white population that had expanded to take in the ethnics, so that the children of the working-class ethnics greatly improved their chances for higher education and social mobility in the 1960s and 1970s. For example, when the City University of New York instituted its open-admissions program in 1970, the major beneficiaries were initially not the blacks and Puerto Ricans for whom the policy was created but working-class whites, primarily from Catholic and Jewish, that is, ethnic, families; they were the ones who were, so to speak, poised to take advantage of new opportunities.[7] When conditions at CUNY deteriorated in the mid-1970s because of financial crises in state and city governments, and tuition was imposed for the first time, many of the whites left; but they did not drop out of higher education. They transferred to other colleges and universities in the region, especially to campuses of the state university system or to the less elite private colleges.

Second, in the decades immediately following the end of World War II large migration streams of southern African Americans as well as Hispanics (Puerto Ricans coming to New York, Mexicans to Chicago) were entering many northern urban areas where the white ethnics were concentrated.[8] They could fill out the bottom strata in many places, relieving the need for white ethnics to take jobs on the bottom rungs. These post–World War II migrations were, I argued earlier, not necessary to the advances made by younger cohorts of ethnics in the two decades following the end of the war, and thus some reordering of ethno-racial boundaries and inequalities would have happened, in any event. But the uplift of the great bulk of the white ethnics seems unthinkable without the presence of other groups to take up the bottom tiers of the labor market. To be sure, there are immigrants coming in large numbers today to many parts of the United States, and they take many jobs on the bottom rungs, in restaurants, food processing, landscaping, and construction. Undoubtedly, they do "push up" some native-born minorities by filling up these rungs and defining some jobs as "immigrant" jobs that those who have grown up in the United States seek to avoid at almost any cost.[9] But because these immigrants belong to the same broad ethno-racial categories as many native workers on the bottom rungs of the labor market, they do not create the kind of ethno-racial distinction between types of job—with some jobs being coded as ones suited only for disadvantaged minorities—that contributed to the repositioning of white ethnics in the critical decades of the mid-twentieth century.

The very different economic context of the early twenty-first century, with income and wealth inequalities that rival those of the Gilded Age, is associated with a steep gradient of life chances that, barring massive changes in the political economy, will prevent a similar incorporation of minorities en masse into the mainstream. If such an incorporation is an unlikely outcome of the mobility opportunities of the next quarter century, then what can be anticipated for racial and ethnic boundaries? It should be remembered in this context that our principal conception of ethno-racial change has been formed from the mid-twentieth-century assimilation of the white ethnics, which not only occurred during a brief span of time but ended with the wholesale erosion of boundaries that initially had ethnic, religious, and racial aspects. Those boundaries have continued to fade in significance ever since, and by the end of the twentieth century, aside from small enclaves of groups that willingly segregated themselves from the mainstream, such as Hasidic Jews, the limits had become relatively minor social distinctions for most white Americans, associated with occasionally expressed voluntary and frequently symbolic identities.[10] What might the outcomes of the looming period of mobility look like if they result in ethno-racial boundary change?

What seems most plausible is that the boundaries that distinguish nonwhites and Hispanics from whites of European descent will become more contingent. Their significance for determining the attitudes and behavior of the ethno-racial majority and the basic life chances of minority individuals—to, for example, obtain professional qualifications or live in a decent neighborhood—will not depend exclusively on phenotype, that is, the historical meaning of race, as exemplified by the infamous "one-drop" rule applied to African Americans. Instead, this significance will depend, as it already does to some extent, increasingly on other social characteristics, especially the socioeconomic position, of minority individuals.[11] For those who possess favorable characteristics, such as high-status occupations, and who interact with whites of equal status at work and in more informal settings, ethno-racial distinctions could fade into the background much of the time. This doesn't mean that they will be entirely forgotten or that such individuals will be immune from the insults of racism. If we could imagine the most favorable outcome, it could be characterized as an increase in the ability of many minority individuals to shape the occasions and manner in which their ethno-racial origins are socially expressed. The balance could shift from ethno-race as a set of limitations and handicaps mainly imposed by the powerful majority on minority-group members to identities that minority individuals have more control over, that they can define in accordance with their own preferences and the needs of their social lives. In a word, race would then become more like ethnicity, as it is found among whites—at least, that is, for some minority-group members.[12]

Phenotypic characteristics are, even in the most optimistic scenario, still likely to matter, to count among the contingencies that affect how minority individuals can position themselves. Despite the one-drop rule, which seems to imply that African Americans all suffer from equivalent disadvantages inherent in racial minority status, "skin tone," the darkness of skin, has been shown to affect strongly life chances among blacks. Those with lighter skin, and possibly those with more European features, have higher average incomes and lower risks of poverty, more education, lower chances of incarceration, and a range of other advantages over their darker-skinned brothers and sisters.[13] A similar phenotypic principle seems to be at work among Latinos—indeed, among them the phenotypic gradient is undoubtedly greater because it is anchored at the light end by individuals who are largely or exclusively of European descent and thus more easily able to merge into the white mainstream when and if they so desire. Skin color, along with European features, has been demonstrated to matter for socioeconomic standing among Hispanics; the research on segregation shows that light-skinned Hispanics are also more likely to be able to enter largely white neighborhoods.[14] As David Lopez and Ricardo Stanton-Salazar note, "those who fit the mestizo/Indian phenotype, who 'look Mexican,' cannot escape racial stereotyping any more than African Americans, though the stigma is usually not so severe."[15] In a scenario with persisting ethno-racial inequality, there is no reason to expect the social significance of phenotype to disappear.

This paradoxical scenario suggests that the United States could shift in the direction of a Latin-American model, away from the "hard" racial divisions historically associated with the black-white divide, the predominant concept of what race means in the United States, and toward greater fluidity for racial distinctions, especially above the bottom of the society. This fluidity in Latin America does not mean that race has lost its paramount status in societies such as Brazil, but it does open up more room for nonwhite individuals to maneuver within a system of racial categories and to escape being pinned to a low social position by their racial origins.[16] One can fairly question how much of an improvement such a system would be over the historical rigidities of the U.S. racial system, with its infamous "one-drop" rule of racial classification. As I have already observed, there will still be a racially based stratification system, and placement within it will matter in the aggregate for the life chances of individuals, as is true of Latin-American societies as well. But I suspect that, for the many more nonwhites who may be able to mix more freely within the mainstream, such a society will seem a decided improvement over the past. For whites, too, the future is likely to look quite different from the past because many fewer will continue to live in an all-white social milieu. A racial system as entrenched as the one in the United States is not going to collapse at a single historical moment; instead, it will weaken gradually as cracks appear and then spread in its foundations.

A question that will undoubtedly arise in the minds of some is: since race is so visibly apparent, how can its significance become less important? But in truth we are aware of numerous social characteristics in our interactions with others—age and gender most obviously, but also cultural affiliations encoded in body adornment, clothing, and characteristic expression—which do not in general possess the determining influence (or the master status, as Robert K. Merton once put it) of race.[17] One way to think about what race could mean may be to recall the significance that religious distinctions between Protestants, on the one hand, and Catholics and Jews, on the other, possessed in mid-twentieth-century America. Because of the importance attached to those distinctions, everyone could not help but be aware of the religious affiliations of the others in their social worlds (but not, granted, of the people they encountered casually in public places): when the great majority attended religious services with some regularity, or on the major holy days, at a minimum, religious affiliations were not hard to decipher, and in any event, they were expressed frequently enough in names. For many Catholics, their religious membership was identifiable from the schools they attended, the black thumbprint on their foreheads on Ash Wednesday, even the college teams they rooted for. During the first half of the twentieth century, the social power associated with religious distinctions remained great and was sufficient to bar Jews, for example, from some settings; for instance, those Jews, few in number, who were admitted as undergraduates to Princeton University before the 1960s were generally prevented from joining the eating clubs that played a central role in the social solidarities of campus life.[18] Yet within a short span of time the social meanings of the distinctions changed fundamentally without the social knowledge about religious memberships declining commensurately. Indeed, the United States remains a very religious society, and hence it is reasonable to assume that many Americans are aware of the religious affiliations of their acquaintances; but the power of this knowledge to fix the degrees of social intimacy among individuals, no less the life chances of religious minorities, is much, much less than it was sixty or so years ago.

It might be objected at this point that race has a visibility in casual interactions, such as those between strangers on the street, that religion does not have; and that visibility exposes nonwhites to racist slights and insults that can prevent them from feeling truly at home in a largely white mainstream. There can be no question about the enormous emotional cost imposed on nonwhites by American racism; as one middle-class black respondent in a study of experiences with racism asserts:

> if you can think of the mind as having one hundred ergs of energy, and the average man uses fifty percent of his energy dealing with the everyday problems of the world—just general kinds of things—then he has fifty percent more to do creative kinds of things that he wants to do. Now that's a white person. Now a black person also has one hundred ergs; he uses fifty percent the same way a white man does, dealing with what the white man has [to deal with], so he has fifty percent left. But he uses twenty-five percent fighting being black, [with] all the problems being black and what it means. Which means he really only has twenty-five percent to do what the white man has fifty percent to do, and he's expected to do just as much as the white man with that twenty-five percent . . . So, that's kind of what happens. You just don't have as much energy left to do as much as you know you really could if you were free, [if] your mind were free.[19]

In all probability, religious membership was also more visible in the past than it seems today, but not as visible as race was and is. Nevertheless, just as the insults based on religious (and associated ethnic) origins have declined as Catholics and Jews in particular have become fully integrated into mainstream settings, it seems likely that the racism possible in casual encounters will also decline or, more precisely, that it will be modulated by other visible social characteristics, especially those connected with social class. As nonwhites become more common in mainstream settings, more and more whites will learn that, at a minimum, there is potentially a large cost to overt racism, because the nonwhites they insult in this way may turn up in other contexts—in workplaces or neighborhoods—and may also possess some degree of countervailing power. Of course, many whites, probably the large majority, will want to act in friendly ways toward those nonwhites who seem to belong, by virtue of education, income, or other characteristics, in the same social milieu as they do. Race boundaries are typically patrolled and enforced by a small minority made up of vehemently racist whites; their freedom of action could be checked by growing numbers of minorities in their midst, who will be less intimidated by racist actions and more supported in their anger about them by many whites.

The changes in the social position of Asian Americans illustrate compellingly that racial visibility is not an insurmountable barrier to increasing social intimacy between the members of a minority and the majority. Although Asians were once subject to vicious forms of racism—in the second half of the nineteenth century, the Chinese on the West Coast were frequently driven out of their homes and businesses by whites and even lynched[20]—today they are increasingly integrated in largely white social milieus. They frequently share residential environments with many whites: analysis of 2000 Census data revealed that the average Asian American resided in a neighborhood where whites were the majority and Asians formed less than a fifth of the population.[21] Neither Hispanics nor blacks typically resided in neighborhoods where they were outnumbered by the white majority. The high rate of intermarriage by young U.S.-born Asian Americans shows that they are also entering into white families.

These changes do not mean a complete ending of racist slights and attacks for Asians. Yet even here one can envision that these expressions of racism will be forced to cede further ground as the integration of Asians, still very fresh in historical terms, continues. One complaint of many Asian Americans is that they continue to be viewed by many other Americans as permanent foreigners: in encounters with strangers, they experience being interrogated on where they "really come from" or complimented on how well they speak English, even when they have been born in the United States and have grown up with English as their mother tongue. Such questions and comments are a form of bias, a prejudgment based on skin color that obscures individual realities. However, these slights, as deplorable as they are, must still be placed in the contemporary context: since Asians represent a small portion of the U.S. population (5 percent in 2006) and Asian adults still are largely foreign born at this point in our history (outnumbering the U.S. born by more than 3 to 1 as of 2006), most other Americans have little or no experience with the U.S.-born generations of Asian Americans. In the not-too-distant future, the Asian population will increase and the proportion of it born in the United States will, too, and many more whites will be able to recognize the diversity among Asian Americans. The integration of Asians into mainstream communities will speed this process.

Also changing the character of relations of minorities with whites will be the growing population of individuals with mixed ancestry.[22] The mixed ancestry engendered by racial intermarriage today is fundamentally different from that in the past, which occurred in the context of the profoundly unequal relations that existed between racial minorities and whites. Thus the racially mixed ancestry found by DNA analysis among African Americans because of past sexual encounters between whites and blacks was mostly produced outside of marriage and not recognized by whites, who as a group held overwhelming power to determine the social place of minority individuals and defined that of mixed-race persons according to the "one drop" rule. Because of it, Thomas Jefferson's white descendants were able to refuse for the better part of two centuries to recognize, even informally, his descendants from his children with the slave Sally Hemings. Many African-American families did retain memories, and frequently bitter ones, of white ancestors, as Malcolm X's memoir attests.[23] But racial intermarriage is today an increasingly common occurrence and now involves 4–5 percent of married whites, with the precise figure depending on whether mixed-race partners are counted as whites or minorities. Most of this intermarriage takes place with Asian or Hispanic partners; intermarriage by whites with African Americans is less common, though it is increasing. Intermarriage, even at such a modest level, has a surprisingly widespread impact on whites' family circles: using a smaller estimate of intermarriage than is found in recent data, the demographer Joshua Goldstein has estimated that one in seven whites possesses a close-kin network that includes at least one non-white.[24] The children of racial intermarriages are by and large not being raised within minority ghettoes, as were the mixed-race children of a century ago, but with access to the family circles of their white and minority parents. This access does not predetermine how they will identify and be identified as adults—those are issues that demand research attention[25]—but whatever that outcome, such individuals are likely to feel comfortable in their social relations with whites as well as with same-minority individuals. They are individuals who have the potential to blur racial boundaries because of their dual-sided membership.

Moreover, the intermarriage rate of whites with minorities is likely to continue to increase. This prediction is supported by the well-known relationship of marriage patterns to population composition: *ceteris paribus,* as the population proportion of potential partners with a given characteristic increases, so does the frequency of marriage with them. The rising percentage of minorities among the young adults of the future is beyond doubt; and unless whites and/or minorities become markedly less willing to marry across boundaries, the percentage of whites marrying nonwhites is destined to rise. This is especially the case for marriages of whites to Asians and Hispanics, the populations that will be expanding most rapidly. (Paradoxically, the same composition principle also leads to the conclusion that the rates of Asians and Hispanics who marry within their ethnic group will increase, as may already be happening. There is no inherent contradiction here because of the changing composition of the population, which involves a decline in the relative number of whites.) There will also almost certainly be a rise in the number of marriages between whites and mixed-race persons, both because of the growing proportion of the latter and because of their unusually high propensity to marry whites.[26] In sum, the proportion of the population who have close family ties in multiple racial groups and who thus blur the boundaries between them seems certain to increase in the future (whether or not these individuals see themselves as part of a mixed-race population and report themselves in this way on the Census).

Boundary Blurring in the Future?

The blurring of major ethno-racial boundaries is a plausible prospect for the near future. Blurring occurs when a zone of ambiguity opens up, when some individuals can successfully present themselves as belonging on both sides of a boundary (not necessarily at the same time, of course). A blurred boundary stands in contrast to a bright one, which is unambiguous and demands that individuals must be located on one side or the other, as historically has held true for the black-white boundary in the United States. A bright boundary is conducive to all-or-nothing assimilation, while a blurred boundary allows for more gradual and partial assimilation, as individuals perceive that they can participate in mainstream settings without having to surrender minority identities and practices.

The victory of Barack Obama in the 2008 presidential election suggests the potential of blurred boundaries for black Americans, the hard case in American race relations. Early on during his race for the Democratic nomination, some commentators suggested that Obama was not "black enough" to obtain the full support of African Americans, presumably necessary to counterbalance the reluctance of many whites to vote for a nonwhite candidate. For example, writing for the e-zine *Salon,* Debra Dickerson opined in early 2007, before Obama's campaign took off:

> "Black," in our political and social reality, means those descended from West African slaves. Voluntary immigrants of African descent (even those descended from West Indian slaves) are just that, voluntary immigrants of African descent with markedly different outlooks on the role of race in their lives and in politics. At a minimum, it can't be assumed that a Nigerian cabdriver and a third-generation Harlemite

have more in common than the fact a cop won't bother to make the distinction. They're both "black" as a matter of skin color and DNA, but only the Harlemite, for better or worse, is politically and culturally black, as we use the term.

Adding to her suspicions at that time was the enthusiasm of liberal whites for Obama's candidacy:

> Whites, on the other hand, are engaged in a paroxysm of self-congratulation . . . Swooning over nice, safe Obama means you aren't a racist. I honestly can't look without feeling pity, and indeed mercy, at whites' need for absolution. For all our sakes, it seemed (again) best not to point out the obvious: You're not embracing a black man, a descendant of slaves. You're replacing the black man with an immigrant of recent African descent of whom you can approve without feeling either guilty or frightened. If he were Ronald Washington from Detroit, even with the same résumé, he wouldn't be getting this kind of love. Washington would have to earn it, not just show promise of it, and even then whites would remain wary.[27]

Yet in the end black voters swarmed to Obama's candidacy, and this happened without a major loss of his white support. His was clearly a new kind of minority campaign for national office.

One key, as Dickerson's essay indicates, is the degree of comfort that many whites feel with Obama's public personality, and that in turn is a function of his ability to bridge the racial divide, to present himself to them in a way that appears to transcend race. This is not to say that his campaign actually overcame the resistance of many whites to the prospect of a black president; his white support was lodged disproportionately among the highly educated and among youth, and many other whites reacted skeptically, to say the least. Yet the degree of enthusiastic support for him among whites exceeded by a good margin that achieved by any prior African-American candidate for national office and, indeed, that which seemed even conceivable but a few years before the 2008 election. The lack of wariness of many whites toward Obama was matched by his confidence in his ability to speak to them. At the same time, he succeeded in convincing the great majority of African-American voters that he is one of them, or at least that he comes close enough that they have a genuine stake in his success. His campaign was an exemplar of blurring boundaries, and its visibility on the national stage potentially gave it paradigmatic significance.

This breakthrough election may have forged a new template with a basis in Obama's own biography. Obama's ability to blur boundaries stems in part from the role of his mixed racial ancestry in his life experience: raised by his white mother and her parents, he early on had loving, intimate relationships with whites, which enabled him to weather the experiences of marginality he subsequently endured as a phenotypically black young man in a racially divided society. That his father was an African immigrant of considerable accomplishment, both in the Western educational system and in his homeland, Kenya, also contributed to Obama's persona by inspiring him with a very positive, if distant, image of what blacks could accomplish (that it was subsequently tarnished by the revelations of his Kenyan half-sister is less important than the early positive imprint). His insightful autobiography, *Dreams from My Father*, reveals a man who, in his youth, felt conflicted about the uncommon mélange of his early-life experiences. Ultimately and probably inevitably, his initially fluid identity crystallized around his black skin, as indicated by his choice to marry an African-American woman and to join an African-American church.

The contrast to Obama's story is that of Anatole Broyard, which illustrates the perilous route of escape from the disadvantages adhering to racial minority membership in a bright-boundary context. A New York literary critic and essayist of the post–World War II period, Broyard lived his adult life as a white man but was posthumously revealed to have been born black, according to the standards of a racially divided society. Broyard had grown up in a racially mixed, Creole family in Louisiana and could pass as white, the only form of mainstream assimilation available to an American with African ancestry in his era. His passing required that he cut himself off from his black relatives, and his children, who did not know of his racial past, only met them at his funeral.[28] "Passing" is the extreme case of assimilation in a bright-boundary context, where assimilation in general requires a jettisoning of membership in one group and assumption of the risks involved in trying to gain acceptance in another. The risks in passing are exceptionally high because of the need to conceal one's origin, perhaps even from those closest to oneself. Bright boundaries can be intimidating to the great majority of a minority group, unwilling to undertake the risks and pain assumed by an Anatole Broyard.

Obama's story is unique, and this fact raises questions about the broader significance of his boundary blurring. This significance will depend more on whether the race-relations template his victory is forging can be generalized than on whether the increasing number of mixed-race individuals can see an approximation to their own life experiences in his and find a suitable model in his identity solutions. That template will reveal its value if more whites are opened to the humanity of nonwhites by the presence of a black First Family in the White House and if more African Americans are inspired to believe that they can overcome the barriers set in their path by a largely white, still racist society. The election of Obama revealed a widespread hunger by Americans of all colors to break apart the logjam of black-white stratification. We will have to see whether this hunger finds a successful resolution.

Yet no matter how significant the breakthrough of the Obama presidency is, the experience of race as a blurred boundary will undoubtedly not hold true for many nonwhites, especially those situated at the bottom of the social ladder. A social system that depends on an unequal distribution of economic resources inevitably creates a group at the bottom, but the stretching out of inequality at the end of the twentieth century and the beginning of the twenty-first has lengthened the already great economic distance separating those at the bottom from the mainstream. According to Census Bureau data, the ratio of income between households located at the eightieth and tenth percentiles—indicative, in the one case, of households that are positioned in the middle of those with earners holding good jobs and, in the other, households in poverty—had climbed by the end of the century to $8.22 to $1, from $7.03 to $1 at the end of the 1960s. Wealth inequalities are far more extreme and only growing more so: the equivalent relative positions on the wealth scale cannot even be formulated in ratio terms because the bottom 17–18 percent of American households have no net worth or are in the red, while households at the eightieth percentile in 2004 had an average net worth of more than $300,000.[29] In the United States, race is a primary sorting characteristic that determines who is placed at the bottom, looking up at a receding economic mainstream. Derrick Bell's metaphor of the "faces at the bottom of the well" is poignantly applicable at the conjunction of nonwhite race and poverty.[30] Blacks and, to a somewhat lesser extent, Hispanics are the groups that have the highest risk of falling to the bottom. According to a 2007 study of the Economic Mobility Project, this risk is high even for the children of middle-class black families, who are more likely than not to wind up at a lower socioeconomic position than their parents occupied, the reverse of the odds for the children coming from white middle-class families.[31] Obviously, many blacks and Hispanics successfully evade this fate, and there are plenty of poor whites, too. However, poor whites are less likely than poor blacks and Hispanics to reside in poor communities, and residence with better-off neighbors probably protects them from the extreme economic and social isolation found in poor minority neighborhoods. Walled off in ghettoes defined by the conjunction of race and poor economic life chances, subject to a high risk of incarceration when they are male, blacks and Hispanics at the bottom have a hard time perceiving realistic opportunities to move upward on the social ladder.[32] Unless there is an economic turnaround that dramatically reduces inequality, raising in particular the bottom of the income distribution, poor minorities will continue to be excluded from the mainstream and its opportunities despite the increasing racial and ethnic diversity in the higher tiers of the labor market. A paradox of the near future will involve the apparent inconsistency between this diversity at the top and the seeming racial homogeneity, more specifically, the relative absence of whites and Asians, at the bottom.

Points of Leverage

The opportunity to alter the ethno-racial boundaries of American society through increasing diversity at its middle and upper levels, achieved by the mobility into these tiers of native minorities and the second generation of contemporary immigrant groups, in the end, is just that: an opportunity, not a predictable outcome. This leads to the obvious next question: What can be done to help bring boundary change about? As I write this conclusion, it is hard to avoid the sense that this may be an especially propitious moment to raise this question because the Obama administration, just installed, is bringing new sensitivities and priorities to Washington, for example, ranking job creation and improvements in education among its most important goals. The analysis of a prior episode of change, in particular the mass assimilation of the white ethnics in the middle of the twentieth century, suggests some points of leverage on the processes involved. I prefer to discuss them as such rather than to embark on a discussion of specific policies, since I claim no special expertise in the substantive domains where they are needed. I leave to the experts the identification of the policies that would exert pressure on the points of leverage in ways that would promote more ethno-racial integration. Public policies will be needed to:

1. Narrow the educational gap between
   white and minority Americans.

The greatest threat to future boundary change lies in the lagging educational attainments of U.S.-born black and Hispanic Americans compared with non-Hispanic whites and Asians. The gap does not loom so large when all forms of postsecondary education are considered, and this fact suggests that minorities are prepared to take advantage in large numbers of opportunities in the middle of the labor force, in those jobs in the second and third quartiles where some degree of postsecondary training will be an advantage or a requirement. However, the gap is quite substantial, on the order of 2-to-1, when it comes to college and university credentials at the baccalaureate level or higher. In addition, U.S.-born Hispanics have substantially higher dropout rates from high school than do white Americans.[33]

The educational gap can be narrowed, if not closed, but it will require national will to do so. The United States has done this before. The educational lag of the children of southern and eastern European immigrants from rural backgrounds, such as the southern Italians, was of the same order of magnitude, yet within a few decades, between 1940 and 1970, the second and third generations of these groups caught up to, even surpassed, white American educational norms.

The "yield" to be expected from even a narrowing of the current gap is large. If the rate of college graduation could be increased for U.S.-born black and Hispanic minorities by just 5 percentage points, it would expand the pool of minority graduates by about a third. But cutting into the gap will take investment at all levels of education. The disparities in ultimate attainment are the consequences of a cumulative set of processes, which, though anchored partly in families and communities, are constructed also through inequalities in educational institutions. Most minority children attend schools that are segregated, that is, largely populated by other minority students; and the ramifications of this segregation are more grave when the children are poor as well as members of minorities. The schools serving minority populations are demonstrably worse than those serving middle-class white children along a number of dimensions, including physical facilities, equipment, and teacher experience and qualifications.[34] The only way such inequalities can be eroded is through investment, especially investment that to some extent compensates for the educational disadvantages that inhere in families whose parents tend to have lower levels of education and in communities that are poorer in resources. I assume, to be sure, that large-scale investment in the schooling of minority children will only be politically acceptable if it occurs within a broader program of educational investment that benefits Americans of all colors and social classes. I have offered the example of teacher recruitment as an instance where a program of investment could make a substantial difference, but experts in educational policy may see other areas where investment could yield large educational improvements.

Such a program of investment makes sense in strictly utilitarian terms given the challenges that the United States will face in coming decades. Comparative educational data from international tests of student achievement reveal that U.S. schoolchildren do not fare well when they are compared in terms of school-taught skills to those in most other economically advanced countries. For several decades, the United States has relied on the recruitment of highly educated immigrants from around the world to make up some of the human-capital deficits left by its school system, but as I have argued earlier, this strategy is likely to become increasing problematic because of the intensifying competition for the elite stratum of immigrants. It is time to rethink basic strategies of populating the top tiers of the labor market.

2. Open channels of mobility wider.

The evidence we have seen throughout indicates indisputably that minorities continue to be disadvantaged in the labor market, even when they have postsecondary education. A variety of research perspectives—for example, studies of managers—converge in finding the privileged position of white males in the labor market. As we saw in Chapter 4,

U.S.-born blacks and Hispanics achieve a lower occupational placement than do native-born whites with similar levels of education, and they earn less than do whites in the same occupations. While to some degree these ethno-racial inequalities could be explained by differences in the quality of the educational institutions attended by whites versus minorities, it is highly improbable that all of them can. A reasonable conclusion is that minorities continue to face discrimination in the labor market.

That being the case, policies of affirmative action are going to continue to be needed during the coming quarter century, which will afford a remarkable opportunity to erode the ethno-racial divisions that have dominated U.S. society for so long. Affirmative action can be narrow in its scope—ensuring, for example, merely that the pool of individuals under consideration for a position is not homogeneous in ethno-racial terms—but undoubtedly more broad-gauge forms of it are going to be required to make large strides in the direction of ethno-racial parity. This means, in other words, that minorities are going to have to be given some degree of preference when they are as qualified as whites. Even if the evidence for discrimination is viewed by some as questionable, there is still a strong rationale for affirmative action in the upper tiers of the labor market, which Orlando Patterson states well:

> The problem with this [color-blind] logic is that it disregards the fact that when firms promote workers they consider not simply the characteristics of employees, but organizational criteria, among the most important of which is the degree to which a candidate for promotion will fit into the upper echelon for which he or she is being considered. And it is precisely here that Afro-Americans lose out because of their small numbers, their ethnic differences, and the tendency of personnel officers to follow the one well-established law of microsociology, first formally propounded by George Caspar Homans.
>
> This very simple principle of human behavior—call it the principle of homyphyly—is that people who share common attributes tend to marry each other, tend to play more together, and in general tend to

get along better and to form more effective work teams. Thus, a non-racist personnel officer, under no pressure to consider ethnic attributes—indeed, under strong misguided pressure to follow a "color-blind" policy—would always find it more organizationally rational to choose a Euro-American person for promotion. There are more than six candidates for every one Afro-American candidate, which means that unless the Afro-American person is a genius of sociability, out-performing Euro-Americans at their own social game, the organizationally rational act will be to select one of the Euro-American candidates. In spite of the technical equality of the Afro-American candidates, the Euro-American person's organizational fit—which comes simply with being Euro-American—will so significantly reduce the cost to the organization of incorporation and training that it would be irresponsible of our ethnically unbiased personnel officer, under orders to select in a color-blind manner, ever to promote an Afro-American person.

Of course, when one introduces one well-known real-world feature of American society to this model of "color-blind" organizational behavior, the cards are even more heavily stacked . . .: this is the fact that Euro-American workers have a hard time taking orders from Afro-American supervisors. There is no need to belabor this fact. This being so, the cost to our non-racist, "color-blind" personnel officer becomes even greater; and it gets worse the more real-world attitudes and behaviors we introduce.[35]

Affirmative action in college admissions, to the extent that it is allowed, will also be critical in narrowing the large overall educational disparity between whites and minorities. Recent studies of admissions to selective institutions indicate that the intensifying competition among white and Asian students, predominantly those coming from upper-middle-class backgrounds who possess strong educational qualifications, would have squeezed out black and Hispanic students except for affirmative action and other policies, such as the top 10 percent policy in Texas, aimed at increasing diversity among students.[36] The United States must seek to expand the pool of educationally qualified minorities if it is to meet successfully the coming challenges of global competition.

Affirmative action will also be necessary to counteract the tendencies in American society to promote the advance of immigrant minorities over that of African Americans. We have observed throughout that the situation of African American seems somewhat less favorable than that of U.S.-born Hispanics—their postsecondary educational attainments are slightly lower than those of Hispanics and, even when their educational credentials are the same, their occupational placements are not as high, for example. There is evidence to indicate that a logic familiar from the postimmigration experiences of impoverished Europeans—namely, that the immigrants and their children soon learn that getting ahead in American society means separating themselves physically and socially from African Americans—is operating today among Latin-American immigrants, too. There is also reason to be concerned that history could repeat itself in this respect, that the advance of Hispanic immigrants and their children could come at the cost of leaving African Americans behind once again. That is a prospect that Americans should guard against, and the best tool available for this purpose is affirmative action, which can be used to make sure that qualified African Americans have a fair chance to advance.

3. Help minorities convert improved socioeconomic
   position into social proximity to whites.

In addition to vertical, socioeconomic mobility, the diminishment of ethno-racial boundaries requires horizontal intergroup relationships of trust and intimacy that perforate boundaries and take the air out of the social distinctions at their core. Mobility for minorities without an increase in equal-status, minority-majority relationships leaves boundaries in place; and since the majority remains ultimately the more powerful group, the socioeconomic gains of the minority are vulnerable. This is true even if the white majority eventually becomes a numerical minority in the United States, as population projections suggest may happen by mid-century (however, as forecasts, the population projections are suspect because they assume ethno-racial categories will have the same meaning in the future as they do today). Research on African Americans continues to reveal the difficulties that successful parents face in passing on their socioeconomic advantages to their children, who in a racially divided society are at greater risk of sliding downward than are comparable white children.[37] Cross-boundary relationships between individuals of unequal status likewise do not diminish boundaries (and perhaps enhance them by validating the stereotypes that are encrusted in their social walls). Such relationships were common enough in the Jim Crow South, for example, where they generally conformed to the social conventions of master-servant relationships.

Social policy obviously cannot force individuals into relationships of friendship and trust. What it can legitimately do, however, is provide access to social contexts where resources are concentrated and where, in the absence of integration, advantages such as high-quality schooling for children are monopolized by dominant social groups. Residential neighborhoods exemplify such contexts. Although the effects of increasing diversity within American communities are currently a matter of debate, the European-American experience demonstrates unambiguously that, given the right conditions, relationships will spring up among individuals from different groups as contexts like neighborhoods become more diverse in their composition.[38] A belief in the moral equality of minority newcomers, similar to that which accompanied the white-ethnic social ascent in the mid-twentieth century, will help to facilitate such linkages.

Residential segregation is one of the most visible manifestations of —and mechanisms for maintaining—ethno-racial inequalities. It is not just that African Americans and others with dark skin are typically confined to neighborhoods where few whites live, but that their neighborhoods have many fewer resources and advantages than do the neighborhoods where comparable whites are found—they feature inferior schools, higher rates of crime, poorer-quality housing, fewer and more expensive stores, and so forth.[39] Many of the resources attached to the neighborhoods where middle-class whites reside are, directly or indirectly, the by-products of public investment (in schools and the police, for example); and this fact alone justifies an interest in opening access to these resources for others. To be sure, nonwhites and Hispanics are not equally affected by residential segregation; it appears that Asians and light-skinned Hispanics are not as constrained in their residential options as are those of visible African or perhaps indigenous ancestry.

The potential impacts of non-zero-sum mobility will be severely limited if upwardly mobile minorities continue to be forced to live largely in segregated neighborhoods. Breaking down the exclusionary barriers to the integration of neighborhoods has for some time been a focus of attention for policymakers interested promoting positive racial change, and so the policies that can ameliorate racial residential segregation have been identified to a significant degree.[40]

Policies can help to bring about ethno-racial boundary change, but pressure in favor of change will need to be generated in other ways as well. Resistance to the social advance of the white ethnics did not end simply because World War II led to a valorization of their moral worth or because the expansion of educational institutions and the middle and upper tiers of the labor market made room for them without reducing the life chances of native-born white Protestants. Barriers had to be dismantled, and effort had to be applied, both by the ethnics and by native white Protestants who believed in the value of a more open society. Jerome Karabel's in-depth analysis of the lowering of restrictive barriers to admission to the Ivy League colleges reveals the complexity of the numerous small-scale struggles that took place along the way.[41]

Since barriers usually do not collapse of their own accord, there will be any number of similar struggles in the near future, even under the best of circumstances, though the precise forms that they will take are impossible to predict. What is predictable is that all resistance to minority advance will not wither away, and therefore there will be a need for organized efforts to overcome it. In recent decades, there has been great interest among sociologists in social movements because of the recognition of the role of human agency in social change.[42] Social movements can help to bring about quite momentous changes, as the successes of the civil-rights movement demonstrate. Yet social movements, as Charles Tilly pointed out, can also have the effect of increasing the salience and resilience of a boundary, since, when the goal is the dismantling of one, they mobilize primarily individuals on one side of the boundary and engender countermobilizations by those on the other side intent on defending it.[43]

Social movements are likely to be most effective when conditions are favorable, when concessions can be made without much apparent effect on the life chances of the members of more privileged groups, and when, therefore, the countermobilization is weaker than it might otherwise be. It does not seem merely coincidental that the greatest achievements of the civil-rights movement came in the mid-1960s, at a time when conditions were also conducive to the mass assimilation of the white ethnics. The non-zero-sum mobility of that period supported the view that gains for disadvantaged groups could be achieved without much sacrifice in the life chances of more advantaged groups. When U.S. economic growth subsequently slowed during the 1970s, some indicators of the progress of African Americans—for example, the ratio of black-to-white family income—stagnated.

We are at the beginning of another period of non-zero-sum mobility, which will be created by the exit of the baby boomers from the labor market. This period is likely to be favorable to concessions made to movements for social justice, which demand, for example, greater representation of minorities and women in positions where they have been rare before.

Yet the scenario of ethno-racial change coupled to non-zero-sum mobility will not help the minority poor very much. To be sure, if there is greater investment in educational institutions and greater opportunity for upward mobility in the labor market, more youngsters who have grown up in poor families and communities will be able to escape poverty than do so now. But the large population of black and Hispanic poor is a consequence of two brute facts: one, the high and growing degree of economic inequality in the United States, which is stretching out distributions of income and wealth and in effect keeping a large population of individuals and families stuck to a bottom that is receding from the middle; the other, the imposition of the greatest risk of falling to the bottom on minority individuals. Neither of these will be affected by the opening up of the labor market engendered by the departure of the baby boomers. The distributions of income and wealth are produced by a set of forces different from those connected with the movements of cohorts through the labor force. In principle, there could be changes to the labor market, expansions and contractions of different tiers, that in turn affect the income and wealth distributions, but they would be difficult to predict. The scenario of non-zero-sum mobility I have posited does not presume such changes, though they could happen. One premise of that scenario, however, is that whites do not experience a significant decline in their life chances. It is hard to imagine that whites would be accepting of minority social gains if they or their children faced a significantly higher risk of falling into poverty.

Thus leverage against the grave problems of poverty will require a different analysis and set of tools than the one presented here. As Orlando Patterson puts it, the required strategies are "bottom up," rather than "top down."[44] One can envision many training- and employment-based strategies that would assist currently poor individuals to improve their chances of lifting themselves out of poverty, and these are worthy of being undertaken. But I find it hard to escape the conclusion that in the contemporary United States, social and economic impoverishment is an unavoidable consequence of great and growing distributional inequality. If we want to reduce this impoverishment, we ultimately have to stare growing inequality in the face and take steps to reduce it, with, for example, more income redistribution through tax and welfare policies and with greater public investment to improve the communities where the poor reside and the institutions that serve them. A cardinal conclusion is that the problems of ethno-racial inequality at the bottom are different from those at other levels of the society. Affecting the latter will do little to improve the former.

In closing, I must point out that the chance to realize substantial ethno-racial change does not come around very often, and periods of fluidity tend to be followed by recrystallizations that lock in whatever changes have taken place and produce new stability for ethno-racial inequalities. In other words, the long-term costs of failing to exploit the foreseeable opportunities of the next quarter century—the predictable non-zero-sum-mobility and the opening it will afford for major ethno-racial realignment—could be high. A wise society will seek to take advantage of such a chance.

NOTES

INDEX

Notes

1. Paradoxes of Race and Ethnicity in America Today

1. Eugene Robinson, "Morning in America," *Washington Post*, November 6, 2008; Thomas Friedman, "Finishing Our Work," *New York Times*, November 5, 2008; Anne Appelbaum, "Whose Race Problem?" *Washington Post*, June 10, 2008.

2. Orlando Patterson, "Jena, O.J. and the Jailing of Black America," *New York Times*, September 30, 2007. On the disputes over the basic facts of the case, see, on the one hand, Craig Franklin, "Media Myths about the Jena 6," *Christian Science Monitor*, October 24, 2007; and, on the other, Clarence Page, "Injustice Is Bigger Than 'Jena 6,'" *Real Clear Politics*, September 25, 2007.

3. For reports and data on the growth and composition of the prison population, see the websites of the Bureau of Justice Statistics (http://www.ojp.usdoj.gov/bjs/prisons.htm#selected) and The Sentencing Project (http://www.sentencingproject.org/Default.aspx). The comparison of the prison-to-college ratio among black males comes from Vincent Schiraldi and Jason Ziedenberg, "Cellblocks or Classrooms? The Funding of Higher Education and Corrections and Its Impact on African American Men," report by the Justice Policy Institute (September,

2002), http://www.justicepolicy.org/images/upload/02–09_REP_Cell-blocksClassrooms_BB-AC.pdf (accessed 8/20/2008).

4. Race and ethnicity have precise, if overlapping, meanings in the social sciences that will be discussed and critiqued in the next chapter.

5. Alexis de Tocqueville, *Democracy in America,* trans. Stephen Grant (Indianapolis: Hackett Publishing, 2000), 155.

6. Camille Zubrinsky Charles, "The Dynamics of Racial Residential Segregation," *Annual Review of Sociology* 29 (2003): 167–207; Ingrid Gould Ellen, *Sharing America's Neighborhoods: The Prospects for Stable Racial Integration* (Cambridge, Mass.: Harvard University Press, 2000); John Logan, Reynolds Farley, and Brian Stults, "Segregation of Minorities in the Metropolis: Two Decades of Change," *Demography* 41 (February, 2004): 1–22; Douglas Massey and Nancy Denton, *American Apartheid: Segregation and the Making of the Underclass* (Cambridge, Mass.: Harvard University Press, 1993); Emily Rosenbaum and Samantha Friedman, *The Housing Divide: How Generations of Immigrants Fare in New York's Housing Market* (New York: New York University Press, 2007).

7. The sources for the data cited are Vincent Parrillo, *Strangers to These Shores,* 8th ed. (Boston: Allyn and Bacon, 2006); U.S. Bureau of the Census, *Income, Poverty, and Health Insurance Coverage in the United States: 2006* (Washington, D.C.: U.S. Department of Commerce, 2007); Dalton Conley, *Being Black, Living in the Red: Race, Wealth, and Social Policy in America* (Berkeley: University of California Press, 1999); Sam Harper, John Lynch, Scott Burris, and George Davey Smith, "Trends in the Black-White Life Expectancy Gap in the United States, 1983–2003," *JAMA* 297 (March 21, 2007): 1224–1232; Becky Pettit and Bruce Western, "Mass Imprisonment and the Life Course: Race and Class Inequality in U.S. Incarceration," *American Sociological Review* (April, 2004): 151–169.

On black-white inequality more generally, see Joe Feagin and Karyn McKinney, *The Many Costs of Racism* (Lanham, Md.: Rowman and Littlefield, 2003); Andrew Hacker, *Two Nations: Black and White, Separate, Hostile, Unequal* (New York: Scribner's, 1992); Melvin Oliver and Thomas Shapiro, *Black Wealth/White Wealth: A New Perspective on Racial Inequality* (New York: Routledge, 1995); Thomas Shapiro, *The Hidden Cost of Being African American* (New York: Oxford University Press,

2003); Bruce Western, *Punishment and Inequality in America* (New York: Russell Sage Foundation, 2006).

8. Cara Hetland, "South Dakota Has Nation's Poorest County," Minnesota Public Radio (October 1, 2002), http://news.minnesota.publicradio.org/ features/200210/02_hetlandc_census-m/ (accessed July 1, 2008); Indian Health Service, *Trends in Indian Health* (Washington, D.C.: U.S. Government Printing Office, 2004).

9. For the data in the paragraph, see Cordelia Reimers, "Economic Well-Being," in Marta Tienda and Faith Mitchell, eds., *Hispanics and the Future of America* (Washington, D.C.: National Academies Press, 2006); Logan, Farley, and Stults, "Segregation of Minorities"; and Joel Perlmann, *Italians Then, Mexicans Now* (New York: Russell Sage Foundation, 2005). For a general overview, see the summary volume of the 2006 National Research Council report, edited by Marta Tienda and Faith Mitchell, *Multiple Origins, Uncertain Destinies: Hispanics and the American Future* (Washington, D.C.: National Academies Press, 2006). The residential patterns of Hispanics are analyzed in depth by John Iceland and Kyle Anne Nelson, "Hispanic Segregation in Metropolitan America: Exploring the Multiple Forms of Spatial Assimilation," *American Sociological Review* 73 (October, 2008).

10. See, e.g., Eduardo Bonilla-Silva, "From Bi-Racial to Tri-Racial: Toward a New System of Racial Stratification in the USA," *Ethnic and Racial Studies* 27 (November, 2004): 931–950; Edward Telles and Vilma Ortiz, *Generations of Exclusion: Mexican Americans, Assimilation, and Race* (New York: Russell Sage Foundation, 2008).

11. For a brief review of the evidence on Asian-American assimilation, see Richard Alba and Victor Nee, *Remaking the American Mainstream: Assimilation and Contemporary Immigration* (Cambridge, Mass.: Harvard University Press, 2003). On intermarriage, see Zhenchao Qian and Daniel Lichter, "Social Boundaries and Marital Assimilation: Interpreting Trends in Racial and Ethnic Intermarriage," *American Sociological Review* 72 (February, 2007): 68–94.

12. John Higham, *Strangers in the Land: Patterns of American Nativism, 1860–1925* (New York: Atheneum, 1970), 212; Lewis Curtis, Jr., *Apes and Angels: The Irishman in Victorian Caricature,* rev. ed. (Washington, D.C.: Smithsonian Institution Press, 1997), 29–67.

13. Curtis, *Apes and Angels*, 58–67. To be sure, caricatures with racist import were widely available for other groups as well. For an example depicting the stereotypical Jew, see Eric Goldstein, in *The Price of Whiteness: Jews, Race, and American Identity* (Princeton: Princeton University Press, 2006), 45.

14. Andrew Greeley, *Ethnicity, Denomination, and Inequality* (Beverly Hills: Sage, 1976), 45; Richard Alba, John Logan, and Kyle Crowder, "White Ethnic Neighborhoods and Spatial Assimilation: The Greater New York Region, 1980–1990," *Social Forces* 75 (March, 1997): 883–912.

15. Michael Hout and Joshua Goldstein, "How 4.5 Million Irish Immigrants Became 40 Million Irish Americans: Demographic and Subjective Aspects of the Ethnic Composition of White Americans," *American Sociological Review* 59 (February, 1994): 64–82.

16. Tom Smith and Glenn Dempsey, "The Polls: Ethnic Social Distance and Prejudice," *Public Opinion Quarterly* 47 (Winter, 1983): 584–600; Parrillo, *Strangers*, 5.

17. See Joane Nagel, "American Indian Ethnic Renewal: Politics and the Resurgence of Identity," *American Sociological Review* 60 (December, 1995): 947–965.

18. The distinction between immigrant-origin groups and minorities that are forcibly incorporated through conquest and enslavement plays an important role in sociological theorizing about race and ethnicity; see, for example, Robert Blauner, *Racial Oppression in America* (New York: Harper & Row, 1972); Stanley Lieberson, "A Societal Theory of Race and Ethnic Relations," *American Sociological Review* 26 (December, 1961): 902–910; John Ogbu, "Immigrant and Involuntary Minorities in Comparative Perspective," in Margaret Gibson and John Ogbu, eds., *Minority Status and Schooling: A Comparative Study of Immigrant and Involuntary Minorities* (New York: Garland, 1991); Michael Omi and Howard Winant, *Racial Formation in the United States: From the 1960s to the 1990s*, 2nd ed. (New York: Routledge & Kegan Paul, 1994).

19. The theory of social boundaries has advanced rapidly in recent years; see Michèle Lamont and Virág Molnár, "The Study of Boundaries in the Social Sciences," *Annual Review of Sociology* 28 (2002): 167–195; Charles Tilly, *Durable Inequality* (Berkeley: University of California Press, 1998); Andreas Wimmer, "The Making and Unmaking of Ethnic Boundaries: A Multilevel Process Theory," *American Journal of Sociology* (February, 2008): 970–1022.

20. James Barrett and David Roediger, "In-Between Peoples: Race, Nationality, and the 'New Immigrant' Working Class," *Journal of American Ethnic History* 16 (Spring, 1997): 3–44. For other examples of the whiteness approach, see Karen Brodkin, *How Jews Became White Folks and What That Says about Race in America* (New Brunswick: Rutgers University Press, 1998); Matthew Frye Jacobson, *Whiteness of a Different Color: European Immigrants and the Alchemy of Race* (Cambridge, Mass.: Harvard University Press, 1998); and David Roediger, *The Wages of Whiteness: Race and the Making of the American Working Class* (New York: Verso, 1991).

21. See, for example, Annette Bernhardt, Martina Morris, Mark Handcock, and Marc Scott, *Divergent Paths: Economic Mobility in the New American Labor Market* (New York: Russell Sage Foundation, 2001); and Kathryn Neckerman and Florencia Torche, "Inequality: Causes and Consequences," *Annual Review of Sociology* 33 (2007): 335–357.

2. The Puzzle of Ethno-Racial Change

1. George Fredrickson, *Racism: A Short History* (Princeton: Princeton University Press, 2002).

2. Stewart Tolnay and E. M. Beck, *A Festival of Violence: An Analysis of Southern Lynchings, 1882–1930* (Urbana: University of Illinois Press, 1995).

3. James Grossman, *Land of Hope: Chicago, Black Southerners, and the Great Migration* (Chicago: University of Chicago Press, 1989); Stanley Lieberson, *A Piece of the Pie: Blacks and White Immigrants since 1880* (Berkeley: University of California Press, 1980); Douglas Massey and Nancy Denton, *American Apartheid: Segregation and the Making of the Underclass* (Cambridge: Harvard University Press, 1993); Olivier Zunz, *The Changing Face of Inequality: Urbanization, Industrialization, and Immigrants in Detroit, 1880–1920* (Chicago: University of Chicago Press, 1982).

4. Joint Center for Political and Economic Studies, "Black Elected Officials: A Statistical Summary 2000": http://www.jointcenter.org/publications_recent_publications/black_elected_officials/black_elected_officials_a_statistical_summary_2000 (retrieved July 4, 2008).

5. Richard Alba, John Logan, and Paul Bellair, "Living with Crime: The Implications of Racial/Ethnic Differences in Suburban Location," *Social*

Forces 73 (December, 1994): 395–434; Massey and Denton, *American Apartheid;* Gary Orfield and Chungmei Lee, "Racial Transformation and the Changing Nature of Segregation," Harvard University, The Civil Rights Project (2006): http://www.civilrightsproject.ucla.edu/research/deseg/Racial_Transformation.pdf.

6. Victor Nee and Jimy Sanders, "The Road to Parity: Determinants of the Socioeconomic Attainments of Asian Americans," *Ethnic and Racial Studies* 8 (January, 1985): 75–93.

7. Victor Nee and Brett de Bary Nee, *Longtime Californ': A Documentary Study of an American Chinatown* (New York: Pantheon Books, 1973); Ronald Takaki, *Strangers from a Different Shore* (Boston: Little Brown, 1989).

8. The story of the 1965 legislation has been told numerous times, and so I do not into details here. See David Reimers, *Still the Golden Door: The Third World Comes to America* (New York: Columbia University Press, 1992).

9. U.S. Census Bureau, *We the People: Asians in the United States, Census 2000 Special Reports* (Washington, D.C.: U.S. Department of Commerce, 2004), http://www.census.gov/prod/2004pubs/censr-17.pdf.

10. Charles Hirschman and Morrison Wong, "Socioeconomic Gains of Asian Americans, Blacks and Hispanics, 1960–1976," *American Journal of Sociology* 90 (November, 1984): 584–607; idem, "The Extraordinary Educational Attainment of Asian-Americans: A Search for Historical Evidence and Explanations," *Social Forces* 65 (September, 1986): 1–27; John Iceland, "Earnings Returns to Occupational Status: Are Asian Americans Disadvantaged?" *Social Science Research* 28 (March, 1999): 45–65; Arthur Sakamoto, Huei-Hsia Wu, and Jessie Tzeng, "The Declining Significance of Race among American Men during the Latter Half of the Twentieth Century," *Demography* 37 (February, 2000): 41–51.

11. On these debates, see Nazli Kibria, *Becoming Asian American: Second-Generation Chinese and Korean American Identities* (Baltimore: Johns Hopkins University Press, 2002); Mia Tuan, *Forever Foreigners or Honorary Whites? The Asian Ethnic Experience Today* (New Brunswick: Rutgers University Press, 1998); Zhen Zeng and Yu Xie, "Asian Americans' Earnings Disadvantage Reexamined: The Role of Place of Education," *American Journal of Sociology* 109 (March, 2004): 1075–1108; Min Zhou and Yang Sao Xiong, "The Multifaceted American Experiences of the

Children of Asian Immigrants: Lessons for Segmented Assimilation," *Ethnic and Racial Studies* 28 (November, 2005): 1119–1152.

12. Zhenchao Qian and Daniel Lichter, "Social Boundaries and Marital Assimilation: Interpreting Trends in Racial and Ethnic Intermarriage," *American Sociological Review* 72 (2007): 79. There is a pronounced gender pattern to Asian intermarriage, with far more Asian females marrying out. Some scholars have argued that this weakens the evidence of intermarriage as an indication of a relaxation of racial boundaries in the Asian case because it suggests that stereotypes about exotic Asian femininity and sexuality are feeding intermarriage. This may be true, but nevertheless the intermarriage of whites and Asians is occurring with much greater frequency than in the past, indicating some sort of change, and has consequences for the racial integration of families and for the degree of racial mixture in the next generation.

13. Richard Alba and Victor Nee, *Remaking the American Mainstream: Assimilation and Contemporary Immigration* (Cambridge: Harvard University Press, 2003), 93.

14. James Barrett and David Roediger, "In Between Peoples: Race, Nationality and the 'New Immigrant' Working Class," *Journal of American Ethnic History* 16 (Spring, 1997): 3–44; Nancy Foner, *From Ellis Island to JFK: New York's Two Great Waves of Immigration* (New Haven: Yale University Press, 2000); Nancy Foner and Richard Alba, "The Second Generation from the Last Great Wave of Immigration: Setting the Record Straight," *The Migration Information Source* (October, 2006): http://www.migrationinformation.org/Feature/display.cfm?id=439; Gary Gerstle, *American Crucible: Race and Nation in the Twentieth Century* (Princeton: Princeton University Press, 2001); Thomas Guglielmo, *White on Arrival: Italians, Race, Color and Power in Chicago, 1890–1945* (New York: Oxford University Press, 2003); Joel Perlmann, *Italians Then, Mexicans Now: Immigrant Origins and Second-Generation Progress, 1890–2000* (New York: Russell Sage Foundation, 2005); David Roediger, *Working toward Whiteness: How America's Immigrants Became White; The Strange Journey from Ellis Island to the Suburbs* (New York: Basic Books, 2005).

15. On the history of anti-Catholicism, see, for example, Philip Jenkins, *The New Anti-Catholicism: The Last Acceptable Prejudice* (Oxford: Oxford University Press, 2003).

16. Quoted in ibid., 23.

17. John Higham, *Strangers in the Land: Patterns of American Nativism, 1860–1925* (New York: Atheneum, 1970); Kenneth Jackson, *The Ku Klux Klan in the City, 1915–1930* (New York: Oxford University Press, 1967); John McGreevey, *Catholicism and American Freedom: A History* (New York: W. W. Norton, 2003).

18. Roediger, *Working toward Whiteness*, 74.

19. Richard Alba, *Italian Americans: Into the Twilight of Ethnicity* (Englewood Cliffs: Prentice-Hall, 1985), 68; Roediger, *Working toward Whiteness*, 37. Noel Ignatiev (*How the Irish Became White* [New York: Routledge, 1995], 61], for instance, displays a cartoon published in 1852, a date well before any appreciable Italian immigration took place, that refers to "de guinea people."

20. Mae Ngai, *Impossible Subjects: Illegal Aliens and the Making of Modern America* (Princeton: Princeton University Press, 2004); Aristide Zolberg, *A Nation by Design: Immigration Policy in the Fashioning of America* (Cambridge, Mass.: Harvard University Press, 2006). Alone among Asian groups, Filipinos, who were at the time U.S. "nationals" since the Philippines was a protectorate of the United States, were still legally able to immigrate until 1934, when the Congress changed the legal status of the Philippines to a commonwealth and set it on a course toward independence; at that time, it also established an annual immigration quota of 50 for Filipinos, far lower than the quotas for other nations allowed to send immigrants (Zolberg, *Nation by Design*, 262).

21. Ngai, *Impossible Subjects*, chap. 1; Zolberg, *Nation by Design*, 263.

22. Stephen Jay Gould, *The Mismeasure of Man* (New York: W. W. Norton, 1981); Higham, *Strangers in the Land;* Lieberson, *Piece of the Pie.*

23. Edward A. Ross, *The Old World in the New* (New York: Century Company, 1914). The quotations can be found in Lieberson, *Piece of the Pie,* 25.

24. Alba, *Italian Americans;* Lieberson, *Piece of the Pie;* Stanley Lieberson and Mary Waters, *From Many Strands: Ethnic and Racial Groups in Contemporary America* (New York: Russell Sage Foundation, 1988).

25. For a fuller discussion, see Richard Alba, *Ethnic Identity: The Transformation of White America* (New Haven: Yale University Press, 1990); Alba and Nee, *Remaking the American Mainstream,* chap. 3; Mary Waters, *Ethnic Options: Choosing Identities in America* (Berkeley: University of California Press, 1990).

26. Hubert Blalock, *Toward a Theory of Minority-Group Relations* (New York: Wiley, 1967).

27. Leonard Covello, *The Social Background of the Italo-American School Child* (Totowa: Rowman & Littlefield, 1973); Joel Perlmann, *Ethnic Differences: Schooling and Social Structure among the Irish, Italians, Jews and Blacks in an American City, 1880–1935* (Cambridge: Cambridge University Press, 1988); Sharon Sassler, "School Participation of Immigrant Youths in the Early 20th Century: Integration or Segmented Assimilation?" *Sociology of Education* 79 (2006): 1–24.

28. Herbert Gans, *The Urban Villagers: Group and Class in the Life of Italian-Americans* (New York: Free Press, [1962] 1982); Nathan Glazer and Daniel Patrick Moynihan, *Beyond the Melting Pot: The Negroes, Puerto Ricans, Jews, Italians, and Irish of New York City* (Cambridge: MIT Press, [1963] 1970); Joseph Ryan, *White Ethnics: Life in Working-Class America* (Englewood Cliffs: Prentice-Hall, 1973); John Skrentny, *The Minority-Rights Revolution* (Cambridge, Mass.: Harvard University Press, 2002).

29. Steven Erie, *Rainbow's End: Irish-Americans and the Dilemmas of Urban Machine Politics, 1840–1985* (Berkeley: University of California, 1988).

30. Richard Alba and Reid Golden, "Patterns of Interethnic Marriage in the United States," *Social Forces* 65 (September, 1986): 203–223; Deanna Pagnini and S. Philip Morgan, "Intermarriage and Social Distance among U.S. Immigrants at the Turn of the Century," *American Journal of Sociology* 96 (September, 1990): 405–432; Paul Spickard, *Mixed Blood: Ethnic Identity and Intermarriage in Twentieth-Century America* (Madison: University of Wisconsin Press, 1989).

31. There is one respect in which the fit is imperfect: there was very little illegal immigration associated with the European immigration of the early twentieth century, since there were, until the literacy restriction enacted in 1917, very few restrictions to breach (see Ngai, *Impossible Subjects*). Illegal or unauthorized immigration creates severe handicaps for many Latin-American immigrants, especially those from Mexico and Central America, and arguably for their U.S.-born children, who grow up in families that suffer from low incomes and other disadvantages. Nevertheless, the children of the undocumented are U.S. citizens when they are born on U.S. soil.

32. Frederik Barth, *Ethnic Groups and Boundaries* (Boston: Little Brown, 1969), 9–38; Stephen Cornell and Douglas Hartmann, *Ethnicity and*

Race: Making Identities in a Changing World, 2nd ed. (Thousand Oaks, Calif.: Pine Forge Press, 2006); Pierre van den Berghe, *Race and Racism: A Comparative Perspective* (New York: John Wiley, 1967).

33. Joane Nagel, "Constructing Ethnicity: Creating and Recreating Ethnic Identity and Culture," *Social Problems* 41 (February, 1994): 101–126; Michael Omi and Howard Winant, *Racial Formation in the United States: From the 1960s to the 1990s,* 2nd ed. (New York: Routledge & Kegan Paul, 1994).

34. Robert Blauner, *Racial Oppression in America* (New York: Harper & Row, 1972); Eduardo Bonilla-Silva, "'This Is a White Country': The Racial Ideology of the Western Nations of the World-System," *Sociological Inquiry* 70 (April, 2000): 188–214; Fredrickson, *Racism;* Omi and Winant, *Racial Formation;* Howard Winant, "Race and Race Theory," *Annual Review of Sociology* 26 (2000): 169–185. The so-called postcolonial literature has also contributed to this vein of thought; see, for example, Edward Said, *Orientalism* (New York: Pantheon Books, 1978).

35. The relevance of the Irish case for critical ethno-racial distinctions in U.S. society is recognized by Richard Williams in *Hierarchical Structures and Social Value: The Creation of Black and Irish Identities in the United States* (Cambridge: Cambridge University Press, 1990). His argument, however, is concerned with how these distinctions were historically established, rather than with how they have changed in recent history. Orlando Patterson, in *The Ordeal of Integration: Progress and Resentment in America's "Racial Crisis"* (New York: Basic Books, 1997), also comments insightfully on the relevance of the Irish case, as does Michael Hechter in *Internal Colonialism: The Celtic Fringe in British National Development, 1536–1966* (Berkeley: University of California Press, 1975).

36. For accounts of this history, see Theodore Allen, *The Invention of the White Race: The Origin of Racial Oppression in Anglo-America* (London: Verson, 1997); James Lydon, *The Making of Ireland: From Ancient Times to the Present* (London: Routledge, 1998); and Lawrence McCaffrey, *Ireland: From Colony to Nation State* (Englewood Cliffs: Prenctice-Hall, 1979).

37. The tendency to racialize the colonized was not limited to the English, of course. Leo Lucassen (in *The Immigrant Threat: The Integration of Old and New Migrants in Europe since 1850* [Urbana: University of Illinois Press, 2005]) argues persuasively that similar tendencies at work in the French colonization of Algeria produced durable stereotypes, which, im-

ported to the French metropole by the *pieds noirs* after Algerian independence, have affected the place of Algerian immigrants.

38. L. P. Curtis, *Anglo-Saxons and Celts: A Study of Anti-Irish Prejudice in Victorian England,* Conference on British Studies, University of Bridgeport, 1968.

39. Ibid., 84.

40. Ibid., 36–36.

41. David Roediger, *The Wages of Whiteness: Race and the Making of the American Working Class* (New York: Verso, 1991), 133; Ignatiev, *How the Irish,* 41.

42. Curtis, *Anglo-Saxons and Celts,* 90.

43. This is hardly my argument alone; see, for example, Stephen Cornell and Douglas Hartmann, "Conceptual Confusions and Divides: Race, Ethnicity, and the Study of Immigration," in Nancy Foner and George Fredrickson, eds., *Not Just Black and White: Historical and Contemporary Perspectives on Immigration, Race, and Ethnicity in the United States* (New York: Russell Sage Foundation, 2004); Patterson, *Ordeal of Integration;* and Andreas Wimmer, "The Making and Unmaking of Ethnic Boundaries: A Multilevel Process Theory," *American Journal of Sociology* (January, 2008): 970–1022.

44. Van den Berghe, *Race and Racism.*

45. Douglas Massey and Garth Lundy, "Use of Black English and Racial Discrimination in Urban Housing Markets: New Methods and Findings," *Urban Affairs Review* 36 (2001): 470–496.

46. David Lopez and Ricardo Stanton-Salazar, "Mexican Americans: A Second Generation at Risk," in Rubén G. Rumbaut and Alejandro Portes, eds., *Ethnicities: Children of Immigrants in America* (Berkley: University of California Press, 2001); Edward Telles and Vilma Ortiz, *Generations of Exclusion: Mexican Americans, Assimilation, and Race* (New York: Russell Sage Foundation).

47. Joseph Ruane and Jennifer Todd, *The Dynamics of Conflict in Northern Ireland: Power, Conflict and Emancipation* (Cambridge: Cambridge University Press, 1996), chap. 3.

48. I am not alone in using this term. David Hollinger also employs it in *Post-Ethnic America: Beyond Multiculturalism* (New York: Basic, 1995).

49. The clever research of David Harris ("In the Eye of the Beholder: Observed Race and Observer Characteristics," Population Studies Center, University of Michigan, 2002) on the identifiability of race in pictures of

faces with mixed racial characteristics demonstrates the lack of certainty that creeps in.

50. Social boundaries have been the focus of considerable attention by sociologists in recent years. See Michèle Lamont and Virág Molnár, "The Study of Boundaries in the Social Sciences," *Annual Review of Sociology* 28 (2002): 167–195; Charles Tilly, *Durable Inequality* (Berkeley: University of California Press, 2004); Wimmer, "Making and Unmaking."

51. Michèle Lamont, *The Dignity of Working Men: Morality and the Boundaries of Race, Class, and Immigration* (Cambridge, Mass.: Harvard University Press, 2000).

52. Tilly, *Durable Inequality.*

53. Jerome Karabel, *The Chosen: The Hidden History of Admission and Exclusion at Harvard, Yale, and Princeton* (New York: Houghton Mifflin, 2006).

54. Cosmetic surgery played a crucial role in diminishing some physiognomic differences, such as the prominent noses of some Jews and other ethnics; see Sander Gilman, *Making the Body Beautiful: A Cultural History of Aesthetic Surgery* (Princeton: Princeton University Press, 1999), chap. 6.

55. McGreevey, *Catholicism.*

56. Richard Alba, "Bright vs. Blurred Boundaries: Second-Generation Assimilation and Exclusion in France, Germany, and the United States," *Ethnic and Racial Studies* 28 (January, 2005): 20–49. The distinction employed here owes a great deal to concepts developed by Rainer Bauböck ("The Integration of Immigrants," Council of Europe, Strasbourg, 1994) and Aristide Zolberg and Long Litt Woon, "Why Islam Is Like Spanish: Cultural Incorporation in Europe and the United States," *Politics & Society* 27 (1999): 5–38.

A recent study of the second generation in New York suggests that its experience is one of blurred boundaries; see Philip Kasinitz, John Mollenkopf, Mary Waters, and Jennifer Holdaway, *Inheriting the City: The Children of Immigrants Come of Age* (New York and Cambridge, Mass.: Russell Sage Foundation and Harvard University Press, 2008).

57. Philip Roth, *The Plot against America* (New York: Houghton Mifflin, 2004).

58. Quoted by Irvin Child, *Italian or American? The Second Generation in Conflict* (New Haven: Yale University Press, 1943), 88.

59. Richard Alba, "Assimilation's Quiet Tide," *The Public Interest* 119 (Spring, 1995): 1–18; Alba and Nee, *Remaking the American Mainstream;* Lieberson and Waters, *From Many Strands;* Joel Perlmann, *Italians Then, Mexicans Now: Immigrant Origins and Second-Generation Progress, 1890–2000* (New York: Russell Sage Foundation, 2005); Joel Perlmann and Roger Waldinger, "Second Generation Decline? Children of Immigrants, Past and Present—A Reconsideration," *International Migration Review* 31 (Winter, 1997): 893–922.

60. Milton Gordon, *Assimilation in American Life* (New York: Oxford University Press, 1964). For a more contemporary statement of assimilation theory, see Alba and Nee, *Remaking;* and Frank Bean and Gillian Stevens, *America's Newcomers and the Dynamics of Diversity* (New York: Russell Sage Foundation, 2003). Also useful in this respect are the essays in Tamar Jacoby, ed., *Reinventing the Melting Pot: The New Immigrants and What It Means to Be American* (New York: Basic Books, 2004); and in Peter Kivisto, ed., *Incorporating Diversity: Rethinking Assimilation in a Multicultural Age* (Boulder: Paradigm Publishers, 2005).

Assimilation has frequently been contested in recent decades. For critiques, see Alejandro Portes, Patricia Fernández-Kelly, and William Haller, "Segmented Assimilation on the Ground: The New Second Generation in Early Adulthood," *Ethnic and Racial Studies* 28 (November, 2005): 1000–1040; Rubén Rumbaut, "Assimilation and Its Discontents: Ironies and Paradoxes," in Charles Hirschman, Josh DeWind, and Philip Kasinitz, eds., *The Handbook of International Migration: The American Experience* (New York: Russell Sage Foundation, 1999); Min Zhou, "Segmented Assimilation: Issues, Controversies, and Recent Research on the New Second Generation," *International Migration Review* 31 (Winter, 1997): 975–1008.

Valuable defenses and revisions have been offered by Elliot Barkan, "Race, Religion, and Nationality in American Society: A Model of Ethnicity—from Contact to Assimilation," *Journal of American Ethnic History* 14 (Winter, 1995): 38–101; Russell Kazal, "Revisiting Assimilation: The Rise, Fall, and Reappraisal of a Concept in American Ethnic History," *American Historical Review* 100 (April, 1995): 437–472; and Ewa Morawska, "In Defense of the Assimilation Model," *Journal of American Ethnic History* 13 (Winter, 1994): 76–87. A survey of evidence about the assimilation of contemporary immigrant groups is given by Mary Waters and Tomás Jiménez, "Assessing Immigrant Assimilation: New Empirical and Theoretical Challenges," *Annual Review of Sociology* 31 (2005): 105–125.

61. Gordon, *Assimilation,* 127–128.

62. Matthew Frye Jacobson, *Roots, Too: White Ethnic Revival in Post-Civil Rights America* (Cambridge, Mass.: Harvard University Press, 2006).

63. Herbert Gans, "Symbolic Ethnicity: The Future of Ethnic Groups and Cultures in America," *Ethnic and Racial Studies* 2 (January, 1979): 1–20.

64. For the whiteness narrative, see Karen Brodkin, *How Jews Became White Folks and What That Says about Race in America* (New Brunswick: Rutgers University Press, 1998); Guglielmo, *White on Arrival;* Ian Haney-Lopez, *White by Law, The Legal Construction of Race,* rev. and updated ed. (New York: New York University Press, 2006); Ignatiev, *How the Irish;* Matthew Frye Jacobson, *Whiteness of a Different Color: European Immigrants and the Alchemy of Race* (Cambridge, Mass.: Harvard University Press, 1998); Roediger, *Wages of Whiteness;* idem, *Working toward Whiteness.* For a valuable critique, see Eric Arnesen, "Whiteness and the Historians' Imagination," *International Labor and Working-Class History* 60 (Fall, 2001): 3–32.

65. Spickard, *Mixed Blood.*

66. Ira Katznelson, *When Affirmative Action Was White: An Untold History of Racial Inequality in Twentieth-Century America* (New York: W. W. Norton, 2005); Roediger, *Working toward Whiteness.*

67. Dalton Conley, *Being Black, Living in the Red: Race, Wealth, and Social Policy in America* (Berkeley: University of California Press, 1999); Melvin Oliver and Thomas Shapiro, *Black Wealth/White Wealth: A New Perspective on Racial Inequality* (New York: Routledge, 1995).

68. Katznelson, *When Affirmative Action;* see also Brodkin, *How Jews.*

69. Katznelson, *When Affirmative Action,* 134.

70. Stanley Lieberson also addresses this question in *Piece of the Pie.*

71. Gerstle, *American Crucible,* 185.

3. Solving the Puzzle: A New Theory of Boundary Change

1. Bernard Rosen, "Race, Ethnicity, and the Achievement Syndrome," *American Sociological Review* 24 (February, 1959): 47–60.

2. Ibid., 52.

3. Herbert Gans, *The Urban Villagers: Group and Class in the Life of Italian-Americans* (New York: Free Press, [1962] 1982); Fred Strodtbeck, "Family Interaction, Values, and Achievement," in David McClelland, Alfred Baldwin, and Urie Bronfenbrenner, eds., *Talent and Society* (Princeton: D. Van Nostrand, 1958).

4. David McClelland with John Atkinson, R. A. Clark and E. L. Lowell, *The Achievement Motive* (New York: Appleton-Century-Crofts, 1953), 277.

5. Gerhard Lenski, *The Religious Factor: A Sociologist's Inquiry* (New York: Doubleday, 1961), 283–284.

6. Peter Binzen, *Whitetown USA* (New York: Vintage, 1970); Michael Novak, *The Rise of the Unmeltable Ethnics* (New York: Macmillan, 1972); Joseph Ryan, *White Ethnics: Life in Working-Class America* (Englewood Cliffs: Prentice-Hall, 1973).

7. Jonathan Rieder, *Canarsie: The Jews and Italians of Brooklyn against Liberalism* (Cambridge: Harvard University Press, 1985). This view reappears in many of the films of Spike Lee, such as *Do the Right Thing* and *Summer of Sam*.

8. For the data on parochial-school attendance, see Andrew Greeley and Peter Rossi, *The Education of Catholic Americans* (Chicago: Aldine, 1966), 33. See also David Lopez, "Whither the Flock? The Catholic Church and the Success of Mexicans in America," in Richard Alba, Albert Raboteau and Josh DeWind, eds., *Immigration and Religion in America: Comparative and Historical Perspectives* (New York: NYU Press, 2008); Robert Putnam, "E Pluribus Unum: Diversity and Community in the Twenty-First Century: The 2006 Skytte Prize Lecture," *Scandinavian Political Studies* 30 (2007): 137–174; Peter Steinfels, *A People Adrift: The Crisis of the Roman Catholic Church in America* (New York: Simon & Schuster, 2003).

9. Ian Baruma, *Murder in Amsterdam* (New York: Penguin, 2006); Nancy Foner and Richard Alba, "Immigrant Religion in the U.S. and Western Europe: Bridge or Barrier to Inclusion?" *International Migration Review* 42 (Summer, 2008): 360–392; Leo Lucassen, *The Immigrant Threat: The Integration of Old and New Migrants in Europe since 1850* (Urbana: University of Illinois Press, 2005).

10. On Brazil, see Edward Telles, *Race in Another America: The Significance of*

Skin Color in Brazil (Princeton: Princeton University Press, 2004); on the Portuguese of Hawaii, see James Geschwender, Rita Carroll-Seguin, and Howard Brill, "The Portuguese and Haoles of Hawaii: Implications for the Origin of Ethnicity," *American Sociological Review* 53 (August, 1988): 515–527. I am grateful to Irene Bloemraad for suggesting the example of the Portuguese to me.

11. Hubert Blalock, *Toward a Theory of Minority-Group Relations* (New York: Wiley, 1967); Herbert Blumer, "Race Prejudice as a Sense of Group Position," *Pacific Sociological Review* 1 (1958): 3–7; Susan Olzak, *The Dynamics of Ethnic Competition and Conflict* (Stanford: Stanford University Press, 1992).

12. For a relevant and recent review of social identity theory, see S. Alexander Haslam, *Psychology in Organizations: The Social Identity Approach* (London: Sage, 2004), chap. 2. Also pertinent to the discussion in the text are Brian Mullen, Rupert Brown, and Colleen Smith, "Ingroup Bias as a Function of Salience, Relevance, and Status: An Integration," *European Journal of Social Psychology* 22 (1992): 103–122; and Jan Stets and Peter Burke, "Identity Theory and Social Identity Theory," *Social Psychology Quarterly* 63 (2000): 224–237. For relevant research inspired by realistic group conflict theory, see Lawrence Bobo, "Prejudice as Group Position: Micro-Foundations of a Sociological Approach to Racism and Race Relations," *Journal of Social Issues* 45 (1999): 445–472; Lawrence Bobo and Vincent Hutchings, "Perceptions of Racial Group Competition: Extending Blumer's Theory of Group Position to a Multiracial Context," *American Sociological Review* 61 (1996): 951–972; Victoria Esses, John Dovidio, Lynne Jackson, and Tamara Armstrong, "The Immigration Dilemma: The Role of Perceived Group Competition, Ethnic Prejudice, and National Identity," *Journal of Social Issues* 57 (2001): 389–412.

13. Rupert Brown, *Prejudice: Its Social Psychology* (Oxford: Wiley-Blackwell, 1995); Putnam, "E Pluribus Unum."

14. Charles Tilly, *Durable Inequality* (Berkeley: University of California Press, 1998).

15. Richard Alba and Roxane Silberman, "The Children of Immigrants and Host-Society Educational Systems: Mexicans in the U.S. and North Africans in France," *Teachers College Record* (2009).

16. Stéphane Beaud, *80% au Bac? Et après? Les Enfants de la Démocratisation Scolaire* (Paris: Éditions La Découverte, 2002).

17. Roxane Silberman, Richard Alba, and Irène Fournier, "Segmented Assimilation in France? Discrimination in the Labor Market against the Second Generation," *Ethnic and Racial Studies* 30 (January, 2007): 1–27.

18. Stephen Steinberg, *The Academic Melting Pot* (New York: McGraw-Hill, 1974); Jerome Karabel, *The Chosen: The Hidden History of Admission and Exclusion at Harvard, Yale, and Princeton* (New York: Houghton Mifflin, 2006).

19. Tilly, *Durable Inequality.*

20. These processes were aptly described as "monopolistic closure" by one of sociology's founders, Max Weber; for an insightful discussion of Weber's ideas on this topic, see Frank Parkin, *Marxism and Class Theory: A Bourgeois Critique* (New York: Columbia University Press, 1979).

21. Kenneth Jackson, *The Ku Klux Klan in the City, 1915–1930* (New York: Oxford University Press, 1967), 18–21.

22. In the literature on social boundaries, the topic of boundary change has not received much attention, as the title of Charles Tilly's book, *Durable Inequality*, suggests. Tilly, for example, claims that boundaries are reinforced by the attempts of disadvantaged groups to overcome their disadvantage because they mobilize along lines defined by the boundary; but he appears to have in mind only a social-movement model of how boundaries are altered.

    Some ideas about boundary change are broached by Andreas Wimmer, "The Making and Unmaking of Ethnic Boundaries: A Multilevel Process Theory," *American Journal of Sociology* (February, 2008): 970–1022.

23. Karabel, *The Chosen*, 245.

24. Ibid.

25. Richard Alba, "Cohorts and the Dynamics of Ethnic Change," in Matilda White Riley, Bettina Huber, and Beth Hess, eds., *Social Structures and Human Lives* (Newbury Park: Sage, 1988); idem, "Assimilation's Quiet Tide," *Public Interest* 119 (Spring, 1995): 1–18.

26. The McCarthy period featured several cross-currents, including a critique by some Irish Catholics, such as McCarthy, of the loyalty of their status superiors at the time, namely high-born WASPs like Alger Hiss and Owen Lattimore. One could argue therefore that the Red Scare of

the 1950s was an attempt at moral and ideological, if not social, ascent by Catholics. This element is highlighted by Gary Gerstle in *American Crucible: Race and Nation in the Twentieth Century* (Princeton: Princeton University Press, 2001), 241–56. However, as he notes, "the percentage of Jews who became Communists, while small in relation to the overall Jewish population, was probably higher than that of any other group" (Gerstle, *American Crucible*, 247). Jews therefore were rightly concerned about the negative impact for them of McCarthy's crusade.

27. Wikipedia, "McCarthyism": http://en.wikipedia.org/wiki/McCarthyism (retrieved 2/29/2008).

28. President's Commission on Law Enforcement and Administration of Justice, *The Challenge of Crime in a Free Society, Task Force Report: Organized Crime* (Washington, DC: U.S. Government Printing Office, 1967), 7.

29. Richard Hofstadter, *The Paranoid Style in American Politics* (New York: Knopf, 1965).

30. The cases of Geraldine Ferraro and Mario Cuomo come readily to mind. In both cases, the suspicions were mobilized when these politicians sought national office but not before. They were also brought to bear on Rudolph Giuliani in the late 1990s, but they were blunted in his case, probably because his many prosecutions of organized-crime figures when he was the U.S. attorney for the New York region made the suspicions implausible. Perhaps also by then, the continuing social ascent of Italian Americans made other Americans more skeptical of the stereotype.

31. Leonard Dinnerstein, *Antisemitism in America* (New York: Oxford University Press, 1994); Gerstle, *American Crucible;* Karabel, *The Chosen;* Charles Silberman, *A Certain People: American Jews and Their Lives Today* (New York: Summit, 1985).

32. Dinnerstein, *Antisemitism,* 151.

33. On religious intermarriage, see Alba, "Cohorts"; Ruby Jo Reeves Kennedy, "Single or Triple Melting Pot? Intermarriage Trends in New Haven, 1870–1940," *American Journal of Sociology* 49 (January, 1944): 331–339; idem, "Single or Triple Melting Pot? Intermarriage in New Haven, 1870–1950," *American Journal of Sociology* 58 (1952): 56–59; Joel Perlmann, "The American Jewish Periphery: An Overview," working

paper, Levy Institute, Bard College: http://www.levy.org/pubs/wp_473.pdf (retrieved 2/29/2008).

34. Hadley Cantril, "Educational and Economic Composition of Religious Groups: An Analysis of Poll Data," *American Journal of Sociology* 48 (March, 1943): 579.

35. Albert Mayer and Harry Sharp, "Religious Preference and Worldly Success," *American Sociological Review* 27 (April, 1962): 227.

36. David Roediger, *Working toward Whiteness: How America's Immigrants Became White; The Strange Journey from Ellis Island to the Suburbs* (New York: Basic Books, 2005); Jeffrey Mirel, "Civic Education and Changing Definitions of American Identity, 1900–1950," *Educational Review* 54 (2003): 143–152.

37. Samuel Huntington, *Who Are We? The Challenges to America's National Identity* (New York: Simon & Schuster, 2004).

38. Claudia Goldin and Robert Margo, "The Great Compression: The Wage Structure in the United States at Mid-Century," *Quarterly Journal of Economics* 107 (February, 1992): 1–34; Claudia Goldin and Lawrence Katz, "Decreasing (and Then Increasing) Inequality in America: A Tale of Two Half-Centuries," in Finis Welch, ed., *The Causes and Consequences of Increasing Inequality* (Chicago: University of Chicago Press, 2001).

39. Douglas Massey, *Categorically Unequal: The American Stratification System* (New York: Russell Sage Foundation, 2007); Thomas Piketty and Emmanuel Saez, "Income Inequality in the United States, 1913–1998," *Quarterly Journal of Economics* 118 (February, 2003): 1–39.

40. Max Weber, "Class, Status, Party," in Hans Gerth and C. Wright Mills, eds., *From Max Weber: Essays in Sociology* (New York: Oxford University Press, 1958); see also the discussion in Parkin, *Marxism and Class Theory.*

41. I intend this as a generalization of a concept that has long been employed in social mobility research: structural mobility, which arises because of changes over time in the distribution of the labor force across occupations or similarly defined positions. Consequently, some degree of intergenerational mobility is "forced," since these changes make it impossible for all children to occupy the same labor-market position as their parents. The concept of structural mobility is usually contrasted

with that of exchange or circulation mobility, which allows upward movement insofar as it is matched by downward movement. (See Michael Sobel, Michael Hout, and Otis Dudley Duncan, "Exchange, Structure, and Symmetry in Occupational Mobility," *American Journal of Sociology* 91 [September, 1985]: 359–372.) Non-zero-sum mobility includes such structurally generated mobility, but it can also arise for demographic reasons, as will become subsequently clear.

42. Karabel, *The Chosen*.

43. Martin Trow, "The Second Transformation of American Secondary Education," *International Journal of Comparative Sociology* 2 (1961): 144–166.

44. Karabel, *The Chosen*.

45. For a detailed analysis of twentieth-century trends in the occupational structure through 1970, see David Featherman and Robert Hauser, *Opportunity and Change* (New York: Academic Press, 1978).

46. Roger Waldinger, "Did Manufacturing Matter? The Experience of Yesterday's Second Generation: A Reassessment," *International Migration Review* (Spring, 2007): 3–39.

47. Herbert Gans, *The Levittowners: Ways of Life and Politics in a New Suburban Community* (New York: Pantheon, 1967), 23–24.

48. Richard Alba, John Logan, and Kyle Crowder, "White Ethnic Neighborhoods and Spatial Assimilation: The Greater New York Region, 1980–1990," *Social Forces* 75 (March, 1997): 883–912; Richard Alba, John Logan, and Brian Stults, "How Segregated Are Middle-Class African Americans?" *Social Problems* 47 (November, 2000): 543–558; Gans, *Levittowners;* Douglas Massey and Nancy Denton, *American Apartheid: Segregation and the Making of the Underclass* (Cambridge: Harvard University Press, 1993); Mary Pattillo-McCoy, *Picket Fences: Privilege and Peril among the Black Middle Class* (Chicago: University of Chicago Press, 1999); Thomas Sugrue, *The Origins of the Urban Crisis: Race and Inequality in Postwar Detroit* (Princeton: Princeton University Press, 1996); Olivier Zunz, *The Changing Face of Inequality: Urbanization, Industrialization, and Immigrants in Detroit, 1880–1920* (Chicago: University of Chicago Press, [1982] 2000).

49. Richard Polenberg, *One Nation Divisible: Class, Race, and Ethnicity in the United States since 1938* (New York: Viking, 1980).

50. Quoted by John Morton Blum, *V Was for Victory: Politics and American*

Culture during World War II (New York: Harcourt Brace Jovanovich, 1976), 63.

51. Gary Gerstle (*American Crucible,* 236–237) makes the same point with a different set of references.

52. An indication of the enlightened attitudes that could be found among elite white Protestants after the war is Digby Baltzell's *The Protestant Establishment: Aristocracy and Caste in America* (New York: Random House), originally published in 1964. Baltzell's book deplores the relatively closed nature of the Protestant elite and argues that an open elite, capable of absorbing talented individuals from non-Protestant backgrounds, is in the best interest of American society.

53. Dinnerstein, *Antisemitism,* 159.

54. Stanley Lieberson, *A Piece of the Pie: Blacks and White Immigrants since 1880* (Berkeley: University of California Press, 1980), 78–81.

55. W. Vance Grant and Leo Eiden, *Digest of Educational Statistics, 1980* (Washington, D.C.: National Center for Educational Statistics, 1980).

56. Thomas Guglielmo, *White on Arrival: Italians, Race, Color, and Power in Chicago, 1890–1945* (New York: Oxford University Press, 2003), 164; also Kenneth Jackson, *Crabgrass Frontier: The Suburbanization of the United States* (New York: Oxford University Press, 1985); Dennis Judd and Todd Swanstrom, *City Politics: Private Power and Public Policy* (New York: HarperCollins, 1994); Massey and Denton, *American Apartheid.*

57. Angus Maddison, *The World Economy: A Millennial Perspective* (Paris: OECD, 2001), Table B-18. Available also at http://www.theworldeconomy.org/publications/worldeconomy/statistics.htm.

58. Lieberson, in *Piece of the Pie,* has done the most to develop the queuing notion to explain ethno-racial inequality.

59. See Charles Hirschman and Ellen Kraly, "Racial and Ethnic Inequality in the United States, 1940 and 1950: The Impact of Geographic Location and Human Capital," *International Migration Review* 24 (Spring, 1990): 4–33. See also, in this context, Stewart Tolnay, "African Americans and Immigrants in Northern Cities: The Effects of Relative Group Size on Occupational Standing in 1920," *Social Forces* 80 (December, 2001): 573–604.

60. Kevin Stainback, Corre Robinson, and Donald Tomaskovic-Devey, "Race and Workplace Integration: A Politically Mediated Process," *American Behavioral Scientist* 48 (2005): 1200–1228.

61. Mary Waters, *Ethnic Options: Choosing Identities in America* (Berkeley: University of California Press, 1990).

4. Contemporary Dynamics of Minority Mobility

1. Herbert Gans, "Second Generation Decline: Scenarios for the Economic and Ethnic Futures of Post-1965 American Immigrants," *Ethnic and Racial Studies* 15 (April, 1992): 173–192; Alejandro Portes and Min Zhou, "The New Second Generation: Segmented Assimilation and Its Variants," *The Annals* 530 (November, 1993): 74–96.
For broad surveys of how the children of contemporary immigrants are faring, see Philip Kasinitz, John Mollenkopf, Mary Waters, and Jennifer Holdaway, *Inheriting the City: The Children of Immigrants Come of Age* (New York and Cambridge, Mass.: Russell Sage Foundation and Harvard University Press, 2008); Alejandro Portes and Rubén Rumbaut, *Legacies: Children of Immigrants in America* (Berkeley: University of California Press, 2001); and Rubén Rumbaut and Alejandro Portes, *Ethnicities: Children of Immigrants in America* (Berkeley: University of California Press, 2001).

2. Annette Bernhardt, Martina Morris, Mark Handcock, and Marc Scott, *Divergent Paths: Economic Mobility in the New American Labor Market* (New York: Russell Sage Foundation, 2001); Jacob Hacker, *The Great Risk Shift: The Assault on American Jobs, Families, Health Care, and Retirement and How You Can Fight Back* (New York: Oxford University Press, 2006).

3. Portes and Rumbaut, *Legacies*.

4. Ron Haskins, Julia Isaacs, and Isabel Sawhill, *Getting Ahead or Losing Ground: Economic Mobility in America* (Washington, D.C.: Brookings Institution, 2008); Kathryn Neckerman and Florencia Torche, "Inequality: Causes and Consequences," *Annual Review of Sociology* 33 (2007): 335–357.

5. Elijah Anderson, *Streetwise: Race, Class, and Change in an Urban Community* (Chicago: University of Chicago Press, 1992); idem, *Code of the Street: Decency, Violence, and the Moral Life of the Inner City* (New York: W. W. Norton, 2000); Kathryn Edin and Maria Kefalas, *Promises I Can Keep: Why Poor Women Put Motherhood before Marriage* (Berkeley: University of California Press, 2005); Douglas Massey, "American Apart-

heid: Segregation and the Making of the Urban Underclass," *American Journal of Sociology* 95 (1990): 1153–1188; William Julius Wilson, *When Work Disappears* (New York: Knopf, 1996).

6. Signithia Fordham and John Ogbu, "Black Students' School Success: Coping with the Burden of 'Acting White,'" *Urban Review* 18 (September, 1986): 176–206; Maria Matute-Bianchi, "Situational Ethnicity and Patterns of School Performance among Immigrant and Nonimmigrant Mexican-Descent Students," in Margaret Gibson and John Ogbu, eds., *Minority Status and Schooling: A Comparative Study of Immigrant and Involuntary Minorities* (New York: Garland, 1991); John Ogbu, "Immigrant and Involuntary Minorities in Comparative Perspective," ibid.; Portes and Zhou, "New Second Generation"; Rubén Rumbaut, "Turning Points in the Transition to Adulthood: Determinants of Educational Attainment, Incarceration, and Early Childbearing among Children of Immigrants," *Ethnic and Racial Studies* 28 (November 2005): 1041–1086.

7. Dowell Myers (*Immigrants and Boomers: Forging a New Social Contract for the Future of America* [New York: Russell Sage Foundation, 2007]) has already called attention to the significance of the baby boomers' retirement for Hispanic immigrants and their children. He emphasizes the economic needs of the boomers arising from their retirement—for workers to generate the national income that will help support them and for young families economically secure enough to buy their homes—and argues for a new "social contract" that will allow the economic advance of immigrant-origin Latinos. This emphasis is consistent with my arguments, but I focus more broadly on the potential for ethno-racial change through the mechanism of non-zero-sum mobility.

8. Full-time workers are defined primarily as those who work at least fifty 35-hour (or more) weeks of the year for pay. For primary- and secondary-school teachers, the minimum number of weeks worked to be considered full-time is dropped to thirty-seven. In order to accommodate workers in other seasonal occupations, anyone who reports working at least 1,820 hours (that is, the equivalent of 52 weeks × 35 hours/week) during the year is also counted as full-time. Except for the last provision, this definition is consistent with the Census Bureau's concept of "year-round full-time worker." In Census data, these definitions are applied to the year prior to the data collection (that is, 1999 in the 2000

Census), which is also the year to which income data refer. In computing the pay of full-time workers, I have included not just their salary and wages but also their self-employment earnings (when these are positive).

9. There are 475 distinct occupational codes in the 2000 Census for which we can measure earnings in the prior year (1999). These occupational codes encompass widely varying numbers of workers, in some cases a few thousand (for example, "subway, streetcar, and other rail transportation workers," a category that included fewer than 10,000 full-time workers in 2000) and in other cases a million or more (for example, "managers, all other," a residual that still included 1.7 million). The average size of the Census occupational categories is about 180,000 thousand workers. The earnings of the full-time workers in these occupations are estimated as the median value of salary and wages plus positive business earnings (if any). There is no way in Census data to be certain that earnings are entirely due to the occupation stated on the form.

10. Frank Parkin, *Class Inequality and Political Order* (London: Paladin, 1971), 18; David Grusky, "Foundations of a Neo-Durkheimian Class Analysis," in Erik Olin Wright, ed., *Approaches to Class Analysis* (New York: Cambridge University Press, 2005), 61. See also David Grusky and Jesper Sørensen, "Can Class Analysis Be Salvaged?" *American Journal of Sociology* 103 (March, 1998): 1187–1234; ChangHwan Kim and Arthur Sakamoto, "The Rise of Intra-occupational Wage Inequality in the United States, 1983 to 2002," *American Sociological Review* 73 (February, 2008): 129–157.

11. Kim Weeden and David Grusky, "The Case for a New Class Map," *American Journal of Sociology* 111 (July, 2005): 187–188.

12. The main alternative to the way I have constructed a ranking of occupations is the standard socioeconomic index of occupations, which is widely used by sociologists (as in, for example, the classic work on social stratification by Peter Blau and Otis Dudley Duncan, *The American Occupational Structure* [New York: Wiley, 1967]). The basis for this scale lies in prestige ratings collected by social surveys, which have been extrapolated to all detailed occupational categories through their correlations with educational attainment and income. Close inspection of the scale, especially in its upper reaches, reveals how problematic it would be for the measurement of the mobility of minorities into the higher tiers of the labor market. The scale gives too much status to occupations on

the basis of their educational requirements or their connections to education, independent of their economic potential. The top occupations, in fact, disproportionately represent education-related professions and teachers. According to the codes listed in Katherine Newman, *Chutes and Ladders: Navigating the Low-Wage Labor Market* (Cambridge, Mass., and New York: Harvard University Press and Russell Sage Foundation, 2006), app. C, the top occupation is "law teacher," which comes two points (on a scale with a range of 76 points) ahead of "lawyer." Executive and financial occupations are placed well down on the scale, which leads to some anomalies that are bothersome: for example, physical education teachers, are placed 5 points ahead of judges, a priority that seems to correspond neither with economic position nor with everyday social status. (The 5-point distance can be given concrete meaning by noting that it is roughly the same difference as is found between maids and some highly skilled trades, such as automobile mechanics.)

13. This is not to deny that intra-occupational income inequality could be increasing (see Kim and Sakamoto, "Rise of Intra-occupational Wage Inequality"). Perhaps students of stratification will devise a measure of labor-market position that is superior to occupation alone, for example, some combination of occupation and industry, but as of now that has not happened.

14. The definitions of the racial and ethnic categories are standard, though not as straightforward as in prior censuses, when mixed-race reporting was not allowed. The Hispanic category includes anyone who reports Hispanic origins regardless of race. Any non-Hispanic who reports black race, regardless of what other races are also checked, is here counted as black, and the Asian category is defined equivalently, to include anyone who reports an Asian race, as long as black race is not also reported. Non-Hispanic whites must report only the white race to be counted as such. The allocations of mixed-race individuals, most of whom are also white, to minority categories is sensible for my purposes insofar as intermarriage with a member of the dominant race is a primary mechanism of assimilation; to lose sight of the children of such intermarriages by placing them in the white category could, in effect, exert a downward bias on the achievements of the members of minority groups. In any event, the same principle has been followed for decades in the measurement of the Hispanic category; and defining the black

category in particular in an equivalent way therefore introduces an appropriate symmetry.

For nativity, one deviation from standard definitions has been made: because migration from Puerto Rico to the mainland is, from a cultural standpoint, similar to a migration across national borders, birth in Puerto Rico (in fact, outside of the fifty states) is counted here as foreign birth, even though it is not legally so.

15. Although I will not address ethno-racial shifts at the most elite levels, diversity is also increasing there; see Richard Zweigenhaft and G. William Domhoff, *Diversity in the Power Elite: How It Happened, Why It Matters* (Lanham, Md.: Rowman & Littlefield, 2006).

16. The knowledgeable reader may notice the one-year offset from the standard range for prime working age, 25–64 years. The shift is required because the determination of full-time employment is based on questions referring to the prior year (that is, 1999 in the 2000 Census); so the population to be analyzed is defined as the 25- to 64-year-olds of 1999, hence the 26- to 65-year-olds of 2000. To reduce confusion in the text, I generally adhere to this age definition throughout this and following chapters.

17. To reduce numbing repetition, I will often refer to U.S.-born blacks as "African Americans" and to U.S.-born Latinos as "Hispanic" or "Latino" Americans. I also sometimes abbreviate "non-Hispanic whites" to just "whites" or "Anglos."

18. Deirdre Royster, *Race and the Invisible Hand: How White Networks Exclude Black Men from Blue-Collar Jobs* (Berkeley: University of California Press, 2003); Roger Waldinger, *Still the Promised City? African-Americans and New Immigrants in Postindustrial New York* (Cambridge, Mass.: Harvard University Press, 1996).

19. The American Community Surveys are annual large-scale surveys of the Census Bureau that have been developed to collect social and economic data about Americans. They have replaced the previous instrument for this purpose, the long form of the decennial Census, which was used for the last time in 2000.

20. My claim of greater interaction as status equals between whites and minorities at higher tiers of the labor market would seem to be contradicted by research on workplace integration, which shows only small improvements since the 1980s. (See Donald Tomaskovic-Devey, Catherine

Zimmer, Kevin Stainback, Corre Robinson, Tiffany Taylor, and Tricia McTague, "Documenting Desegregation: Segregation in American Workplaces by Race, Ethnicity, and Sex, 1966–2003," *American Sociological Review* 71 [August, 2006]: 565–588.) However, for two reasons, there is not a contradiction. First, that research relies mainly on the well-known index of dissimilarity, the principal tool in segregation research. One reason that the index is so widely used is that it is not very sensitive to shifts in composition. However, as will shortly be made evident, the shifts in minority representation in top tiers have come about mainly through changes in composition, that is, growing numbers of minorities in the underlying population and throughout the workforce. Hence the shifts do not register well in the index of dissimilarity. The other reason is that the workforce changes are occurring among younger workers. The research on workplace integration is not able to control for worker age and thus cannot focus on the critical younger age groups.

21. Despite their small size, the changes are also statistically significant. For instance, in the case of the very small increase in the African-American share among 1965–1974 cohort workers in the top decile, the z statistic is 2.19, significant at the .05 level in a two-tailed test. Other comparisons cited in the paragraph are also significant.

22. The one risk they do not take into account, since they are on the basis of the number of surviving members of a cohort at a given point in time, is that of early death.

23. Eric Grodsky and Devah Pager, "The Structure of Disadvantage: Individual and Occupational Determinants of the Black-White Wage Gap," *American Sociological Review* 66 (August, 2001): 542–567.

24. Apart from recency, an advantage of using the ACS data is that they allow me to avoid a degree of circularity in the analysis, since a key variable, occupational earnings, is a construction based on individual earnings in the 2000 Census data. This advantage will become particularly important as the analysis continues, leading to a regression model predicting individual-level earnings in part based on occupational earnings. By applying this analysis to a fresh sample, we avoid the circularity that would arise from having each individual's earnings appear twice, once as the dependent variable and the other as a component (granted, very tiny because of the sample size) of the median earnings of an occupation.

25. The logged form of the dependent variable and the dummy-variable

format of the key independent variables, the ethno-racial/nativity categories, allow a simple conversion into relative percentage differences. Straightforward algebra shows that the percentage change in the dependent variable associated with a one-unit change in any of the dummy variables is given by: $100(e^b - 1)$, where b is the regression coefficient. This formula can be used to estimate the expected percentage difference of any minority category relative to the native-born non-Hispanic white one, with other variables held constant.

26. Kasinitz et al., *Inheriting the City.*
27. William Bowen and Derek Bok, *The Shape of the River: Long-term Consequences of Considering Race in College and University Admissions* (Princeton: Princeton University Press, 1998).
28. See, for example, Grodsky and Pager, "Structure of Disadvantage"; Melvin Thomas, Cedric Herring, and Hayward Horton, "Discrimination over the Life Course: A Synthetic Cohort Analysis of Earnings Differences between Black and White Males," *Social Problems* 41 (1994): 608–628; and Donald Tomaskovic-Devey, Melvin Thomas, and Kecia Johnson, "Race and the Accumulation of Human Capital across the Career: A Theoretical Model and Fixed-Effects Application," *American Journal of Sociology* 111 (July, 2005): 58–89.
29. Thomas, Herring, and Horton, "Discrimination over the Life Course"; Tomaskovic-Devey, Thomas, and Johnson, "Race and the Accumulation of Human Capital."
30. By a statistical device known as an interaction effect, the lower salary scales for highly placed workers in public employment are also factored in.
31. Grodsky and Pager, "Structure of Disadvantage."
32. For brief histories, see Frank Dobbin and Frank Sutton, "The Strength of a Weak State: The Rights Revolution and the Rise of Human Resources Management Divisions," *American Journal of Sociology* 104 (September, 1998): 441–476; and Kevin Stainback, Corre Robinson, and Donald Tomaskovic-Devey, "Race and Workplace Integration: A Politically Mediated Process," *American Behavioral Scientist* 48 (2005): 1200–1228. A more extended discussion is by John Skrentny, *The Minority-Rights Revolution* (Cambridge, Mass.: Harvard University Press, 2002). For an innovative analysis of the conditions under which discrimination charges arise and the processes through which they are resolved, see C. Elizabeth Hirsh and Sabino Kornrich, "The Context of

Discrimination: Workplace Conditions, Institutional Environments, and Sex and Race Discrimination Charges," *American Journal of Sociology* 113 (March, 2008): 1394–1432.

33. Barbara Reskin, *The Realities of Affirmative Action in Employment* (Washington, D.C.: American Sociological Association, 1998), 5,6.

34. Sigal Alon and Marta Tienda, "Diversity, Opportunity and the Shifting Meritocracy in Higher Education," *American Sociological Review* 72 (August, 2007): 487–511; Bowen and Bok, *Shape of the River;* Eric Grodsky, "Compensatory Sponsorship in Higher Education," *American Journal of Sociology* 112 (May, 2007): 1662–1712; Douglas Massey, Camille Charles, Garvey Lundy, and Mary Fischer, *The Source of the River: The Social Origins of Freshmen at America's Selective Colleges and Universities* (Princeton: Princeton University Press, 2002).

35. Stainback, Robinson, and Tomaskovic-Devey, "Race and Workplace Integration."

36. Harry Holzer and David Neumark, "Assessing Affirmative Action," *Journal of Economic Literature* 38 (September, 2000): 483–568.

37. Ibid., 504–508; Justin McCrary, "The Effect of Court-Ordered Hiring Quotas on the Quality and Composition of Police," *American Economic Review* 97 (March, 2007): 318–353; Reskin, *Realities of Affirmative Action,* 52.

38. Stainback, Robinson, and Tomaskovic-Devey, "Race and Workplace Integration."

39. Holzer and Neumark, "Assessing Affirmative Action."

40. Alon and Tienda, "Diversity."

41. Waldinger, *Still the Promised City?;* Roger Waldinger and Michael Lichter, *How the Other Half Works: Immigration and the Social Organization of Labor* (Berkeley: University of California, 2003).

42. Donald Tomaskovic-Devey et al.,"Documenting Desegregation."

43. Herbert Blumer, "Race Prejudice as a Sense of Group Position," *Pacific Sociological Review* 1 (1958): 3–7; Hubert Blalock, *Toward a Theory of Minority-Group Relations* (New York: Wiley, 1967).

44. John Logan, Reynolds Farley, and Brian Stults, "Segregation of Minorities in the Metropolis: Two Decades of Change," *Demography* 41 (February, 2004): 1–22.

45. Saskia Sassen, *The Global City: New York, London, Tokyo* (Princeton: Princeton University Press, 1991).

46. Kasinitz et al., *Inheriting the City.*

47. The relative advantages of blacks of West Indian descent constitute a long-standing theme in research on African Americans; see Kyle Crowder, "Residential Segregation of West Indians in the New York/New Jersey Metropolitan Area: The Roles of Race and Ethnicity," *International Migration Review* 1 (Spring, 1999): 79–113; Nancy Foner, *Islands in the City: West Indian Migration to New York* (Berkeley: University of California Press, 2001); Matthis Kalmijn, "The Socioeconomic Assimilation of Caribbean American Blacks," *Social Forces* 74 (March, 1996): 911–930; Suzanne Model, *West Indian Immigrants: A Black Success Story?* (New York: Russell Sage Foundation, 2008); Mary Waters, *Black Identities: West Indian Immigrant Dreams and American Realities* (Cambridge, Mass.: Harvard University Press, 1999).

On the overrepresentation of immigrant-origin blacks among the beneficiaries of affirmative action at elite colleges, see Douglas Massey, Margarita Mooney, Kimberly Torres, and Camille Charles, "Black Immigrants and Black Natives Attending Selective Colleges and Universities in the United States," *American Journal of Education* 113 (February, 2007): 243–271; Sara Rimer and Karen Arenson, "Top Colleges Take More Blacks, but Which Ones?" *New York Times,* June 24, 2004.

5. An Extraordinary Opportunity: The Exit of the Baby Boomers

1. Dowell Myers, *Immigrants and Boomers: Forging a New Social Contract for the Future of America* (New York: Russell Sage Foundation, 2007).

2. The 15 million figure is based on a projected growth of full-time employment by 18 percent between 2000 and 2030. The projection, it must be admitted, is no more than a rough guesstimate, whose basis will be explained subsequently.

3. Claude Fischer and Michael Hout, *A Century of Difference: How America Changed in the Last One Hundred Years* (New York: Russell Sage Foundation, 2006).

4. U.S. Census Bureau, "2008 National Population Projections": http://www.census.gov/population/www/projections/2008projections.html (retrieved 8/15/08).

5. For the back-of-the-envelope calculations I employ some reasonable approximations of the depletion of these younger cohorts of workers due to mortality and retirement as they age over the thirty-year period of the

projection. These approximations are based on standard mortality rates and current retirement data. For instance, the 26- to 34-year-old group can be expected to lose about 10 percent of its members through death by the time it is 56 to 65 years old; this follows from the most recent life tables, which show that 90 percent of 30-year-olds are expected to survive to age 60. (See Elizabeth Arias, "United States Life Tables, 2004," *National Vital Statistics Reports* 56 [December 28, 2007], table B.) According, moreover, to the retirement data summarized subsequently in Figure 5.3, 37 percent of 56- to 65-year-olds can be expected to be employed full time. The mortality and retirement data combined imply that, after thirty years, about 33 percent (that is, 0.9 of 37 percent) of the original cohort is employed full time. Applied to the population data, that is, the number of 26- to 35-year-olds in 2000, this percentage projects about 13.5 million full-time workers for this cohort in 2030, half of whom are assumed to be in the top half of the workforce. This represents a reduction of more than 50 percent from the number who held good jobs in 2000. A similar calculation indicates a fall-off of more than 90 percent in the number employed full time in good jobs for the 36- to 45-year-old cohort of 2000.

6. Bureau of Labor Statistics, "Tomorrow's Jobs," 2003: http://www.bls.gov/oco/oco2003.htm (retrieved 10/3/07).

7. For Census Bureau population estimates, see http://www.census.gov/popest/states/NST-ann-est.html.

8. My assumption is that full-time employment growth closely tracks labor-force growth, but it should be noted that, by definition, the labor force includes part-time workers and the unemployed, as well as full-time workers. The 18 percent figure comes about by, first, assuming measured employment growth (6.8 percent) between March 2000 and March 2008 (see the BLS data at http://data.bls.gov/cgi-bin/surveymost [accessed 8/1/2008]) and, then, applying to subsequent years the annual growth rates projected by the BLS. For those rates, see http://www.bls.gov/opub/working/page1b.htm (accessed 8/1/2006). Since the U.S. economy is in a severe downturn as I complete this book, it is unlikely to experience anything like these growth rates for the time being; I am assuming therefore that, when the recession eventually ends, there will be catch-up growth, so that over the whole period job growth will approximate the rate projected for it.

For further analysis of labor-force growth, see Mitra Toosi, "Employment Outlook 2006–2016: Labor Force Projections to 2016: More Workers in Their Golden Years," *Monthly Labor Review* (November, 2007): 33–52.

9. U.S. Census Bureau, *Statistical Abstract of the United States: 2006* (Washington, D.C.: U.S. Government Printing Office, 2005), table 576.

10. In particular, for whites I am assuming that their probabilities of entrance into different tiers of the labor market are given by the proportions of the white population in these tiers among 26- to 55-year-olds in the 2000 Census. For immigrants (and the small group of those of "other" race), I am assuming that their absolute numbers in different tiers are the same as in the 26–35 group in the 2000 Census; these individuals mainly entered the labor market during the 1990s.

11. The point that a declining share of white workers provides an opening for the mobility of minority groups has been made before. Roger Waldinger has analyzed the impact of such a change on the ethno-racial stratification in the New York region during the latter decades of the twentieth century—see his "Changing Ladders and Musical Chairs: Ethnicity and Opportunity in Post-Industrial New York," *Politics and Society* 15 (1986/87): 369–401; and *Still the Promised City? African-Americans and New Immigrants in Postindustrial New York* (Cambridge, Mass.: Harvard University Press, 1996).

12. Randy Ilg and Steven Haugen, "Earnings and Employment Trends in the 1990s," *Monthly Labor Review* 123, no. 3 (March, 2000): 21–32.

13. I have combined the two years to create greater stability in the estimates. The comparison of decennial Census data with the American Community Survey is not ideal, I must admit. The decennial Census data is collected at a single time point (on April 1), while the ACS data are collected continuously throughout a year. At this point in the young history of the ACS, no one can say with confidence how much the data are affected by this design feature.

14. Alan Blinder, "How Many U.S. Jobs Might Be Offshorable?" CEPS working paper no. 142, March, 2007. I am grateful to Tim Smeeding for bringing this paper to my attention.

15. For a discussion of how the BLS arrives at its occupational projections, see James Franklin, "Employment Outlook: 2006–2016: An Overview of BLS Projections to 2016," *Monthly Labor Review* (November, 2007):

3–12. The BLS also issues forecasts of contraction and expansion by industry. However, an analysis of these forecasts for a detailed cross-classification of occupations and industries would be a very complex task, which I do not attempt here.

16. Runjuan Liu and Daniel Trefler, "American Jobs and the Rise of Service Outsourcing to China and India," *NBER Digest* (February, 2009): http://www.nber.org/digest/feb09/w14061.html (accessed 2/21/09).

17. Bureau of Labor Statistics, *Occupational Outlook Handbook, 2008–2009*, http://www.bls.gov/oco/home.htm (retrieved 3/20/08).

18. Admittedly, some of these jobs are moving to India. See the report by Heather Timmons, ". . .India's Role Is Growing," *New York Times* (August 12, 2008), sect. C, p. 1. According to one of her informants, "Theoretically, as much as 40 percent of the research-related jobs on Wall Street, tens of thousands of jobs, could be sent off-shore, . . . though the reality will be less than that."

19. Leora Friedberg, "The Recent Trend Towards Later Retirement," Center for Retirement Research, Boston College, March 2007: http://www.bc.edu/centers/crr/issues/wob_9.pdf (retrieved 3/1/08).

20. Full-time and part-time status are calculated on the basis of the work history of the prior year, 1999. Full-time status is defined in the same way as in Chapter 4, while regular part-time work is defined as working less than full time but more than 160 hours in 1999. To prevent the part-time estimate from becoming inflated by the presence of individuals who worked for a portion of 1999 and then retired, an additional stipulation is that individuals must still be in the labor force in 2000 to be counted in the estimates.

21. Friedberg, "Recent Trend."

22. Alicia Munnell and Steven Sass, *Working Longer: The Solution to the Retirement Income Challenge* (Washington, D.C.: Brookings Institution Press, 2008).

23. This scenario is implemented by shifting the year-by-year probability of full-time employment, so that the assumed probability of employment at any age is equal to what it previously was for individuals three years younger. Such a shift is equivalent to adding three years to the average age of retirement from the full-time workforce. The percentages are then recomputed for different age groups and applied to compute the relevant columns of departures in Table 5.3.

24. Jacob Hacker, *The Great Risk Shift: The Assault on American Jobs, Families, Health Care and Retirement and How You Can Fight Back* (New York: Oxford University Press, 2006).

25. Annette Bernhardt, Martina Morris, Mark Handcock, and Marc Scott, *Divergent Paths: Economic Mobility in the New American Labor Market* (New York: Russell Sage Foundation, 2001).

26. David Card and John DiNardo, "Skill-Based Technological Change and Rising Wage Inequality: Some Problems and Puzzles," *Journal of Labor Economics* 20 (October, 2002): 733–783.

27. ChangHwan Kim and Arthur Sakamoto, "The Rise of Intraoccupational Wage Inequality in the United States, 1983 to 2002," *American Sociological Review* 73 (February, 2008): 129–157.

28. Ted Mouw and Arne Kalleberg, "Occupations and the Structure of Wage Inequality in the United States, 1980s-2000s," Department of Sociology, University of North Carolina, Chapel Hill, April, 2007; Kim Weeden, Young-Mi Kim, Matthew Di Carlo, and David Grusky, "Social Class and Earnings Inequality," *American Behavioral Scientist* 50 (January, 2007): 702–736.

29. In fact, the analysis by Bernhardt and her colleagues that found negative labor-market changes was deliberately limited to non-Hispanic whites.

30. David Hollinger, *Post-Ethnic America: Beyond Multiculturalism* (New York: Basic, 1995).

31. Paul Krugman, "Who'll Stop the Pain?" *New York Times,* February 19, 2009.

32. National Bureau of Economic Research, "US Business Cycle Expansions and Contractions": http://wwwdev.nber.org/cycles/cyclesmain. html (accessed 2/21/09); Bureau of Labor Statistics, "Databases, Tables, and Calculators by Subject": http://data.bls.gov/PDQ/servlet/ SurveyOutputServlet?data_tool=latest_number&series_ id=LNS14000000 (accessed 2/21/09).

6. The Contingencies of Change

1. Migration Policy Institute, "Proposed Points System and Its Likely Impact on Prospective Migrants," *Immigration Backgrounder* 4 (May, 2007): http://www.migrationpolicy.org/pubs/PointsSystem_051807.pdf (accessed 8/1/2008).

2. George Borjas, *Heaven's Door: Immigration Policy and the American Economy* (Princeton: Princeton University Press, 1999).

3. For details, see the web site of U.S. Citizenship and Immigration Services, the agency that replaced INS: http://www.uscis.gov/portal/site/usciss. For a review of current patterns according to categories of admission, see Gretchen Reinemeyer and Jeanne Batalova, "Spotlight on Legal Immigration to the United States," *Migration Information Source* (November, 2007): http://www.migrationinformation.org/USFocus/display/.cfm?ID=651.

4. See Maia Jachimowicz and Deborah Meyers, "Temporary High-Skill Migration," *Migration Information Source* (November, 2002): http://www.migrationinformation.org/USFocus/display.cfm?ID=69 (accessed 8/1/2008); and Muzaffar Chishti and Claire Bergeron, "USCIS Receives 163,000 H-1B Applications for Fiscal Year 2009," *Migration Information Source* (April, 2008): http://www.migrationinformation.org/USFocus/display.cfm?ID=678 (accessed 8/1/2008).

5. Lawrence Burton and Jack Wang, "How Much Does the U.S. Rely on Immigrant Engineers," National Science Foundation, NSF 99–327 (February 11, 1999): http://www.nsf.gov/statistics/issuebrf/sib99327.htm (accessed 1/30/2008).

6. Berlin Institute for Population and Development, "Europe's Demographic Future: Growing Imbalances," report, 2008: http://www.berlin-institut.org/fileadmin/user_upload/Studien/Europa_e_Kurzfassung_sicher_o_B.pdf (accessed 8/30/08).

7. Stephen Castles and Mark Miller, *The Age of Migration,* 3rd ed.(The Guilford Press, 2003).

8. Open Doors, *Open Doors Report, 2007.* Institute of International Education (November 12, 2007): http://opendoors.iienetwork.org/ (accessed 1/31/2008).

9. Jeanne Batalova, "The 'Brain Gain' Race Begins with Foreign Students," *Migration Information Source* (January, 2007): http://www.migrationinformation.org/Feature/display.cfm?ID=571 (accessed 8/1/2008); Aisha Labi, "Europe Challenges U.S. for Foreign Students," *Chronicle of Higher Education* (September 28, 2007).

10. Ira Katznelson, *When Affirmative Action Was White: An Untold History of Racial Inequality in Twentieth-Century America* (New York: W. W. Norton, 2005).

11. Claude Fischer and Michael Hout, *A Century of Difference: How America Changed in the Last One Hundred Years* (New York: Russell Sage Foundation, 2006).

12. In addition to the data shown earlier, see ibid., chap. 2.

13. Leora Friedberg, "The Recent Trend towards Later Retirement," Center for Retirement Research, Boston College (March, 2007): http://www. bc.edu/centers/crr/issues/wob_9.pdf (accessed 5/1/2008).

14. On the labor-force patterns of professional women, see Christine Percheski, "Opting Out? Cohort Differences in Professional Women's Employment Rates from 1960 to 2005," *American Sociological Review* 73 (June, 2008): 497–517. On the different child-rearing patterns in middle- and working-class families, see Annette Lareau, *Unequal Childhoods: Class, Race, and Family Life* (Berkeley: University of California Press, 2003). The burdens on working women are addressed by Jerry Jacobs and Kathleen Gerson, *The Time Divide: Work, Family, and Gender Inequality* (Cambridge, Mass.: Harvard University Press, 2004); and Pamela Stone, *Opting Out? Why Women Really Quit Careers and Head Home* (Berkeley: University of California Press, 2007).

15. On the educational gap in the case of Mexican Americans, see Tomás Jiménez and David Fitzgerald, "Mexican Assimilation: A Temporal and Spatial Reorientation," *Du Bois Review* 4 (September, 2007): 337–354; James Smith, "Assimilation across the Latino Generations," *AEA Papers and Proceedings* 93 (May, 2003): 315–319; Edward Telles and Vilma Ortiz, *Generations of Exclusion: Mexican Americans, Assimilation, and Race* (New York: Russell Sage Foundation, 2008).

16. Claudia Goldin and Lawrence Katz, *The Race between Education and Technology* (Cambridge, Mass.: Harvard University Press, 2008), 257–258.

17. Ibid., 347.

18. Dowell Myers, *Immigrants and Boomers: Forging a New Social Contract for the Future of America* (New York: Russell Sage Foundation, 2007). See also Robert Haveman and Timothy Smeeding, "The Role of Higher Education in Social Mobility," *The Future of Children* 16 (Fall, 2006): 125–150; and Jennifer Hochschild and Nathan Scovronick, *The American Dream and the Public Schools* (New York: Oxford University Press, 2003).

19. Myers, *Immigrants and Boomers.*

20. Leonard Covello, *The Social Background of the Italo-American School Child* (Totowa, N.J.: Rowman & Littlefield, 1972); Joel Perlmann, *Ethnic Differences: Schooling and Social Structure among the Irish, Italians, Jews and Blacks in an American City, 1880–1935* (Cambridge: Cambridge University Press, 1988); Stephen Steinberg, *The Academic Melting Pot* (New York: McGraw-Hill, 1974).

21. Richard Alba and Victor Nee, *Remaking the American Mainstream: Assimilation and Contemporary Immigration* (Cambridge, Mass.: Harvard University Press, 2003), chap. 3.

22. Hochschild and Scovronick, *American Dream*, 79.

23. John Logan, Reynolds Farley, and Brian Stults, "Segregation of Minorities in the Metropolis: Two Decades of Change," *Demography* 41 (February, 2004): 1–22; Gary Orfield and Chungmei Lee, *Racial Transformation and the Changing Nature of Segregation*, The Civil Rights Project, Harvard University: http://www.civilrightsproject.ucla.edu/research/deseg/Racial_Transformation.pdf (accessed 1/15/2008).

24. Orfield and Lee, *Racial Transformation*, 29. On the physical threat to students, see, for example, Mary Waters, *Black Identities: West Indian Immigrant Dreams and American Realities* (Cambridge, Mass.: Harvard University Press, 1999). On the "toxic" schools attended by many children from immigrant families, see Carola Suárez-Orozco, Marcelo Suárez-Orozco, and Irina Todorova, *Learning a New Land: Immigrant Students in American Society* (Cambridge, Mass.: Harvard University Press, 2008), chap. 3.

25. Hochschild and Scovronick, *American Dream*, 61. On funding inequalities, see also Jonathan Kozol, *Savage Inequalities: Children in America's Schools* (New York: Crown, 1991); Dennis Condron and Vincent Roscigno, "Disparities Within: Unequal Spending and Achievement in an Urban School District," *Sociology of Education* 76 (2003): 18–36.

26. Hochschild and Scovronick, *American Dream*, 62.

27. National Center for Educational Statistics, *The National Assessment of Education Progress: The Nation's Report Card: Reading 2005:* http://nces.ed.gov/nationsreportcard/pdf/main2005/2006451.pdf (accessed 5/1/2008).

28. Myers, *Immigrants and Boomers*.

29. Tamar Lewin, "Race Preferences Vote Splits Michigan," *New York Times,* October 31, 2006; Douglas Massey, Margarita Mooney, Kim-

berly Torres, and Camille Charles, "Black Immigrants and Black Natives Attending Selective Colleges and Universities in the United States," *American Journal of Education* 113 (February, 2007): 243–271; Peter Schmidt, "UCLA Reverses Decline in Black Admissions but Rejects More Asians," *Chronicle of Higher Education* (April 20, 2007); on affirmative action in admissions to selective universities, see also Douglas Massey, Camille Charles, Garvey Lundy and Mary Fischer, *The Source of the River: The Social Origins of Freshmen at America's Selective Colleges and Universities* (Princeton: Princeton University Press, 2002); Sigal Alon and Marta Tienda, "Diversity, Opportunity and the Shifting Meritocracy in Higher Education," *American Sociological Review* 72 (August, 2007): 487–511.

30. Lareau, *Unequal Childhoods.*

31. As I am finalizing this chapter in January 2009, President Obama's economic stimulus bill (the first of a series, perhaps) is under consideration by Congress. The bill contains a massive increase in federal spending on education. However, it appears that most of this increase will go for maintaining school systems rather than improving them—that is, the money will be used to fill the holes in state education budgets that have opened because of the major recession that began in 2008. See Sam Dillon, "Stimulus Plan Would Provide Flood of Aid to Education," *New York Times,* January 27, 2009.

32. Goldin and Katz, *Race,* 327–328.

33. Hochschild and Scovronick, *American Dream,* 2.

34. For summaries of this evidence, see Sean Corcoran, William Evans, and Robert Schwab, "Women, the Labor Market, and the Declining Quality of Teachers," *Journal of Policy Analysis and Management* 23 (Summer, 2004): 449–470; Hamilton Lankford, Susanna Loeb, and James Wyckoff, "Teacher Sorting and the Plight of Urban Schools: A Descriptive Analysis," *Educational Evaluation and Policy Analysis* 24 (Spring, 2002): 37–62.

35. See Corcoran, Evans, and Schwab, "Women."

36. Goldin and Katz, *Race,* 347.

37. Fischer and Hout, *Century of Difference.*

38. Devah Pager, "The Mark of a Criminal Record," *American Journal of Sociology* 108 (March, 2003): 937–975. On the expansion of incarceration and its impact on ethno-racial inequalities, see also Becky Pettit and Bruce Western, "Mass Imprisonment and the Life Course: Race and

Class Inequality in U.S. Incarceration," *American Sociological Review* (April, 2004): 151–169, and the reports of The Sentencing Project, available at its Web site: http://www.sentencingproject.org/Default.aspx.

39. This involvement has been documented for the Irish, Italians, and even for eastern European Jews. On the Jewish record in crime, see Stephen Steinberg, *The Ethnic Myth: Race, Ethnicity, and Class in America* (Boston: Beacon, 1989).

40. Vincent Schiraldi and Jason Ziedenberg, "Cellblocks or Classrooms? The Funding of Higher Education and Corrections and Its Impact on African American Men," report by The Justice Policy Institute (September, 2002): http://www.justicepolicy.org/images/upload/02-09_REP_CellblocksClassrooms_BB-AC.pdf (accessed 8/20/2008)

41. Jeffrey Passel, "Size and Characteristics of the Unauthorized Migrant Population in the U.S.: Estimates Based on the March 2005 Current Population Survey," Pew Hispanic Center Report (March, 2006): http://pewhispanic.org/reports/report.php?ReportID=61 (accessed 8/15/08). Though Passel's estimates are derived from 2005 CPS data, the numbers given in the text are his updates to March, 2006.

42. Susan Brown, Frank Bean, Mark Leach, and Rubén Rumbaut, "Legalization and Naturalization Trajectories among Mexican Immigrants and Their Implications for the Second Generation," forthcoming in Richard Alba and Mary Waters, eds., *Dimensions of Second Generation Incorporation.*

43. Douglas Massey, Jorge Durand, and Nolan Malone, *Beyond Smoke and Mirrors: Mexican Immigration in an Era of Economic Integration* (New York: Russell Sage Foundation, 2003).

44. For some sensible proposals about American immigration policies, including what I view as the appropriate emphasis on the need for bilateral solutions, see Alejandro Portes, "The Fence to Nowhere," *American Prospect* (September 24, 2007): http://www.prospect.org/cs/articles?article=the_fence_to_nowhere (accessed 9/1/08).

45. Alba and Nee, *Remaking.*

46. Xavier de Souza Briggs, "'Some of My Best Friends Are. . .': Interracial Friendships, Class and Segregation in America," *City & Community* 6 (December, 2007): 263–290.

47. Donald Tomaskovic-Devey, Catherine Zimmer, Kevin Stainback, Corre Robinson, Tiffany Taylor, and Tricia McTague, "Documenting Desegregation: Segregation in American Workplaces by Race, Ethnicity, and

Sex, 1966–2003," *American Sociological Review* 71 (August, 2006): 565–588. This research depends on the reports that large employers (100 employees or, in the case of federal contractors, 50) must file annually with the Equal Employment Opportunity Commission (EEOC). Obviously, then, it cannot cover small firms, where segregation is probably much higher. Employers must file a separate racial/ethnic and gender tabulation for each "establishment," which is defined by the EEOC as generally a "single physical location" "engaged in one, or predominantly one, type of economic activity" (from the instruction booklet; see http://www.eeoc.gov/eeo1survey/2007instruct.html).

48. That is to say, the index of dissimilarity, the main measurement tool of segregation researchers, is a measure of "unevenness" of distribution. When changes, like increases in the numbers of minority-group members throughout a distribution, do not alter that unevenness, then they will not register in the dissimilarity index. They are likely to be altering the probabilities that members of different groups are interacting, however. See Douglas Massey and Nancy Denton, "The Dimensions of Residential Segregation," *Social Forces* 67 (1988): 281–315.

49. Kevin Stainback and Donald Tomaskovic-Devey, "Long-Term Trends in Managerial Representation for Black and White Women and Men in Private Sector U.S. Firms," forthcoming in the *American Sociological Review.*

50. Fischer and Hout, *Century of Difference.*

51. Douglas Massey, "Ethnic Residential Segregation: A Theoretical Synthesis and Empirical Review," *Sociology and Social Research* 69 (April, 1985): 315–350; see also Richard Alba, John Logan, and Kyle Crowder, "White Ethnic Neighborhoods and Spatial Assimilation: The Greater New York Region, 1980–1990," *Social Forces* 75 (March, 1997): 883–912.

52. Richard Alba, John Logan, and Brian Stults, "How Segregated Are Middle-Class African Americans?" *Social Problems* 47 (November): 543–558; Camille Charles, *Won't You Be My Neighbor? Race, Class and Residence in Los Angeles* (New York: Russell Sage Foundation, 2006); Douglas Massey and Nancy Denton, *American Apartheid: Segregation and the Making of the Underclass* (Cambridge, Mass.: Harvard University Press, 1993); Mary Pattillo-McCoy, *Black Picket Fences: Privilege and Peril among the Black Middle Class* (Chicago: University of Chicago Press, 1999).

53. Richard Alba, John Logan, and Brian Stults, "The Changing Neighborhood Contexts of the Immigrant Metropolis," *Social Forces* 79 (December, 2000): 587–621; Susan Brown, "Delayed Spatial Assimilation: Multi-Generational Incorporation of the Mexican-Origin Population in Los Angeles," *City & Community* 6 (2007): 193–209; Camille Charles, "The Dynamics of Racial Residential Segregation," *Annual Review of Sociology* 29 (2003): 167–207; John Logan, Richard Alba, and Wenquan Zhang, "Immigrant Enclaves and Ethnic Communities in New York and Los Angeles," *American Sociological Review* 67 (April, 2002): 299–322; Scott South, Kyle Crowder, and Erick Chavez, "Migration and Spatial Assimilation among U.S. Latinos: Classical versus Segmented Trajectories," *Demography* 42 (August, 2005): 497–521.

54. John Iceland, "Beyond Black and White: Metropolitan Residential Segregation in Multi-Ethnic America," *Social Science Research* 33 (June, 2004): 248–271; idem, *Coming Together or Living Apart? Immigration and the Racial and Ethnic Transformation of America's Neighborhoods* (Berkeley: University of California Press, 2009); Logan, Farley, and Stults, "Segregation of Minorities."

55. Logan, Farley, and Stults, "Segregation of Minorities." Some analysts of segregation have claimed to find larger declines than this (for example, Fischer and Hout, *Century of Difference;* David Cutler, Edward Glaeser, and Jacob Vigdor, "The Rise and Decline of the American Ghetto," *Journal of Political Economy* 107 [1999]: 455–506). However, they typically compare whites and blacks without separating out Hispanics. This is an analytical mistake, in my view, because it confounds possible changes in the segregation of African Americans with the immigration upsurge from Latin America. That is, since Latinos are a racially heterogeneous population, their increasing numbers create the appearance of more residential integration of blacks in general. This occurs because the neighborhoods in which Latinos reside generally mix individuals who in racial terms are white, black, and "other." It should be apparent that this "integration" can increase without any change in the extent of residential separation between non-Hispanic whites and blacks.

56. See Nancy Denton and Richard Alba, "The Decline of the All-White Neighborhood and the Growth of Suburban Diversity," presented at the conference on Suburban Racial Change, Harvard University, March 28 (1998).

57. Samantha Friedman, "Do Declines in Residential Segregation Mean

Stable Neighborhood Racial Integration in Metropolitan America? A Research Note," *Social Science Research* 37 (September, 2008): 920–933.

58. William Frey, "Immigration, Domestic Migration, and Demographic Balkanization in America: New Evidence for the 1990s," *Population and Development Review* 22 (December, 1996): 741–763.

59. Ingrid Gould Ellen, *Sharing America's Neighborhoods: The Prospects for Stable Racial Integration* (Cambridge, Mass.: Harvard University Press, 2000).

60. Paul Spickard, *Mixed Blood: Ethnic Identity and Intermarriage in Twentieth-Century America* (Madison: University of Wisconsin Press, 1989).

61. Zhenchao Qian and Daniel Lichter, "Social Boundaries and Marital Assimilation: Interpreting Trends in Racial and Ethnic Intermarriage," *American Sociological Review* 72 (February, 2007): 68–94. See also Sharon Lee and Barry Edmonston, "New Marriages, New Families: U.S. Racial and Hispanic Intermarriage," *Population Bulletin* 60 (2005) (Washington, D.C.: Population Reference Bureau).

62. Minjeong Kim and Angie Chung, "Consuming Orientalism: Images of Asian American Women in Multicultural Advertising," *Qualitative Sociology* 28 (2005): 67–91.

63. Qian and Lichter, "Social Boundaries."

64. Ibid., table 2.

65. Telles and Ortiz, *Generations of Exclusion,* 179–180.

66. Maria Krysan, "Prejudice, Politics, and Public Opinion: Understanding the Sources of Racial Policy Attitudes," *Annual Review of Sociology* 26 (2000): 135–168.

67. Lawrence Bobo and Cybelle Fox, "Race, Racism, and Discrimination: Bridging Problems, Methods, and Theory in Social Psychological Research," *Social Psychology Quarterly* 66 (December, 2003): 319–333.

68. Howard Schuman, Charlotte Steeh, Lawrence Bobo, and Maria Krysan, *Racial Attitudes in America: Trends and Interpretations* (Cambridge, Mass.: Harvard University Press, 1997).

69. Krysan, "Prejudice."

70. See ibid. for a good overview.

71. Lawrence Bobo, "Prejudice as Group Position: Microfoundations of a Sociological Approach to Racism and Race Relations," *Journal of Social Issues* 55 (1999): 447. This theory is inspired by Herbert Blumer, "Race

Prejudice as a Sense of Group Position," *Pacific Sociological Review* 1 (1958): 3–7.

72. Krysan, "Prejudice," 144.

73. Logan, Farley, and Stults, "Segregation of Minorities."

74. Roger Waldinger, *Still the Promised City? African-Americans and New Immigrants in Postindustrial New York* (Cambridge, Mass.: Harvard University Press, 1996); Roger Waldinger and Michael Lichter, *How the Other Half Works: Immigration and the Social Organization of Labor* (Berkeley: University of California, 2003).

75. See, for example, Waldinger and Lichter, *How the Other Half.*

76. Jacqueline Villarrubia, Nancy Denton, and Richard Alba, "Gateway State, Not Gateway City: New Immigrants in the Hudson Valley," presented at the annual meeting of the Population Association of America, 2007. For similar findings from North Carolina, see Helen Marrow, "Reconceptualizing Discrimination and Hierarchy in the Multiethnic Rural U.S. South," forthcoming in Charles Gallagher, ed., *Below the Belt: Race, Ethnicity, Labor, and Politics in a Changing Sunbelt* (Athens: University of Georgia Press).

77. For example, Thomas Guglielmo, *White on Arrival: Italians, Race, Color and Power in Chicago, 1890–1945* (New York: Oxford University Press, 2003).

78. For example, Herbert Gans, "The Possibility of a New Racial Hierarchy in the Twenty-First Century United States," in Michèle Lamont, ed., *The Cultural Territories of Race* (Chicago: University of Chicago Press, 1999). See also Jennifer Lee and Frank Bean, "America's Changing Color Lines: Immigration, Race/Ethnicity, and Multiracial Identification," *Annual Review of Sociology* 30 (2004): 221–242; idem, "Reinventing the Color Line: Immigration and America's New Racial/Ethnic Divide," *Social Forces* 86 (December, 2007): 561–586.

7. Imagining a More Integrated Future

1. For example, Douglas Massey, *Categorically Unequal: The American Stratification System* (New York: Russell Sage Foundation, 2007); Thomas Piketty and Emmanuel Saez, "Income Inequality in the United States, 1913–1998," *Quarterly Journal of Economics* 118 (February, 2003): 1–39.

2. Robert Pear, "Gap in Life Expectancy Widens for the Nation," *New York Times,* March 23, 2008.

3. Douglas Massey and Mary Fischer, "How Segregation Concentrates Poverty," *Ethnic and Racial Studies* 23 (2000): 670–691.

4. Herbert Gans, *The Urban Villagers: Group and Class in the Life of Italian-Americans* (New York: Free Press, [1962] 1982); Nathan Glazer and Daniel Patrick Moynihan, *Beyond the Melting Pot: The Negroes, Puerto Ricans, Jews, Italians, and Irish of New York City* (Cambridge: MIT Press, [1963] 1970).

5. Claudia Goldin and Lawrence Katz, *The Race between Education and Technology* (Cambridge, Mass.: Harvard University Press, 2008), 44, 46.

6. On the so-called Great Compression, see Claude Fischer and Michael Hout, *A Century of Difference: How America Changed in the Last One Hundred Years* (New York: Russell Sage Foundation, 2007), 143; Claudia Goldin and Lawrence Katz, "Decreasing (and Then Increasing) Inequality in America: A Tale of Two Half-Centuries," in Finis Welch, ed., *The Causes and Consequences of Increasing Inequality* (Chicago: University of Chicago Press, 2001).

7. David Lavin, Richard Alba, and Richard Silberstein, *Right versus Privilege: The Open Admissions Experiment at the City University of New York* (New York: Free Press, 1981).

8. On the African-American migration northward, see Stewart Tolnay, "The African American 'Great Migration' and Beyond," *Annual Review of Sociology* 29 (2003): 209–232. The evolving place of racial minorities in New York City's labor market during the second half of the twentieth century is addressed by Roger Waldinger, *Still the Promised City? African-Americans and New Immigrants in Postindustrial New York* (Cambridge, Mass.: Harvard University Press, 1996).

9. Philip Kasinitz, John Mollenkopf, Mary Waters, and Jennifer Holdaway, *Inheriting the City: The Children of Immigrants Come of Age* (New York and Cambridge, Mass.: Russell Sage Foundation and Harvard University Press, 2008).

10. Richard Alba, *Ethnic Identity: The Transformation of White America* (New Haven: Yale University Press, 1990); Mary Waters, *Ethnic Options: Choosing Identities in America* (Berkeley: University of California Press, 1990).

11. William Julius Wilson, in his famous book *The Declining Significance of*

Race (Chicago: University of Chicago Press, 1978), argued that class was increasingly replacing race as the basis for black-white stratification in the contemporary era. My argument is related to his but also differs in that I am suggesting that the social meaning of race is increasingly coming to depend on the social-class position of minority individuals. For those nonwhites on the lower rungs of the socioeconomic ladder, race remains a powerful constraint on their social lives.

12. I am grateful to Ira Katznelson for suggesting the "ethnicity" formulation to me, but I am certainly not alone in imagining it as a possibility. See David Hollinger, *Post-Ethnic America: Beyond Multiculturalism* (New York: Basic, 1995).

13. Cedric Herring, Verna Keith, and Hayward Horton, *Skin Deep: How Race and Complexion Matter in the "Color Blind" Era* (Chicago: University of Illinois Press, 2004); Jennifer Hochschild and Vesla Weaver, "The Skin Color Paradox and the American Racial Order," *Social Forces* 86 (December, 2007): 643–670.

14. Richard Alba, John Logan, and Brian Stults, "The Changing Neighborhood Contexts of the Immigrant Metropolis," *Social Forces* 79 (December, 2000): 587–621; Edward Murguia and Edward Telles, "Phenotype and Schooling among Mexican Americans," *Sociology of Education* 69 (October, 1996): 276–289; Edward Telles and Edward Murguia, "Phenotypic Discrimination and Income Differences among Mexican Americans," *Social Science Quarterly* 71 (1990): 682–696.

15. David Lopez and Ricardo Stanton-Salazar, "Mexican Americans: A Second Generation at Risk," in Rubén G. Rumbaut and Alejandro Portes, eds., *Ethnicities: Children of Immigrants in America* (Berkeley: University of California Press, 2001), 72.

16. On Brazil, see Anthony Marx, *Making Race and Nation: A Comparison of South Africa, the United States, and Brazil* (New York: Cambridge University Press, 1997); and Edward Telles, *Race in Another America: The Significance of Skin Color in Brazil* (Princeton: Princeton University Press, 2004). Eduardo Bonilla-Silva, "From Bi-racial to Tri-racial: Towards a New System of Racial Stratification in the USA," *Ethnic and Racial Studies* 27 (November, 2004): 931–950, and Gregory Rodriguez, *Mongrels, Bastards, Orphans, and Vagabonds: Mexican Immigration and the Future of Race in America* (New York: Pantheon, 2007), also argue for the emergence of an increasingly Latin-American-style racial system in the

United States, partly as a result of the impact of Latinos on U.S. society. The problematic relationship of Latinos to U.S. racial categories is addressed by Clara Rodríguez, *Changing Race: Latinos, the Census, and the History of Ethnicity in the United States* (New York: New York University Press, 2000); and the fluidity of racial categories in Puerto Rico is analyzed by Mara Loveman and Jeronimo Muniz, "How Puerto Rico Became White: Boundary Dynamics and Intercensal Racial Reclassification," *American Sociological Review* 72 (December, 2007): 915–939.

17. Robert K. Merton, *Social Theory and Social Structure* (New York: Free Press, [1948] 1968). For an elegant analysis of what the lower emphasis on race in a society similar to the U.S. means, see Irene Bloemraad, *Becoming a Citizen: Incorporating Immigrants and Refugees in the United States and Canada* (Berkeley: University of California Press, 2006), chap. 4.

18. Jerome Karabel, *The Chosen: The Hidden History of Admission and Exclusion at Harvard, Yale and Princeton* (New York: Houghton Mifflin, 2006).

19. Joe Feagin, "The Continuing Significance of Race: Antiblack Discrimination in Public Places," *American Sociological Review* 56 (February, 1991): 115.

20. Jean Pfaelzer, *Driven Out: The Forgotten War against Chinese Americans* (New York: Random House, 2007).

21. Lewis Mumford Center, "Ethnic Diversity Grows, Neighborhood Integration Lags Behind," report issued April 3, 2001: http://mumford.albany.edu/census/WholePop/WPreport/MumfordReport.doc (retrieved 3/26/2008).

22. Frank Bean and Gillian Stevens, *America's Newcomers and the Dynamics of Diversity* (New York: Russell Sage Foundation, 2003); Jennifer Lee and Frank Bean, "America's Changing Color Lines: Immigration, Race/Ethnicity, and Multiracial Identification," *Annual Review of Sociology* 30 (2004): 221–242; idem, "Reinventing the Color Line: Immigration and America's New Racial/Ethnic Divide," *Social Forces* 86 (December, 2007): 561–586.

23. Felicia Lee, "Famous Black Lives through DNA's Prism," *New York Times,* February 5, 2008; Malcolm X, *The Autobiography of Malcolm X* (New York: Penguin Books, 1973); David Shipler, *A Country of Strangers: Blacks and Whites in America* (New York: Knopf, 1997); Paul Spick-

ard, *Mixed Blood: Ethnic Identity and Intermarriage in Twentieth-Century America* (Madison: University of Wisconsin Press, 1989).

24. Joshua Goldstein, "Kinship Networks That Cross Racial Lines: The Exception or the Rule?" *Demography* 36 (August, 1999): 399–407; Zhenchao Qian and Daniel Lichter, "Social Boundaries and Marital Assimilation: Interpreting Trends in Racial and Ethnic Intermarriage," *American Sociological Review* 72 (February, 2007): 68–94. One limitation to Goldstein's analysis is the exclusion of Hispanics. This probably has offsetting effects, though possibly their omission leads to an overstatement of the racial diversity among the close kin of whites. That is because Hispanic whites are more likely than other whites to have kin of other races, given the racial diversity within some of the major Hispanic groups. Nevertheless, the omission of white-Hispanic intermarriages also produces some degree of understatement of kin diversity.

25. See, as a start, the essays collected by Joel Perlmann and Mary Waters in *The New Race Question: How the Census Counts Multiracial Individuals* (New York: Russell Sage Foundation, 2002).

26. Qian and Lichter, "Marital Assimilation."

27. Debra Dickerson, "Colorblind," *Salon* (January 22, 2007): http://www.salon.com/opinion/feature/2007/01/22/obama/ (retrieved 2/12/2008).

28. Henry Louis Gates, Jr., "The Passing of Anatole Broyard," in *Thirteen Ways of Looking at a Black Man* (New York: Vintage, 1998); Broyard is reputed to be the basis for the main character in Philip Roth's 2000 novel *The Human Stain.*

29. U.S. Census Bureau, "Historical Income Inequality Tables": http://www.census.gov/hhes/www/income/histinc/ineqtoc.html (retrieved 2/4/2009). Fischer and Hout, *Century of Difference*, 143–148; Edward Wolff, "Recent Trends in Household Wealth in the United States: Rising Debt and Middle-Class Squeeze," Levy Institute, Bard College (June, 2007): http://www.levy.org/pubs/wp 502.pdf (retrieved 2/4/2009).

30. Derrick Bell, *Faces at the Bottom of the Well: The Permanence of Racism* (New York: Basic, 1993).

31. Julia Isaacs, "Economic Mobility of Black and White Families," report of the Economic Mobility Project (November 13, 2007): http://www.economicmobility.org/assets/pdfs/EMP_Black_White_Families.pdf (retrieved 2/12/2008). See also Ron Haskins, Julia Isaacs, and Isabel

Sawhill, *Getting Ahead or Losing Ground: Economic Mobility in America* (Washington, D.C.: Brookings Institution, 2008).

32. William Julius Wilson, *When Work Disappears* (New York: Knopf, 1996).

33. Richard Alba and Roxane Silberman, "The Children of Immigrants and Host-Society Educational Systems: Mexicans in the U.S. and North Africans in France," *Teachers College Record* (2009): http://www.tcrecord. org/Content.asp?ContentId=15340; Edward Telles and Vilma Ortiz, *Generations of Exclusion: Mexican Americans, Assimilation, and Race* (New York: Russell Sage Foundation, 2008).

34. Jennifer Hochschild and Nathan Scovronick, *The American Dream and the Public Schools* (New York: Oxford University Press, 2003); Gary Orfield and Chungmei Lee, *Racial Transformation and the Changing Nature of Segregation,* 2006 report of The Civil Rights Project, Harvard University: http://www.civilrightsproject.ucla.edu/research/deseg/Racial_Transformation.pdf (retrieved 3/1/2008).

35. Orlando Patterson, *The Ordeal of Integration: Progress and Resentment in America's "Racial Crisis"* (New York: Basic Books, 1997), 161–162.

36. Sigal Alon and Marta Tienda, "Diversity, Opportunity and the Shifting Meritocracy in Higher Education," *American Sociological Review* 72 (August): 487–511.

37. See Haskins, Isaacs, and Sawhill, *Getting Ahead.*

38. The debate arises because of Robert Putnam's provocative findings about the negative impact of diversity on social capital—see his essay "E Pluribus Unum: Diversity and Community in the Twenty-First Century: The 2006 Skytte Prize Lecture," *Scandinavian Political Studies* 30 (2007): 137–174.

39. Douglas Massey, "American Apartheid: Segregation and the Making of the Urban Underclass," *American Journal of Sociology* 95 (1990): 1153–1188; Douglas Massey and Nancy Denton, *American Apartheid: Segregation and the Making of the Underclass* (Cambridge, Mass.: Harvard University, 1993).

40. See, for example, Emily Rosenbaum and Samantha Friedman, *The Housing Divide: How Generations of Immigrants Fare in New York's Housing Market* (New York: NYU Press, 2007); Gregory Squires and Charis Kubrin, *Privileged Places: Race, Residence, and the Structure of Opportunity* (Boulder: Lynne Rienner Publishers, 2006).

41. Karabel, *The Chosen.*

42. For example, Doug McAdam, John McCarthy, and Mayer Zald, *Comparative Perspectives on Social Movements: Political Opportunities, Mobilizing Structures, and Cultural Framings* (Cambridge: Cambridge University Press, 1996); Doug McAdam, *Political Process and the Development of Black Insurgency, 1930.*

43. Charles Tilly, *Durable Inequality* (Berkeley: University of California Press, 1998).

44. Patterson, *Ordeal*, 155, 184–188.

Index